The Treachery of Realities

Studies in Critical Social Sciences Book Series

Haymarket Books is proud to be working with Brill Academic Publishers (www.brill.nl) to republish the *Studies in Critical Social Sciences* book series in paperback editions. This peer-reviewed book series offers insights into our current reality by exploring the content and consequences of power relationships under capitalism, and by considering the spaces of opposition and resistance to these changes that have been defining our new age. Our full catalog of *SCSS* volumes can be viewed at https://www.haymarketbooks .org/series_collections/4-studies-in-critical-social-sciences.

THE TREACHERY OF REALITIES

Safeguarding Truth in the Age of Science Denial

SAL RESTIVO

Haymarket Books
Chicago, IL

First published in 2025 by Brill Academic Publishers, The Netherlands
© 2025 Koninklijke Brill NV, Leiden, The Netherlands

Published in paperback in 2026 by
Haymarket Books
P.O. Box 180165
Chicago, IL 60618
773-583-7884
www.haymarketbooks.org

ISBN: 979-8-88890-789-4

Distributed to the trade in the US through Consortium Book Sales and
Distribution (www.cbsd.com) and internationally through Ingram Publisher
Services International (www.ingramcontent.com).

This book was published with the generous support of Lannan Foundation,
Wallace Action Fund, and the Marguerite Casey Foundation.

Special discounts are available for bulk purchases by organizations and
institutions. Please call 773-583-7884 or email info@haymarketbooks.org for more
information.

Cover design by Jamie Kerry and Ragina Johnson.

Printed in the United States.

Library of Congress Cataloging-in-Publication data is available.

In memory of my Brooklyn born working class father, Phil Restivo (1901–1985), a second-generation Sicilian, who taught me to embrace reality fearlessly, and who lived his teaching to the very end. He was not a believer. And in memory of my mother Mafalda Volpicelli Restivo (1915–2003), born in Calabria, Italy and renamed "May" by Ellis Island officials, Her unconditional love overrode her untutored Catholic beliefs and provided a scaffolding for my fearless embrace of reality. Favorite quotes: "I'm number one;" but: "I will do anything for my family" (Phil). "What does the Pope know" (May). Somehow, my "Catholic" family got the impression that Pope Paul VI had said it was ok to eat meat on Friday (not quite, but my mother didn't care).

∴

Civilizations die from suicide, not from murder.
ARNOLD TOYNBEE

∴

Contents

PART 3
Evolution, Culture, and Survival Wisdom

PART 4
Paradigm for Transition

Acknowledgments

A graduate student once said that arguing with me was like arguing with a brick wall. That brick wall was the critical realism demanded by the natural order. It's true that after a certain point it was difficult for people to break through that wall. It was possible, but you had to be extraordinary. The philosopher Cliff Hooker was one of the first people I learned new and interesting things from once I was inside my brick wall. His influence on my critical realism is everywhere in this book. The physicist David Bohm sat across from me in my living room and we taught each other physics and causality, but not symmetrically; he was a master of literate quantum mechanics and relativity theory and a dialectically sophisticated, Marx inspired, investigator of causality. Randall Collins, friend and sometime collaborator, and Mary Douglas in her writings and face-to-face taught me about the ubiquity of rituals and their function in our emotional lives. Donald Campbell, friend and champion, introduced me to the mysteries of methods. Everett Rogers shared his thoughts on communication in theory and in practice with me over numerous dinners. Joseph Needham combined a profound reservoir of scholarship across the intellectual spectrum with a kindness and generosity that fueled our years of conversations about the history of Chinese science and politics. My contributions to the sociology of the brain and mind owe an enormous debt to the writings of and my friendship with Leslie Brothers. Jean Paul Van Bendegem, a philosopher with his head and feet firmly planted on planet Earth, has been a friend, teacher, and collaborator since he met me at the airport in Brussels in 1984, microphone and tape recorder in hand. I am indebted to other Belgian friends and colleagues, notably Rik Pinxten, Bart Van Kerkhove, Karen François, Michéle Pieters (a dream and a nightmare), Michael Byrnes and Tamara Van Hahn. The theologian Nancey Murphy has challenged but not overcome my spiritual wickedness and she has done this with love and humor. I can say the same for my friends in the ministry, Peter Denton and Sarah Voss. I am obliged at every opportunity to thank my teachers, mentors, and educators for showing me the pathway to meaning and value in a senseless universe: Marie Delio, Mr. Sanders, James Quinn, Aaron Noland ("I am a Proudhon man"), Bernard Rosenberg, Leo Hamalian, Burt Aginsky, and John Useem. They were aided in this respect by my friends and colleagues in the Science for the People and Radical Science Movements, notably Rita Arditti, Jerry Ravetz, Les Levidow, and Hilary and Steven Rose. I owe am also indebted in various ways to feminist theorists Donna Haraway, Elizabeth Fee, Leone Burton, and Evelyn Fox Keller. David Bloor provoked and Mario Bunge, Dirk Struik, and Chandler

Davis encouraged my explorations in the sociology of mathematics. That work led to enduring friendships and collaborations with my graduate student in Lisbon, Monica Mesquita, and ethnomathematics founder Ubi D'Ambrosio. Nick Mullins, Daryl Chubin, Karin Knorr-Cetina, and Steve Woolgar helped shape my early career trajectory in science and technology studies with friendship, advice and tolerance. I am also grateful to feminist sociologist and my companion for twenty years Julia Loughlin, my students Jennifer Croissant, Wenda Bauchspies, Sabrina Weiss, Rachel Dowty, and Colin Beech, and for entirely different reasons Natalie DiPaolo, Susan Kagan, Marilynn Sue Jones, Jennifer Verlander, and Emily Juliano; Michelle of Moose Jaw and the ladies of the rails; and Louisa Earp and the ladies of the road. And for my "foster daughters" Lia and Katie. Among those scholars who continue to teach me I am privileged to name Jens Egede Høyrup and Lewis Pyenson. My RPI friends and colleagues Linnda Caporael, Ellen Esrock, and Langdon Winner also influenced my thoughts on mind, brain, and technology. As ever, my sons David and Daniel continue to educate me, as do my siblings Emily and Nancy. And finally, special thanks to Lorena Valentin for her help in preparing the manuscript for this book for final submission. This acknowledgement reflects a slogan I introduced in my study of Einstein's brain; give me a genius and I will show you a social network. The more general slogan applicable here is; give me an individual and I will show you a social network. In a deeply profound sense, I am my social network.

Preface

Speciations in weird urban habitats, viruses chasing hosts around the globe, and the greatest challenge life on Earth has faced for two million years: this is the fascinating and sobering ecology of the Anthropocene. Rebecca Wragg Sykes, author of *Kindred*.

> 2020: from the book's backmatter

∴

Merriam Webster's word of the year for 2023 was "Authenticity." Editor Peter Sokolowski said 2023 represented a crisis of authenticity. This is one indication for why this is a critical time to turn our attention to safeguarding truth. The importance of safeguarding truth is different today because our very existence as a species depends on our ability to identify and try to develop solutions to the multiplying existential threats that threaten human life and the planetary ecology. Humanity is well into the Anthropocene (bracketing controversies for the moment), the proposed new geological epoch. This epoch is defined by human pressures that have put the Earth on a trajectory moving rapidly away from the stable Holocene state of the past 12,000 years. This is the epoch that has sustained the life of humanity as we know it. Rapid changes to our planet are undermining the critical life-support systems that crystallized in the Holocene. Significant societal impacts of these changes are already being felt, and they could lead to triggering tipping points that irreversibly destabilize humanity and the Earth. These changes are mostly driven by social and economic systems run on unsustainable resource extraction and irrational consumption patterns. The consequences of changes in the planetary ecology vary greatly across social groups and countries. Given these interdependencies between inclusive human development and a stable and resilient Earth, an assessment of safe and just boundaries is required that accounts for planetary resilience and human well-being in an integrated framework (Rockstrom, Gupta, et al., 2023: 102).

1   Contemporary Science Denial: The Context

Science denial is not new. For centuries germ theory had to contend with the idea that poisonous vapors in the air caused disease (miasma theory). Percivall Potts discovered a link between chimney sweeping and lung cancer in the late

1770s but it took more than a century to overcome resistance to coal reforms. In the 1840s, Semmelweis' hygienic practices (e.g., hand washing) and contagion concepts were resisted in some hospitals. In 1904, the introduction of a mandatory vaccination law in Brazil aimed at the working poor caused public riots protesting government control. In the modern period, the history of tobacco has a claim on giving us the basic paradigm for science denial. And if we wanted to pinpoint the most recent instance of science denial we need only look to the disregard of science during the COVID-19 pandemic.

The tobacco denial and disinformation campaign came in the wake of an era of science heroics. Physicists were among the heroes in the defeat of the Nazis; DuPont gave us "better things for better living through chemistry;" General Electric scientists and engineers "brought good things to life." These were more than mere slogans in a post-War world measurably improving lives through science and technology. What's different about the 21st century is the convergence of post-truthism, an ideology of alternative facts, and outright lies as part of the political toolkit of populist and authoritarian politicians. They have mobilized a pathological version of "freedom" to market their fascist policies. The result is a virulent form of science denial that has provoked an emerging genre of books defending science. These books are written by authors from a variety of disciplinary backgrounds and rather than thinking of them as competitors I prefer to think of them as a science defending bloc, all of them reinforcing the defense against the attacks on science, reason, objectivity and truth. The bloc is divided according to whether the authors are focused on documenting existential threats (e.g., Vox, Ord, and Anderson) or on the specific defense of science (e.g., Goddard and Dalgleish, Kakutani, Jackson and Jamieson, and McIntyre). Among the most prominent authors in the existential threat section of this bloc are historian Lisa Vox (2017), philosopher Ord (2020), and risk management consultant David Anderson (2018). The science defenders are medical professionals such as the contributors to Goddard and Dalgleish (2023), literary critic Michiko Kakutani (2018), the journalist and communications professor collaborators Brook Jackson and Kathleen Hall Jamieson (2007), and notably philosopher Lee McIntyre (2015; 2018; 2019; 2021). Keeping my own aims in mind, I am especially interested in the science defenders.

Goddard and Dalgleish (2023: 11–12) paint a dark picture of science "lying on its death bed" while an unbridled technology gallops forward led by artificial intelligence technologies that even its developers can't explain. Science denial is blamed on complacency and the rapid spread of fake news and propaganda via social media. This has led to the dangerous idea that all ideas are equally valid. This idea is often linked to simplistic notions of freedom of speech. Science is tied to a business model that runs on the profit motive; it is viewed as a lower form of thinking by comparison with the arts and literature; and it is considered corrupted by the ideology of political correctness and the dictates of managerial principles. The result is a brain drain of scientists from areas like medicine to the arms industry. And there are reasons for science denial at the individual level such as the pursuit of pleasure and ambition. The crises of science denial can be avoided only by rekindling a passion for science, fostering science literacy, and ensuring that policymaking is based on scientific consensus. The real change has to be at the collective level, a change in society and culture and the social form of science.

Science itself has been burdened by a lack of good science in health care, climatology, cosmology, and other areas. The medical science perspective that drives the arguments in Goddard and Dalgleish (2023) sees the solution to science denial in better science and "good, nuanced argument." Life is a matter of varying greys not black and white choices: "At times we must embrace the order but at other times, the chaos." The authors also recommend writing letters to editors to voice opposition to science deniers (Goddard and Dagleish, 2023: 333). The recommended solutions tend to be individually based and not guided by a robust sociological imagination. This is the basic flaw in the arguments to save science we get from physical and natural scientists, philosophers, journalists, and humanity scholars.

Jackson and Jamieson (2007: vii) open their book by announcing "We live in a world of spin ... Millions are deceived every day, buying products, voting for candidates, supporting policies and even wars – all because of spin ... a polite word for deception." They conclude their introduction by quoting the late senator from New York, Daniel Patrick Moynihan: "You are entitled to your opinion. But you are *not* entitled to your own *facts*." Following the usual path in books protecting science and truth, documenting various lies, falsehoods, and deceptions across our culture, their proposal for staying "UnSpun" is this: "When confronted with a claim, keep an open mind, ask questions, cross check, look for the best information, and then weigh the evidence; ... Respect facts" (Jackson and Jamieson, 2007: 179, 184). Again, the lack of a sociological imagination leads them to put the onus for protecting science and truth on the individual's assumed capacity for reasoning things through. The problem is that our sense of what reason is comes to us through the voices of our cultural leaders and institutions, leaving us at the mercy of their power to define the nature and limits of reason, of science, of objectivity, and of truth. We are a nation in which we have relegated the intellectual reins of leadership in the world of ideas to our journalists. While many of them have PhDs, their arguments tend to rely on clever, catchy writing in small bites. And those with academic credentials tend to veil them in a misguided effort to avoid the "egg head" label. Philosophers can be more profound but they too tend to victimize their readers with clever catchy writing in bigger bites. Clever catchy writing tends to be weighed more heavily than the factual grounds of arguments by our more prestigious authors and publishers. What kind of peer review, for example, allowed Christian philosopher Alvin Plantinga (2000: 207–208) to publish a book with Oxford University Press in which he claims that "the doctrine of original sin ... has been verified in the wars, cruelty and general hatefulness that have characterized human history from its very inception to the present?" This kind of "academic freedom" (if that's what it is; see Van Bendegem's explanation in Restivo, 2024: 102–103) actually contributes to science denial.

Americans don't have time for serious robust science based scholarship. It should not come as a surprise that Pulitzer Prize journalist Michiko Kakutani's *The Death of Truth* (2018) was a *New York Times* bestseller published with endorsements from our leading magazines and newspapers (e.g., *Rolling Stone, Esquire, the Financial Times*) and leading public intellectuals (e.g., Walter Isaacson, Fareed Zakaria). David Grann of the *New Yorker* said her book was "destined to become the defining treatise of our age" (front cover endorsement on the paperback edition).

Kakutani's citing circle comes mainly from news sources, novelists (e.g., Margaret Atwood), and a scattering of public intellectuals (e.g., Jean Baudrillard, Stanley Fish). Her writing is bold, accessible, and has the pugilistic elegance of a Muhammad Ali. She begins (Kakutani, 2018: 11) by defining our contemporary cultural Trumpian landscape as one of the two "most monstrous regimes in human history," the other one being that of the Nazis. The defining characteristic of these regimes, in the words of Hannah Arendt (1972: 474), is a "people for whom the distinction between fact and fiction (i.e., the reality of experience) and the distinction between true and false (i.e., the standards of thought) no longer exist."

Donald Trump is at the center of the contemporary discourse on science denial, but our age of unreason has earlier markers in history near and far. I've already noted some historical examples of science denial. Science denial in our near pre-Trump history was documented by Susan Jacoby (2008: 307). She traced the descent of reason into infotainment addiction, religious fundamentalism, the popular notion that intellectualism was liberal and at odds with traditional values, and an educational system that "does a poor job of teaching not only basic skills but the logic underlying those skills."

Kakutani then gives us an account of the new culture wars, the world of "moi" and the rise of subjectivity, the vanishing of reality in a world where it has become difficult to tell the difference between satirical *Onion* headlines and CNN headlines, a world in which "surreal" and "chaos" are "invoked hourly by journalists trying to describe daily reality in America" (Kakutani, 2018: 77). Language is co-opted to spread distrust, discord, and tribalism. Technology is harnessed to the process of undermining objectivity, and we find ourselves in a world dominated by propaganda and fake news. She concludes her final chapter, "The Schadenfreude of the Trolls" by essentially blaming our age of science denial on postmodernism, a claim that underlines the way relativism promoted alternative facts as a way of adding to the conversation and the deep nihilism of deconstruction. From this perspective, postmodernism lays down and lights up a path to believing that reason is outdated. Its earlier function as an antidote to the hypocrisy and smugness of the 1950s world of TV's *Leave it to Beaver* had, from my perspective, been paved over by its lower sensibilities. Postmodern irony became our environment (Kakutani, 2018: 160–163). In the end, Kakutani puts her faith in "commonly agreed-upon facts;" With her last words she returns us to our founders, Jefferson (the young republic assumed that we could be governed by reason and truth) and Madison (government of the people requires popular information without which government is a prologue to farce or tragedy or both): "Without truth democracy is hobbled" (Kakutani, 2018: 173). And so we are left with erudition and insight, but very little substance in terms of policies for structural change. But this book helps to raise our collective awareness of the dangerous era we are living in politically.

Of all the authors under consideration, McIntyre is the most familiar with the social sciences. McIntyre's books on reality and science deniers, including *On Disinformation: How to Fight for Truth and Protect Democracy* (2023; and 2015, 2018, 2021), are important parts of the defense of science bloc. *On Disinformation* offers individual and governmental strategies for defending science, from resisting polarization to pressuring our Congress to regulate social media – as well as the important steps a rightly elected government must take. The approach is more notable for raising consciousness than for the profundity of its proposed solutions. His earlier book, *The Scientific Attitude* is less impressive and the one I focus on here.

McIntyre is a philosopher and historian to conjure with. But it takes him only 20 pages (McIntyre, 2019: 20) to demonstrate the sociological poverty of his philosophy by linking social construction and the sociology of science to relativists and postmodernists responsible for allegedly dismantling the rationality and truth telling of science. This is itself a kind of science denial, a denial of the empirical findings of the sociologists and anthropologists of science who have demonstrated in ethnographic detail the actual practices of the sciences. These practices do not match the non-empirical idealist philosophies of science as a self-correcting autonomous system uncovering the secrets of an unseen reality, reality in itself. Science doesn't work this way in practice but the way it works in practice does lead to fallible, corrigible, tentative truths with practical implications.

McIntyre makes another common mistake. He assumes science is made by fallible humans whose biases contaminate science. And he "understands" that science is an institution and assumes that human biases are corrected at the institutional level. But he doesn't look to the sociologists for a perspective on scientific knowledge as a "public possession," but to philosopher Helen Longino (1990: 74) who actually gets the words right but not the concept: "Objectivity ... is a characteristic of a community of practice ...," from which McIntyre (2019: 90, 112) draws a. psychological conclusion: it is "fidelity to the scientific attitude as community practice that makes science special as an institution;" "science is more objective as an institution than its practitioners" In a sense, he "corrects" the myth of the individual scientist with the myth of the individual institution. What he doesn't understand is that institutions are subject to biases too, arising for example from professionalization and bureaucratization. In fact, the science of the present is corrected by way of the intersubjective testing over historical time by generationally linked networks of scientists and their collaborating inquirers. His criticisms of the science in sociology are carried out as in similar philosophical contexts by ignoring the best and most scientifically robust sociology of practitioners like Randall Collins and Dalton Conley. I will come back to this in later chapters.

McIntyre's approach to the problem of science denial is to help the reader understand science. He devotes most of his time to lecturing the reader on what science is but does this in a way that is not helpful because his approach is a philosophy of science that eschews the sociology of science and the sociological imagination. Trump is once again at the center of our troubles in this book. The book's subtitle shows his aim: Defending Science from Denial, Fraud, and Pseudoscience. The utility of the book is that it brings out the community practice nature of science. But this is offset by a sociologically flawed understanding of what this means, limiting the usefulness of the book as a guide to a more reasoned political future. Nonetheless, I would include it in my bloc for its defense, however flawed, of science.

My book has a distinct advantage compared to McIntyre's writings and other contributions in this emerging market. First, I bring an unusually interdisciplinary perspective to the issues. I was originally trained in electrical engineering, theoretical physics, and mathematics; my PhD is in sociology with a strong anthropological emphasis (and with specializations in social psychology and historiography). My sociology is radically interdisciplinary, classically rooted in the works of Karl Marx, Peter Kropotkin, Nietzsche, Gumplowicz, and Emile Durkheim and in the modern contributions of, among others, W.E.B. DuBois,

Peter Berger, C. Wright Mills, Dorothy Smith, Emma Goldman, Mary Douglas, and Randall Collins. Second, I draw attention to the widely misunderstood or ignored relevance of the social sciences to our problems.

It is hard for me to imagine many people who could have written or wanted to write this book. I associate my book with E.O. Wilson's works (2012, 2014, 2016) and perhaps Bernie Sanders (2023). We continue to rely on technological fix strategies that assume all of our problems can be solved by technology, or by physics. Widely touted and funded STEM programs are just another technological fix strategy. Finally, I bring half a century of empirical and theoretical research on science and scientific practice to my project.

This book is the work of an angry old man. It's not the kind of anger that raises your blood pressure. It's a more stoic anger, one bathed in the soothing salve of Marcus Aurelius' (121–180CE) observation that we were born for better things. It is the work of a man who has spent a lifetime trying to figure things out only to find himself on the edge of being cast unceremoniously into an endless void no more enlightened than he was when he was unceremoniously dragged out of that void more than 80 years ago. And for good reason. Everything we humans have achieved has been for naught in the long run. Nothing will survive time, not even time (even if only for a time before another "Big Bang" occurs). But I have found myself playing a game within a small arena of space and time in a small corner of the universe that has lit up my life. And I find myself playing this ultimately but not immediately meaningless game to the very end in this book. Given this context, my time might have been better spent playing music and having as much sex as possible.

It is an indictment of "the rational animal," *homo sapiens*, that I have had to write two books in the 21st century to demonstrate why religion is real and god is not. I am tired of the reign of stupidity in Washington and in governments around the world. I.F. Stone (MacPherson, 2006) warned us that all governments lie and none should ever be believed. I am tired of the glorification of entrepreneurship, professionalism, productivity, and the rule of money in a world being destroyed by the ideology of capitalism. Capitalism is the economy that never was, isn't, and never will be; see Chapter 10. Why do so many people need life coaches? Why are there so many people who want to be life coaches. Why is everyone acting as if it's perfectly normal for billions of dollars (precious natural and human resources) to be used for war machines most of which will never be used? Why does a lack of compassion for living, breathing human beings guide politics, the economy, and everyday life? What's fueling the rampant Floridian ignorance about education and science? Of course education and science are liberal, left wing, radical, and after all anarchism should be the ordinary language of politics and scieince.

Our species does not seem to be able to keep its noses out of each other's business or to stifle being offended by everything from sexual choices to food preferences. That's understandable on one level; we are a radically social species. But we are a petty, fearful species and we have taken monitoring each other to hellish levels. I have a job for the coaches: lighten up and teach others to lighten up. We are an existential threat to each other. We need to stop giving political power to people who claim that stripping women of rights is more important than political gains, or that abortion is evil, or that the Constitution established a Christian nation. That cultural evolution has damaged our potential for reason and critical realism is evident every day in the antics of our politicians, and the failure of Americans to see the virtues in our flawed but still brilliant Constitution. Some parts of the world are doing better. But they are threatened by a rampant pandemic of know-nothingness and a hunger for masters and gods.

2   Interlude: How Bad Are Things Really?

2.1 *Wake Up and Smell Eternity*

A POEM, inspired by *L'art de guillotiner les procréateurs: Manifeste anti-nataliste*, T. de Giraud (2006)

> Ode to de Giraud
> Hear ye Hear ye cried the voices of old
> puncture, cut, break up and fold
> Ice is better once it melts
> better if it were something else
> if it had chosen never to be frozen
> 冰之凝，不若其釋也，又況不為冰乎
> "The condensation of ice is not as good as its release,
> let alone ice."
> Did Buddha too embrace the Tao?
> Did he too insist that we desist?
> That when you see a birth in mind be kind,
> Inclined to what can be foreseen?
> Then bring the guillotine ...
> to Act One of the last scene ...
> Time to end the celebration
> for the act of procreation
> Let freedom ring and voices sing

We light the last cocktail
hoping darkness will avail
the Tao to end and to prevail.

I am overwhelmed in these waning years by the absolute futility of life, even of a life well-lived. At the same time, I have been driven all my life to Diogenes' lamp like a moth to the flame of virtue, truth, and reason, to science. And this book is the last hurrah of the kind of human being Diogenes was searching for.

3   Why It's Important That a Sociologist Is Writing This Book

This is a very personal book that is rooted in a lifetime of a variety of experiences, studies and thoughts that go beyond any discipline. And yet, since I discovered sociology in college, it has invaded every aspect of my life. I am, like many sociology students of my generation, imbued with the sociological imagination expressed in the writings of C.Wright Mills. In a 1956 letter to Harry and Bette Swados, he described himself as "a goddamned anarchist" (Mills, 1959/2000: 232). The relationship between the sociological imagination and anarchism already shows up in Kropotkin's mutual aid anarchism. This is part of the reason anarchism will inevitably emerge as my chapters unfold.

That aside, the importance of sociology has recently been expressed in the response of American Sociological Association president Joya Misra's (2024) reply to Florida's elimination of sociology from the university core curriculum. The sociological imagination is the key to linking personal experiences to societal forces and historical trends. For example, losing your job isn't a personal failure but a function of the business cycle (e.g., waves of unemployment due to recessions). Sociologists can help to identify the causes of catastrophes and strategies for avoiding them in the future. Their research has helped identify ways to support people with breast cancer, demonstrated that jobs with unpredictable schedules are a health hazard, that homicide rates tend to increase as inequality grows, and shown how to create more inclusive workplace cultures. The Medical College Admission Test emphasizes sociological concepts because it's important for doctors to have the means to engage effectively with their patients.

Moreover, to extend Dr. Misra's remarks, sociology has notably advanced our knowledge of the nature and foundations of reason, science, belief, mathematics, logic, and objectivity, the most fundamental grounds which give us access to sociological knowledge and to scientific knowledge in general. There are reasons for sociology's history as a thorn in the sides of ruling elites. It has a

tendency to de-bunk, de-mystify, and de-mythify. In addition, there is an anarchist agenda at its core that makes it difficult or impossible to defend individualism and free will. Consider Mills (1959/2000: 6–7) list of questions prompted
by the sociological imagination:

1. What is the structure of this particular society as a whole? What are
   its essential components, and how are they related to one another?
   How does it differ from other varieties of social order? Within it, what
   is the meaning of any particular feature for its continuance and for its
   change. ... for the development of humanity as a whole?
2. How does any particular feature we are examining affect, and how
   is it affected by, the historical period in which it moves? And this
   period – what are its essential features? How does it differ from other
   periods? What are its characteristic ways of history-making?
3. What varieties of men and women now prevail in this society and in
   this period? And what varieties are coming to prevail? In what ways
   are they selected and formed, liberated and repressed, made sensitive and blunted? What kinds of human natures are revealed in the
   conduct and character we observe in this society in this period? And
   what is the meaning for human nature of each and every feature of
   the society we are examining?

The sociological imagination requires that we distinguish between personal
troubles of milieu and public issues of social structure (Mills, 1959/2000: 10).
Our experiences in various and specific milieus can often be traced to structural changes. The sociologist is tasked with translating "personal troubles into
public issues, and public issues into the terms of their human meaning for a
variety of individuals" (Mills, 1959/2000: 187). The sociological imagination
promises the realization of the values of truth, reason, and freedom: "The role
of reason in human affairs and the idea of the free individual as the seat of
reason are the most important themes inherited by twentieth-century social
scientists from the philosophers of the Enlightenment" (Mills, 1959/2000: 167).
Freedom does not mean "free will" or the capacity to do anything you wish at
any time independent of the social and cultural forces operating at the intersection of personality, biography, history, and society: "Within an individual's
biography and within a society's history, the social task of reason is to formu-
late choices, to enlarge the scope of human decisions in the making of history"
(Mills, 1959: 174). On realizing the anarchist promise of the sociological imagination see Rafael (2018).

About the Path of This Book

Science and the academy are used to clear, linear, logical lines of theses and arguments. These have proven to be the best forms of theses and arguments for solving problems in a rational context. However, these forms eventually become routinized – the routinization of rationalities – and increasingly useless in the face of novel non-linear events. By the middle of the 20th century, issues and problems in science were becoming increasingly complex and scientists found it necessary to rely more and more on non-linear, fractal, and chaotic methodologies and mathematics. The transition from routine methods and mathematics required a certain loosening of the canons of rigor. This is the case for the narrative I am about to unfold. We will be entering a world of problems where the routinization of rationalities is breaking down the power of reason to deal with increasingly non-linear and chaotic existential threats. We are obliged therefore to set out on this journey with the expectation that we will not always be able to find our way by sticking to conventional linear canons of narrative. We can still count on them but we will find it hard to avoid non-linear and chaotic pathways. This is also a consequence of the multiple audiences this book is addressed to. It is designed primarily for academic audiences oriented to critical sociological theory. The narrative, however, is relatively open to more public audiences. It also provides guidelines for academics who wish to reach wider audiences on contemporary existential threats.

Overture

The World Economic Forum (WEF) surveyed 1,490 risk experts worldwide from September 4 to October 9, 2023. Of those surveyed, almost two-thirds said they expected an elevated chance of global catastrophes in the next decade. About 30% said they expect the same in the next two years. The experts identified disinformation as the most severe risk over the next two years, followed by extreme weather events. Over the next decade, environmental concerns are at the forefront. The top five risks are extreme weather events, critical change to Earth systems, biodiversity loss and ecosystem collapse, natural resource shortages, and misinformation and disinformation (Dienes, 2024a).

> I told you so. You damned fools.
> H.G. WELLS

PART 1

The Sociology of Reality

..

CHAPTER 1

A World of Post-truths, Lies and Alternative Facts

Strands of anti-intellectualism and anti-science are not new in America or the world at large. But, with our focus on American society, there are moments that stand out and grab our attention and we rational ones think: Oh oh! Something is afoot. Staying within the time of my own memory, one of those moments was the 1950s. Richard Hofstadter (1963: 3) wrote:

> During that decade the term anti-intellectualism, only rarely heard before, became a familiar part of our national vocabulary of self-recrimination and intramural abuse. In the past, American intellectuals were often discouraged or embittered by the national disrespect for mind, but it is hard to recall a time when large numbers of people outside the intellectual community shared their concern, or when self-criticism on this count took on the character of a nation-wide movement.

McCarthyism brought home the fact that the critical mind in American culture had reached a "ruinous discount." Intellectuals weren't McCarthy's only target but they were "in the line of fire." On January 22, 2017, we witnessed another moment in this history, one that in the context of a "regime of post truth" (Harsin, 2015) and the election of Donald J. Trump to the American presidency was more momentous. The background for this moment was the new White House press secretary Sean Spicer's first press conference on January 21st. Spicer claimed that Trump's inaugural ceremony had drawn the largest inauguration audience ever witnessed in person and worldwide. Aerial imagery and D.C. Metro police statistics demonstrated that Spicer's claim was patently and visually false. The next day Trump's counselor Kellyanne Conway was challenged by *Meet the Press* host Chuck Todd on Spicer's provably false statement. Her reply raised visions of Orwell's *1984* and the concept of doublethink: Spicer, she said, was giving "alternative facts." Some of us could already see that Spicer, Conway, and especially Trump were revealing the vulnerabilities of our limited and fragile democracy.

The emergence of an era of alternative facts, notably in America, should not have been surprising. We have a history of anti-intellectualism. The historian Richard Hofstadter told this story in 1963 when he documented American Protestantism's value of spirit over intellectualism. Unlike their European cousins, Americans have a history of resenting the life of the mind. They have sung the praises of the common man with a sound and fury that has drowned out science and reason. The learned class has been portrayed as "immoral, dangerous, and subversive." In 1962, columnist Stewart Alsop introduced the word "eggheads" which Republicans began to toss at presidential candidate Adlai Stevenson and the intellectuals and professors who supported him. Senator Eugene McCarthy was called a "sardonic intellectual" in 1968. By the time Nixon reached office, his vice president Spiro Agnew was feeding on "egg-head" steroids and transforming it into "nattering nabobs of negativity." This epithet was widely interpreted to apply to journalists but Norman Lewis (2010) argued that it was meant for Nixon's political enemies. But the anti-intellectual tone was certainly not impossible to hear given Agnew's cognitive credentials. And 1972 Presidential hopeful George Wallace blamed America's problems on "pointy-headed intellectuals."

There may have been moments in American political life when something like a positive view of the life of the mind had its day. Even Pat Robertson, the conservative Christian politico, boasted about his Yale law degree. Mario Cuomo stood on his "bookish learning," Jack Kemp was an "idea" man, Gary Hart was the "new ideas" politician, and Jeane Kirkpatrick's reputation as a "steely-willed intellectual" was a political asset. Some politicians readily and publicly called on support from "think tanks." These episodes are blips in a history that does not raise the life of the mind above the hymns to the common man and at worst supports a common denominator citizenship paradigm. And if you have any questions about this follow the money. How much money and support do we provide for teachers and schools and how much for athletics and entertainment? How much for bread, and how much for circuses? Our educational system needs a complete overhaul as part of the process of addressing the existential threats of our time.

The most difficult problem America has to face, in a sense, is leaving childish things behind when it comes to religion. They are already being left behind not only by their European counterparts but by the theologians and religious leaders themselves. Our general abilities to confront the existential threats to our species and our planet will not be up to the task if we continue to live as if it is not simply 1776 or 1791 but 1500.

1   The Post-truth Regime

The term "regime of post-truth" entered our vocabulary in 2015 (Harsin, 2015). The term encompassed many aspects of post-truth politics and captured a shift from regimes of truth to regimes of post-truth. We now began to hear once again about "truth markets" (Foucault, 1976/1997: 145):

> Each society has its regime of truth, its 'general politics of truth.' That is, the types of discourse which it accepts and makes function as true; the mechanisms and instances which enable one to distinguish true and false statements, the means by which each is sanctioned; the techniques and procedures accorded value in the acquisition of truth; the status of those who are charged with saying what counts as true.

Regimes of truth circulate through the controlling machinery of cultural institutions (academic, religious, economic, political, military, media, and information). References to regimes of post-truth, like references to post-industrial, post-modern, and post-capitalist reflect the growing awareness that conventional regimes of rationality are no longer functioning as effective foundations for problem solving. I speak here of the "routinization of rationality." Liminal eras are characterized by the routinization of rationality(ies) and the decline in the efficacy of conventional categories and classifications. This is a recurring feature of history in motion, and such eras are characterized by the loosening of canons of logic and reason which permits the proliferation of new strategies for renewing categories, classifications, and rationalities capable of dealing with a new realm of issues and problems. Most students of our post-truth era have relied on a narrow explanatory framework that at its widest point goes back as far as the 1600s and the breakdown of the Westphalian order. But as recurring intellectual strategies, post-truth regimes are ubiquitous throughout civilized history.

From a historical perspective, post-truthism is only new in terms of depth and scope. It was characteristic of political and media practices in eighteenth and nineteenth century America (Pazzanese, 2016). "Pamphlet wars" of the 1600s and thereafter represented a kind of material Internet propelled by printing technologies. Slander and vitriol traveled easily and fomented dissent, wars, and revolutions. Its resurrection around the world in contemporary society must be attributed in part to the globalization of an out-of-control "information" system driven by the Internet.

America's anti-intellectual tradition nourishes "fake news." Internationally, cynicism about the political process has made a mockery of politics, a process already underway in the post-war period (Londsdale, 1957). Facts, understood properly and in context, nourish our survival, feed our curiosity, form a dynamic, dialectically and paradoxically flexible concrete foundation on which we build, mobilize, and use the tools, technologies, techniques, and cognitive devices we require to solve problems of every type we encounter in our lives, in our history, on our planet. An increasingly substantial segment of the world's population, with America leading the way, has morphed rational skepticism into an irrational skepticism, rational freedom from unbridled authority into an irrational defense of absolute freedom. This has been done under the umbrella of the myth of individualism. The "people" have had enough of experts, and have come to view facts as negative, pessimistic, and unpatriotic (Deacon, 2016).

Post-truthers live off and spread conspiracies (Boston, 2016). Examples of how conspiracism breeds violence have become all too common, notably in America (Kang and Goldman, 2016). One of the pathologies of democratic thinking sometimes linked to the politics of freedom of speech is that everyone is entitled to an opinion. Every school room from pre-school to graduate school should have a flag emblazoned with Wittgenstein's (1922/1990: 189) last words in the *Tractatus*: "Whereof one cannot speak, thereof one must be silent."

What are the key factors at work in transforming cultures to post-truth regimes? They are part of the strategy of managing perceptions and beliefs in populations segmented by the dynamics of modern technological-industrial society: microtargeting (which relies in part on strategically using rumors and lies); the fragmentation of media and media gatekeepers in an economy of information overload and acceleration, user-generated content, and the collapse of a core of societal authorities entrusted with monitoring the borders that separate truths from falsehoods. We can encapsulate these developments within two terms: tabloidization (Esser, 1999) and infotainment. This is not simply a matter of post-truth politics but a regime of post-truth.

Our contemporary situation has publicized the problems of mis- and disinformation. Little or no attention has been given to the problem of "over-information," of the "over-informed" society. Our social media access technologies from iPhones, iPads, and computers to TVs and paper media flood us daily with information from disparate sources from across the world. This flood of information from the sciences, humanities, and arts and from legitimate sources with legitimate aims to intentional and unintentional deceivers overwhelms our conventional filters, which vary from fine-grained to coarse cross cultural categories such as class, ethnicity, and gender. My seventh grade teacher in 1953 was able to demonstrate the meaning and nature of ideological perspectives on contemporary events simply by holding up copies of the New York Times front page coverage of President Truman firing General MacArthur (April 11, 1951) side by side with copies of coverage of the event in the New York and Chicago tabloids. Today, the variety of ideologies and information overload make the task of teaching young people and adults how to separate what is true from what is false in a timely manner practically impossible. This is compounded by the fact that truth and falsity have been pluralized by the two-prongs of postmodernism – the one prong exposing the practical complexities of truth telling, the other prong facilitating the relativistic demolition of the very possibility of truth telling.

We cannot leave out the consequences of the anti-democratic anti-American activities of foreign private and public agents (Pomerantsev, 2015, 2019; Drezner, 2016). We are living in an age of misinformation where everyone feels equally qualified to make claims. The situation is exacerbated by the fact that a survey industry is constantly asking people their opinions about everything from "Do you think O.J. is guilty?" to "Do you approve of the president's economic policies?" The problem is that we don't associate the people we ask with any information about their credibility. The anti-expert mongers see this in distorted "power to the people" terms. But they have different standards depending on the context and frame of reference for the questions. Everyone is entitled to express an opinion about O.J.Simpson's guilt or innocence; and we'll even ask public opinion questions about pandemic policies. But we wouldn't base our own actions regarding open heart surgery on public opinion, although I'm sure some people will seek second opinions from family, friends, and quacks.

So we encourage opinions and not studied, educated, fact based statements. Many of my students considered their opinions about sociology and even about my specialties equal in value to my own. In America, more than anywhere else, an anti-intellectual cultural predisposition combined with the distortion of the principle of free speech into the slogan "everyone is entitled to h/her own opinion" has produced a least common denominator school system. This is as much to blame for the emergence of a post-truth regime as any of the other factors I've mentioned. We are in an age of misinformation where limits of plausibility have vanished and where everyone feels equally qualified to make claims that are easily shared and propagated (Helfand, 2017).

Anti-intellectualism in America may seem like the foundation for the post-truth era. But in terms of our history, and in the context of a wider view of world history, we have always lived in a post-truth world. Steve Tesich, a Serbian-American playwright introduced the term "post-truth" in 1992. The new century became marked by post-truth messaging. Keyes (2004) introduced the term "post-truth era." In the wake of misleading statements by the post-9/11 Bush administration, Alterman (2004: 305) wrote about a "post-truth political environment" and "the post-truth presidency." Crouch (2004) used the term "post-democracy," an environment of public electoral politics managed by spin doctors. "Post-truth politics" looked like it was taking its lessons from the advertising business.

In 2016, the German Language Society named "postfaktisch" (post-factual) the word of the year. They followed many other journalistic and scholarly sources by linking it to the rise of right-wing populism. "Post-truth" was named Word of the Year in 2016 by the Oxford English Dictionary where it is defined as "Relating to or denoting circumstances in which objective facts are less influential in shaping public opinion than appeals to emotion and personal belief." Trump's election occurred in the midst of this troubling worldwide phenomenon. Already by the 1990s, the term "post-democracy" was showing up more and more in the writings of sociologists. There were examples of forged evidence and historical revisionism in India (Gopalakrishnan (2016). Snodgrass (2017) wrote about distrust of academics in South Africa. Arron Banks, founder of the Leave EU campaign in the UK, said that you had to learn from Trump's success and connect with people emotionally, not by relying on facts. Earlier I drew attention to I.F. Stone (MacPherson, 2006): "Every government is run by liars." This suggests something more pervasive and pernicious than what standard ideas about the "post-truth society" point to.

The United States historically has generated various forms of denialism. The modern forms include the anti-vaxxers, resistance to evolutionary theory and genetically modified foods, birtherism, climate change denialism, and the promulgation of dietary strategies and health products unregulated and with very little attention to expert counterevidence. In every case, counter-vailing factual evidence has been extensive and readily available.

Counter-vailing forces are coming "on-line." These include new and improved fact checking technologies, giving scientists more visibility, and state-led efforts to oppose fake news (which come with a dangerous potential for censorship). In March 2017, the United Nations Special Rapporteur on Freedom of Opinion and Expression, the Organization for Security and Cooperation in Europe, and the Organization for American States issued a Joint Declaration on "Freedom of Expression and Fake News, Disinformation and Propaganda" to warn against the effects of fake news but, at the same time, condemned any attempts at state-mandated censorship (United Nations, 2017).

As a philosophical and political concept the term *post-truth* is relatively recent. The concept can be traced back to earlier moral, epistemic, and political debates about relativism, postmodernity, and mendacity in politics, including untruthfulness, lies, deception, and deliberate falsehoods (Arendt, 1972). This perspective makes it possible to creates a false link to science and technology studies. In spite of its general alignment with the conventional principles of science, it did serve to complicate issues and problems around the manufacture of knowledge and the social construction of scientific facts. Post-truth writers who have identified Nietzsche as one of the chief fashioners of the concept fail to recognize that his arguments about the human creation of concepts anticipated the science studies movement. In his 1873 essay, "Truth and Lying in an Extra-Moral Sense," Nietzsche holds that humans create truths about the world through their use of metaphor, myth, and poetry. He writes,

> If someone hides an object behind a bush, then seeks and finds it there, that seeking and finding is not very laudable: but that is the way it is with the seeking and finding of "truth" within the rational sphere. If I define the mammal and then after examining a camel declare, "See, a mammal," a truth is brought to light, but it is of limited value. I mean, it is anthropomorphic through and through and contains not a single point that would be true and universally valid, apart from man. The investigator into such truths is basically seeking just the metamorphosis of the world into man; he is struggling to understand the world as a human-like thing and acquires at best a feeling of assimilation.

This, along with Marx and Durkheim on the social construction of facts, is less about a post-truth agenda and more about an emerging argument against purist and Platonic conceptions of science. Revealing the messy realities of scientific practice was taken by some careless observers to mean that science could not be trusted.

We also need to pay attention to the argument that facts and values are separate and distinct realms of experience, a position Max famously advocated in his essay on *Science as a Vocation* (1918/1946). The philosopher Leo Strauss (1965: 35–80) worried that if we accept Weber's viewpoint then we are left no way to evaluate scientific truths according to ethical standards. Strauss was too strong in his claim that Weber was trying to isolate reason from opinion. But he was right in arguing that the "ought" ought to be within reach of human reason. For somewhat different reasons, philosophers as different as Foucault, Derrida, and Latour express skepticism about the traditional division between facts and values.

Hannah Arendt (1972: 6–7) distinguished defactualization from falsehood and lying. She wrote (Arendt, 1972: 12):

> What these problem-solvers have in common with down-to-earth liars is the attempt to get rid of facts and the confidence that this should be possible because of the inherent contingency of facts.

Deception and self-deception are meaningless in a defactualized world which destroys the distinction between truth and falsehood. In a defactualized environment, the individual (Arendt, 1972: 36) "loses all contact with not only his audience, but also the real world, which will still catch up with him because he can remove his mind from it but not his body." The Vietnam era problem solvers led us to defactualization by "translating all factual contents into the language of numbers and percentages" and by being divorced from the facts of "given reality" (Arendt, 1972: 11, 18). They eagerly reduced factual reality to formulae "expressed in a pseudo-mathematical language." Her definition of post-truth did not rely on the triumph of emotions over facts and evidence. Defactualization identified hyper-rationality as the mechanism that blurred fact and fantasy.

Enter Steve Fuller (2018), the most prominent Science and Technology Studies (STS) scholar writing on post-truth. As an STS scholar, Fuller is especially well-placed to understand that putting "facts" in scare quotes is a recognition that facts are socially constructed, contextual, and networked. All this is fine, but Fuller's work is a "gonzo" melding of erudite philosophy, counter-narratives, and shocks to the social solar plexuses of elites. The empirical grounds of our critical and even radical understanding of social injustice and social inequality are overshadowed by self-indulgent philosophy seasoned with sociologisms and a self-righteous sense of having become king of the hill. To put this in less combative terms, he could be seen as standing at one end of a continuum that defines one axis in science studies, the one that has the late Bruno Latour as king of the hill at the other end. These opposite poles are both weakly charged and tend to collapse into each other.

Like Latour, Fuller is a self-styled "game changer" and what goes with that is active self-promoting, staking out of territory and ignoring like-minded thinkers. There is every reason not to put our full faith and promise in the hands of unquestioned authorities and experts, and this is a position Fuller exploits with all his might. He sees a "culture of intellectual deference" where I see "anti-intellectualism." The two can co-exist, but my position is that anti-intellectualism, certainly in the American context, is the proximate source of modern post-truthism, which is not new but has only become more public and more virulent. But there is a broader context for understanding post-truthism as I will show.

Fuller and I certainly agree that knowledge has an ethical component. I reach this point through the results of empirical studies by a community of researchers in science studies. Fuller knows and uses these same results but his path to enlightenment is through the philosopher Karl Popper and an Athenian concept of democracy. He boils down the debates about facts and values and facts and alternative facts to a conflict between technocrats and rhetoricians. Using the Brexit vote as a case study he argues like a good Athenian that the rhetoricians are more democratic; and of course it is democracy we should wish for. Skipping over all the erudition and Latourian word play, Fuller and I can agree that education is the key to achieving a common humanity. An academy with an interest in promoting the public good should be an academy that educates us in what we should desire (shades of Aristotle and Kant!). I will also skip over the relevance and accuracy of his Brexit case analysis, which is brought into question, for example, by Peter Mair (2013).

In what sounds like a variation on Latour's "we have never been modern," Fuller argues that "we have always been post-truth." If his intention is to argue that politics, like sex, is everywhere, he is at one with many thinkers over the centuries. And the more you read, the more Fuller sounds like the inventor of Plato 2.0. And without bulldozing all of the subtleties and complexities of ancient philosophy, it is precisely the adjective "ancient" that should worry us as we read Fuller. Because at the end of the day, he is a mirror image of Latour asking us to buy a good story and ironically given the way he trashes the academy give him a gold star for academic excellence.

Arguments about whether post-truth politics is here to stay or not (e.g., Fuller versus Hewitt, 2020) miss the point that post-truth eras are a recurring feature of history which consists of cycles of crystallizing, routinizing, and loosening canons of rationalities. Periods of routinization in which the strategic and survival values of conventional categories and classifications begin to fail enliven a proliferation of innovative candidates for a new configuration of rationality, a new order of categories and classifications. This is rarely a wholesale revolution but comes close to that in liminal times. Liminal times require paradigm shifts, changes in worldviews. Such times give birth necessarily to post-truth regimes as segments of post-rationality regimes. The novel quality of our liminal era is that we face more and greater existential threats to humanity and planet Earth than at any time in the era of the human species. This helps explain the virulence of contemporary post-truth regimes.

Fuller's sociological pretensions are belied by the main sources he draws on which are inevitably philosophers. This tends to ground his already questionable ideas in philosophical fantasies rather than sociological realities. Societies do not "get used to" post-truth regimes and the routinization of rationalities. That is a pathway to civilizational decline and in our current state a path to a more rapid than necessary extinction. Populism and post-truth politics are not a pathway to greater democratization in science and society. That is an Athenian fantasy. There is something pathologically STS in the way the oppositions between Latour and Fuller are both nourished by an overabundance of

Platonism. My answer to the question "For whom does the bell toll in science, knowledge, and thinking" has for a long time been "It tolls for thee, Plato."

Fuller identifies common post-truth tropes. In abbreviated form and in my own words they are that (1) scientific research in process is unsettled, (2) settled science is by convention demonstrated in the scientific paper; (3) truths, consensus, and normative epistemic categories are all contingent. These well-established STS tropes are not, as Fuller contends, endorsements for post-truthism anymore than they entail relativism or anti-science sentiments. In his review of Fuller (2018), Sismondo (2017) offers a list of more appropriate tropes:

1. The emotional resonances and feelings generated by statements are coming to matter more than their factual bases.
2. Opinions, especially if they match what people already want to believe, are coming to matter more than facts.
3. Public figures can make statements disconnected from facts, without fear that rebuttals will have any consequences. Significant segments of the public display an inability to distinguish fact and fiction.
4. Bullshit, casual dishonesty and demagoguery are increasingly accepted parts of political and public life; this should not, however, be confused with ordinary lying, which is nothing new.
5. There has been a loss of power and trust in traditional media, leading to more fake news, news bubbles and do-it-yourself investigations.

There is still a sense in the post-truth critical literature that post-truthism has roots in modern culture rather than that it is a recurring intellectual strategy in the history of ideational structures. It is widely believed that post-truthism was born in post-modern epistemology and the cultural debates of the 1960s–1970s (e.g., Baer and Hennefeld, 2017) that makes it an easy matter to connect it to STS. One has to take a wider look around to get a more realistic perspective on the social and historical forces at work here. But Fuller has pathologized the connection to STS as a way of gaining attention and claiming a share of the market in ideas. Fuller takes Kuhn's ideas on paradigm shifts and normal science literally and as accurate descriptions of scientific practice. Based on this questionable view of science he criticizes the very idea of consensus in science, labelling it "cognitive authoritarianism" (Fuller, 1988). This traps him into erasing the boundary between fact and fiction. STS gets absurdly linked to reducing nature to a linguistic fiction, and embedding truth into the empty concept of a "free market" no longer taken seriously by critical realist economists. He defends a caricature concept of economic man "homo homini lupus." What this all comes down to is a pathologized version of critical science

studies. He wanders blinded by idiosyncratically embraced ancient philosophers into a maze of pseudo-STS defenses of climate denial, creationism, and
other nonsense.

Like Latour, Fuller has set himself an agenda that involves mobilizing attention at all costs. He has a distorted set of assumptions about the democratization of knowledge and information. The Fuller-Internet that has made all
this possible is not the Internet we know to be influenced by commercial and
monopolistic interests and goals but rather a Platonic form. Laissez-faire,
Fuller cries, building a "free market" for truth and expertise on the model of
Friedrich Hayek's economic models, not to mention a widely distorted version
of Adam Smith's empty notion of an "invisible hand." Elites and power contaminate all aspects of science and society in Fuller's Pareto-influenced version of
STS, and in his defense and generalization of neo-liberal economic models. He
wants to disabuse us of an absolutist view of science that Bloor, Restivo, and
others in STS dismissed long ago with a view of "relativism" that did not mean
"anything" and "everything" goes but "disinterested inquiry." Are we going to
join Herman Kahn and begin to "think the unthinkable"? Surely you're joking,
Mr. Fuller? Omodeo (2019: 10–11) writes:

> At no point in *Post-Truth: Knowledge as a Power Game* can the reader be
> enlightened on the most pressing questions of today. ... At no point does
> *Post-Truth: Knowledge as a Power Game* step back from its paradoxical
> partisanship and provocation in order to address the more compelling
> historical development behind these contemporary slogans, beginning
> with the breakdown of the Westphalian order and the catastrophic envi-
> ronmental problems of the age that we are currently living through. We
> fail to pay attention to this at our peril.

2   Conclusion

We are faced with the problem of restoring belief in democracy in the face of
elites that go unchallenged and in fact become objects of worship. Citizens
are reduced to subjects who are too weak or too jaded or too dumbed down to
be enraged except in ways that invite authoritarianism. Now the ghost of the
1930s arrives, bringing with it insufficient strategies for dealing with problems
far more serious and global in their reach. The masses are trapping themselves
and the rest of us into frameworks that benefit their owners and blind them to
the realities of existential threats or transform them into militant survivalists.

Both technology companies and governments have started to make efforts to tackle the challenge of "post-truth politics." In an article for the journal *Global Policy*, professor Nayef Al-Rodhan (2017) suggested four particular responses:

1. Improve the technological tools for fact checking. For example, Germany has already asked Facebook to introduce a fake news filtering tool.

2. Greater involvement and visibility for scientists and the scientific community. The UK, for instance, has a series of Parliamentary committees at which scientists are called to testify, and present their research to inform policy-making. Similarly in Canada the role of Chief Science Advisor was re-established and each department with even a small scientific capability was required to develop a policy for scientific integrity. In countries such as the Czech Republic, new units have been set up to tackle fake news. The most important challenge here is to ensure that such state-led efforts are not used as tools for censorship.

3. Securitizing fake news. It is important to treat post-truth politics as a matter of security and devise global efforts to counter this phenomenon.

Let's add to this list President Biden's resurrection of the role of the science advisor and its elevation to Cabinet status. These are all short-term solutions that may play out to our benefit if they help to reconstruct our rationalities, our categories, and our classifications.

CHAPTER 2

The Iron Laws of Reality

Few people have the imagination for reality: Goethe.
Humankind cannot bear very much reality: T.S. Eliot.
Delulu: The idea that our thoughts can attract a specific desired reality. Delulu is mostly about seeing life through a rose-tinted, excessively romanticized lens. Thinking realistically is never good, according to TikTok user @romaneexvirgara, a business coach and dedicated delulu spreader.
The world is everything that is the case.
   WITTGENSTEIN

• • •

Reality is all that there is.
   RESTIVO

• • •

No one will ever figure out why there is anything at all. As for the rest of it, it's cosmic accidents all the way down.
   RESTIVO

• •
• •
•

1   Introduction

2   Epistemic Vigilance versus Machiavellian Vigilance

Epistemic vigilance (Thomson, 2023) hypothesizes that humans possess a tool kit they can draw on for identifying and calling out lies (Sperber et al., 2010). But Shieber (2023) challenges this idea, arguing that research shows that we're not very good at detecting deception. We may have a built-in bullshit detector but it's not very accurate, it's often not on, and it's easily distracted. Shieber argues for what he calls "The Nietzsche Thesis." Our conversations are not oriented to acquiring truths but to "self-presentation." We don't have epistemic vigilance we have Machiavellian vigilance. This is bolstered by the prevalence of conspiracy theories and echo-chamber nonsense. Inquiring, investigating, being curious, and seeking explanations are "hugely important components of human happiness," Benson and Stangroom (2006: 179–180) tell us. But these do not seem too popular in today's world:

> Public rhetoric tends to aim much lower for some reason. It seems to see us all as hunkered down, and settling. Settling for minimal, parochial, almost biological satisfactions – family, safety, money. But that underestimates us. We want more than that. We want to ask questions, we want to learn, we want to understand. That's a very human taste and pleasure. ... real enquiry presupposes that truth matters. ... We like games, but we also like genuine enquiry. That's why truth matters.

One caution: Benson and Stangroom (2006: 180), like many others who value truth and science, blame postmodernists for creating the rhetoric characteristic of a hunkered down public. This is only true to the extent that some postmodernists went too far, became too relativist, in their efforts to challenge the damaging consequences of reigning systems of categories and classifications, too far in criticizing the routinization of rationalities. As a counterpoint to their critique of postmodernists, Benson and Stangroom (2006: 180–181, citing Ridley) also draw attention to the mythology of the Romantic poets who taught us "that science gets rid of mysteries." Yet, as Ridley notes, Einstein's thought experiments, Newton's insights on deep space, Darwin's explorations of deep time, and Crick and Watson's discovery of the mysteries of deep encoding "are far more otherworldly, elusive, thrilling and baffling than anything dreamt up by poets ... To get rid of those insights would be to reduce the world's stock of awe." I am obviously sympathetic to these views, but I don't see why we have to enchant science with words like "mysteries" and "awe." That sort of thinking puts us on the doorstep of the gods and dictators.

3   Through the Cultural Looking Glass

If everything about life awes you, you will never see the world the way it is. You will be distracted by sunsets, and daffodils, eclipses, and snow covered mountains and ignore the more important lessons that earthquakes and volcanoes, hurricanes and floods, poverty and inequalities teach us. The real world and its cosmic home are not beautiful; they are terrifying. The caveat here is that what is beautiful and what is terrifying may be two sides of the same coin. A deep dive into the relationship between beauty, terror, and the sublime is beyond the scope of this book. It is sufficiently relevant to the worldview issues I am concerned with to require some brief attention.

4   Beauty, Terror, and the Sublime

In his *Poetics*, Aristotle argues that objects that are terrifying in everyday life can be beautiful when elevated to the realm of art. Kant engages this idea in his aesthetic philosophy. Angels, for example, are perceived as beautiful, but we can't control them so that makes them dangerous. The danger of a beautiful thing depends on how powerful it is. For the poet Rainer Maria Rilke (1876–1925; 2021), "beauty is nothing but the beginning of terror." Rilke's angels are not the angels of religion. They are intimate parts of being itself and internal to the self. They are something like Jung's "unconscious." What Rilke is after is help for our pain and if we seek help from these lyrical angels their power could overwhelm us. In the end we cannot be consoled; we can only help ourselves; there are no angels to come to our aid. We must accept the chaos of existence and try to find solace in everything beautiful and everything ugly. These references provide some of the scaffolding for Donna Tartt's *The Secret History* (1992: 41–45) in which her characters tell us that "Death is the mother of beauty;" "It's a very Greek idea. ... Beauty is terror;" "Genuine beauty is always quite alarming."

The deeper foundations of this theme take us into the third century Greek notion of the sublime. In this context, the sublime on one interpretation means great beauty. From a different perspective (e.g., the 1st century Greek writer Longinus), the sublime connects beauty and terror. The problems of beauty, terror, and the sublime are tied to spiritual realms of philosophical and theological discourse and enigmas in our experience of the liminal. Kant (1764/2003) described three types of sublimity: the awful, the lofty and the splendid (Salier, 2002; MacGregor-Reid, 2020):

> The passion caused by the great and Sublime in nature, when those causes operate most powerfully astonishment, and astonishment is that state of the soul in which all its motions are suspended, with some degree of horror. No passion so effectually robs the mind of all its power of acting and reasoning as fear.
>
> EDMUND BURKE, 1757

5   A Child of the Book

This book was as hard to write as it has been hard to live; and it has been as easy to write as it has been easy to live. It has been hard to write because the lesson it teaches is that in order to protect humanity and the Earth, we must prioritize disenchantment and set enchantment aside. It has been easy to write because I have experienced meaning and love in the midst of disenchantment, and because of the ease with which I embraced what things are like freed of the constraints of hopes, wishes, beliefs, and prayers. It has been hard to write because while I have sat contemplating great works of art in museums and libraries, and while I sit now comfortably writing on my computer listening to the music of Mozart, Bach, Beethoven, and The Grateful Dead, the world is now as ever immersed in mayhem. It has been easy to write because I have since childhood been comfortable with the awareness that the Emperor has no clothes, and later with the realization that there wasn't even an Emperor. I can't tell you why but perhaps growing up with a mother who was an untutored believer and a father who didn't believe in anything but who knew things holds the answer. In a working-class household in Brooklyn, New York, a home without books, not even a Bible, I became a child of the book. In one of my classes during my years in the academy, one of my students asked my teaching assistant why she didn't believe in God. "I read books," she told him.

Perhaps ignoring the plights of humanity and the planet is the most rational answer to how terrifying everything is or becomes once you realize that you are going to die. Wouldn't it make sense then to dedicate yourself to immersing yourself in all of the pleasurable experiences that are available to you – especially the sexual ones – and ignoring as much as possible all the junk life throws at you, from people who threaten you to people who tax you, from racist cops with batons and guns to dictators who would brutalize you? If not suicide, and leaving that option open, hedonism might be our best response, our most realistic response, and in a way it has been mine. I considered suicide as a college student. I developed an axiomatic answer to the question, "Does life make sense?" and if not how should one respond as a rationalist. I called the system, in a burst of collegiate enterprise, existential utilitarianism. I concluded based on such axioms as "There is no God," and "There is no after life," that suicide was the logical choice for a rational being. A protoplasmic will to live kept me from following through on this, though I have kept the option in my back pocket until this very day. But I have lived with a concern for social justice and a sense of doing the right thing that I learned from my parents but also from Superman, Batman, Wonder Woman, and the Lone Ranger. I also developed a sense of the futility, the absurdity of it all that I learned from life, the universe and everything, not to mention Woody Allen and Fellini.

My sense of social justice has led me to view everyday realities in non-ordinary ways. For example, most of us take for granted the presence of dogs and cats in our everyday environments. In some homes they are considered part of the family. I think we should reconsider our association with pets. To grasp people's relationships with dogs and cats one must be something I could never be. Americans spend about $100 billion dollars a year on all things pet. The official poverty rate in 2021 was 11.6 percent, with 37.9 million people in poverty. It is roughly unchanged today. It has been estimated that we could end poverty in America at a cost of $350 billion dollars. We could do it for $100 billion if we loved the poor more than our pets. Globally, current estimates suggest that we need donor governments to invest around $37 billion every year until 2030 to tackle both extreme and chronic hunger. I inject this note to underscore that what is at stake in our race against existential threats is our collective abilities to enact a radical restructuring and re-envisioning of our relationship to the world in ways we have not been prepared to contemplate because they are so concretely rooted in what we take for granted.

My concerns about pets in the context of existential threats are not idiosyncratic. For 500 years pets have been endangering hundreds of threatened animals around the world. Domestic cats have contributed to the elimination of the Stephens Island wren of New Zealand and the Hawaiian crow. Dogs have been linked to the elimination of numerous species. Cats, dogs, and other pets are responsible for dwindling wildlife across the globe. Too many of us are choosing to have animals in our lives rather than visiting them in theirs (Christie, 2024).

This book is the story of what I learned from Superman, Batman, and the Lone Ranger about truth and justice. Of course, my parents and teachers helped with this once you strip away those teachers who taught patriotism, religiosity, and the myth of American exceptionalism. Hedonism was an echo in the background of these lessons. But unfettered hedonism does not solve problems of life and death, it is not an answer to existential threats. It was recognizing this and the broader issues of the injustices that are baked into our social structures that led me to the Marxists and the anarchists. I think I became a Marxist the day I visited the shoe factory my dad worked in. I was ten years old. I was hit by the realization that my father left our house every morning to go to this dirty, smelly, dusty, dark place with pictures of naked women on the walls next to the workstations. Some fifteen years later, I began advocating for Science for the. People and the Radical Science Movement.

My path to bringing the radicalism of science into the classroom took me through the Science for the People and Radical Science Movement activities of the 1960s. I didn't have the right temperament for the streets; I was always exceptionally cerebral in engaging the world. If I couldn't consistently take the revolution to the streets I could take it to the classroom. And I did, skirting challenges and threats from faculty, students, parents, and administrators long enough to have a fifty-year career punctuated by three successful administrative efforts to shut me down.

This book, independently of how I have or have not lived my own life, is about what if anything we can do about existential threats, threats that may mean hedonists will have to turn their attention to problems of survival in this moment for them to continue to pursue their hedonistic lifestyles or life at all. But hedonism should not be ignored by those who choose to live as activists in the world of everyday and existential threats. My defense of realistic hedonism has nothing in common with rational hedonism. Classically, it draws on Epicurus' views on avoiding a life of untamed appetites and opting for a life of moderation and respect for others. To the extent that it is normative, it is so in the context of a community. I do not subscribe to motivational or egotistical hedonism. Nor do I subscribe to the modern idea of rational hedonism as a religion of individual indulgences. I will consider a form of hedonism rooted in my defense of science and realism in Chapter 14.

I understand the sense of awe that can overcome you, drug you, when you look up into the night sky, stand in the center of one of the great Gothic cathedrals, or watch a sunset from Gates Pass in Tucson, Arizona. These "looking up" behaviors can readily convince you there is meaning, and perhaps a God, "up there." I recall Nietzsche's (1886/1989: 80) aphorism, "As long as you still experience the stars as something "above you" you lack the eye of knowledge." I have written poems and songs about experiencing awe. But I have been able to write this book because even in those moments, I never stopped thinking. Disenchantment is necessary for survival; but it can also bring beauty and the sublime into our lives. What I ask of the reader in this book is not easy. But there is no alternative to disenchantment if you want to save humanity and the world, sustain them for a little bit longer. In the long run what we do or don't do is irrelevant. The destiny of life, the universe, and everything is extinction.

6   The Road to Reality

A great part of humanity, including rich and poor, educated and uneducated, ancient and modern have been and continue to be guided by millennia-old fallacies. These have become increasingly dangerous as our world has become more and more like a village. They are dangerous because they violate the basic laws of reality. Since the start of the industrial age in the nineteenth century, the networks of transportation, communication, and exchange have been reaching out across the globe. These networks, interlinked with the networks of the digital revolution, have linked virtually all the peoples and cultures of the world in an emerging global culture. On the one hand we have become a global village; on the other hand old enmities, demographic and geographic barriers, and recalcitrant differences have given us a fractured global village. In this context, we are confronted on all sides by existential threats to humanity and the planet, from climate change to potential artificial intelligence singularities. The situation has provoked sustainability and survival strategies as well as an anti-natalist movement dedicated to ending humanity. For those who would like us to continue to bridge differences and fix fractures it has never been more important to ground ourselves in the way the world really is. Beliefs, opinions, hopes, prayers, and wishes will not save us. Lies, post-truths, and alternative facts simply stress existing fractures. Our only hope is unfettered inquiry and a commitment to truths, no matter the extent to which they violate millennia old assumptions, beliefs, and faiths. This book is a guide to the real world crying out for our help. In this chapter, I will introduce some non-obvious facts to start the conversation. In Chapter 5 I will consider the reality humans ignore at their peril, and problems with the very ideas of "reality" and what is "real."

This book has a fail-safe button: There is no justification for investing any scientific claim or any claim at all with positive or absolute belief, or absolute conviction; everything is in flux, and subject to criticism and change. The inventor of this fail-safe button is Cliff Hooker (1995). Science, skepticism and disobedience are vaccines; they do not block behavior, they make behavior a little safer. Let's explore some of the key myths and fallacies that are themselves existential threats.

7   Free Will

Consider that, as individuals, we do not experience the earth in motion. Yet it spins on its axis wobbling in precession; at any point along the equator it is rotating at about one thousand miles per hour; it travels around the sun at a speed of 67,000 miles per hour; and it is part of a solar system orbiting the center of the Milky Way. The Milky Way is part of a cluster of galaxies (The Local Group) traveling toward the center of the cluster, and The Local Group itself is speeding through space at three hundred and seventy miles a second. None of this motion is accessible to individual experience. Yet we have knowledge of these motions through the collective generationally linked intersubjectively tested experiences of scientists. Here and elsewhere I will use "scientist" to refer to any systematic inquirer using broadly rational natural methods to try to figure out how the world works.

What if this is true of all of our experiences; that they cannot be trusted to reveal truths about how things work in the real world? What if the intro-spectively accessed free-willing self is as much an illusion of individual expe-rience as is a stationary earth? Part of the reality of everyday life includes this fact: our experiences are not a good indicator of what the world is really like. They do not give us privileged access to what is really going on in and around us. Experiences and feelings are not trustworthy ways of interrogating and knowing the real world. Moreover, they're not even strictly speaking *our* expe-riences. Already by the late decades of the nineteenth century, social theorists had proposed that it is the social community that thinks not the individual. That is, the individual's thoughts are not h/ers but those of the spirit of the times, of the culture. In other words, you can only think things that your social environment concentrates upon your brain.

> It is not the individual who thinks but the spirit of his age and social group, his social community ... The source of his thoughts is in the social medium in which he breathes, and he cannot think anything else other than what the influences of his social environment concentrating upon his brain necessitate.
>
> LUDWIG GUMPLOWICZ (1885/1990: 240)

By the late twentieth century, we had enough accumulated evidence in the social sciences to confirm that ideas arise in social networks and "speak" through the voices of individuals. This is not so strange if you consider that humans arrive on the evolutionary stage as the most radically social of the social species, more social than the apes and social in a different way than ants and bees. Humans have social selves, social brains, and social genes (Restivo, 2023). Once we understand this we are less likely to succumb irrevocably and without recourse to illusions. We will be less likely to be the victims of per-sistent, recalcitrant mistakes in identifying the causes of our thoughts, emo-tions, and behaviors. We will also be more likely to avoid profound distortions in logic and reason that can lead to such social pathologies as conspiracy theo-ries and belief in gods, ghosts, and angels.

We can, of course, learn to trust our experiences to the extent that we are taught how to negotiate our everyday world. We can learn and act on things autonomously like crossing the street safely, shopping, going to school and coming home. These experiences are a different order than what is required to learn the movements of the Earth.

One of the features of reality is that there are no transcendental worlds, supernatural worlds, worlds of souls, spirits and ghosts, gods, devils, and angels, heavens and hells. They are symbolic of the ways in which we organize our social lives. There is nothing beyond our material, organic, and social worlds. Death is final; there is no soul, there is no life after death. I refer to such beliefs as parts of a general transcendental fallacy (see Appendix 1). Before we explore this aspect of our everyday reality let's take a moment to consider the origin of our feeling that we are free-willing agents.

8 Open and Closed Systems

Think of the real world as organized in systems. A system is a group of interacting interrelated elements that act according to a set of rules to form a more or less unified, more or less functioning whole. Systems operate along a continuum from efficient functioning to dysfunctional. This applies to the system as a whole and to its elements. Here we assume an efficiently functioning system. This is the way ideal systems work. In practice, we are confronted by various sources of perturbations that impact predictable and efficient functioning. As long as these perturbations are not too grand, we can have some control over the system.

A system, surrounded and influenced by its environment, is described by its boundaries, structure and function and expressed in its operation. Imagine all the features of your life, from objects to other bodies, from organizations to group activities arranged as systems along a continuum from open to closed. The boundaries of open systems are permeable and such systems can interact with other systems; the boundaries of closed systems are impermeable, and they cannot interact with other systems. The more open a system is the harder it is to predict and control its behavior; the more closed a system is the easier it is to predict and control its behavior. The solar system is a complexly open system. However, it is sufficiently closed to allow us to predictably land rockets on the moon or on Mars and control the flight of probes through the system. Scientists in laboratories create closed systems that allow them to control and predict the behavior of chemicals, particles, and other matter as well as human interactions. There is no such thing as a completely closed system. All systems vary in the extent to which they are deterministic. The more open the system, the less deterministic it is. All systems, however, are lawful (Bohm, 2016).

Smaller, less complex societies are relatively more closed than modern industrial societies. Human behavior is more restricted and predictable in the former, less restricted and predictable in the latter. The more a society approaches the openness of a modern industrial society, the more its individual members experience themselves as free willing agents. Free will is an open systems illusion. This experience is possible in ancient societies to the extent that they are technologically and structurally complex, diversified, and offer a variety of ways of satisfying needs and desires. Choice behavior is the reality behind the illusion of free will. Computers illustrate the fact that choice behavior does not entail free will.

9   The Rejection of Transcendental Realities

Let's go back now to the most dramatic implication of the fact that there are no transcendental or supernatural worlds. There is no God. You've no doubt heard everyone from your teachers and friends to distinguished scientists and philosophers say that you can't prove or disprove God. That claim is true in the context of the philosophical reading of the core sciences of physics, biology, and chemistry. Even then, it is supported more by ideology than by logic or science. But once you add the social sciences to the mix it becomes possible to prove there is no God. The reason is that God is actually a social phenomenon, a social reality, a symbol of the community or society that gives birth to the God myth. If we leave our home, our street, our neighborhood, our city, our country, our culture, and finally our time, and have a wider look around we notice some interesting things about God. In brief, if we adopt the comparative method and look at God across history and cultures we find, for example, that warlike societies produce Gods of war, agricultural societies produce fertility gods, and patriarchal societies give us male gods. Xenophanes (560–478BCE) had already observed that "the gods of Ethiopians were inevitably black with flat noses while those of the Thracians were blond with blue eyes." The very idea of God changes systematically with changes in society. And "immortal gods" die; they disappear when the societies they symbolize decline and die out (see Mencken's essay on the graveyard of the gods, "Memorial Service," 1982: 295–297).

Monotheism is associated with societies that have three or more hierarchical levels of power (e.g., clan, city, empire); polytheism is associated with societies dominated by classes; ancestor worship is found in societies organized around the extended family; and reincarnation is associated with small village communities in which individuals experience intense face-to-face interaction. Belief in a Creator God concerned with human moral conduct shows up in about four percent of hunter/gatherer societies, ten percent of simple horticultural societies, fifteen percent of advanced horticultural societies, and sixty four percent of agrarian societies. This demonstrates that there is a relationship between the evolution of social complexity and the cultural evolution of the concept of an engaged Creator God.

Anywhere in history we find believers, we also find skeptics and non-believers. Seventeenth century Europe witnessed the beginnings of the rational study of the Bible, Jesus, and Christianity. Religious rationalism emerged in this period in France and Germany. By the middle of the nineteenth century religious rationalism began to evolve into the sociological study of religion and an important theory emerged: projection theory. Basically, projection theorists claimed that God was a projection of social causes to an imagined outside force that satisfied the need for a causal explanation of certain emotional experiences in groups. Over thousands of years, this imagined force solidified into various forms of a God. By the early twentieth century we had an explanation for this phenomenon. It's a phenomenon that we can all experience.

Imagine you are standing in line waiting to get into an arena to hear your favorite rock and roll group. I might be in line, for example, to see The Rolling Stones or The Grateful Dead. What are you feeling standing in line? What kinds of anticipations and emotions are welling up inside you and the people around you? Now you're inside the arena, the concert is going full blast. You and the rest of the audience are acting like a single organism reacting to the music and its beats, and you are sharing in an emotional high. Those emotions and the feeling that you are part of a communal organism might even be enhanced by drugs. What is causing the emotions you feel? Is it being caused by the audience's shared experience, or is it coming from outside the group? The earliest humans had this kind of experience during their rituals, which involved singing, dancing, chanting, music, and drums. They didn't know what we know; that their experiences were being generated by the group's collective actions. This had to be a consequence of some cause. Since they didn't know enough to look to their own activities, they projected the cause to an outside force which eventually solidified into a powerful God. The technical term for this phenomenon is collective effervescence. A religion comes into being and is legitimated through the accumulation of these moments of collective effervescence. The process of finally coming to believe in "other worlds" and gods takes thousands and thousands of years.

Collective effervescence refers to moments in social life when a group of individuals come together in order to engage in a ritual. If this is true, then you should experience different emotions in different group settings. So now imagine you're in line waiting to attend a performance of Mozart's compositions. You feel differently in line than you did waiting to get into the rock and roll concert, don't you? And your experience inside the concert hall once the music starts is dramatically different than it was at the rock and roll concert, isn't it? You're also dressed differently. The settings are different, the music – the rhythms, the beats – are different and so you experience a different form of collective effervescence. This, in brief, is the clue to the origin of belief in God.

10   Religion

God is not real in the way a table, the sun, or you are real. It's culturally real, a symbol. Religion, on the other hand, is real in a different way. It's not real in exactly the same way as a table, the sun, or you; it's socially real, like God, but it is more directly phenomenal. It is a social institution, supported and sustained by the actions of real people and with rules, regulations, and sanctions that direct how people behave in organizational settings. While these actions are also at work in sustaining belief in God, social institutions have physical organizational manifestations that can be viewed, visited, worked in, and so on.

The reality that is the subject of this book, in the simplest decomposition, has basically four levels: physical, chemical, biological, and social. The social level has observable and measurable causes and consequences just like the other levels. Religion is part of that social reality. It is that part of society that organizes and defends what social and cultural evolution has produced and identified as good and bad, right and wrong. Religion is the "glue" that holds society, the community, the family, and even the individual together. This is as much as I can say here without getting into complicated social science theories. The bottom line is: Religion is real, God is not.

Don't take the theologians seriously or those philosophers who spend thousands of hours and make careers out of endless commentaries on ontological and other so-called "proofs" for the existence of God. Schopenhauer (1813/ 2015: 15) already pointed out that "Considered in the light of day and impartially, this famous ontological proof is now actually a most beloved piece of nonsense." Schiller (1798–99/2017) described the proof as "extraordinarily stupid." And yet this nonsense and stupidity underwrites endowed chairs and academic honors for the Plantinga's of the world. Alvin Plantinga is a prominent Christian analytic philosopher; see, for example, Plantinga (1974). We must wonder at theologians like Hans Küng (1978: 666) who proclaim: "Now, without having to give up his reason, man encounters a God he can pray and offer sacrifice, again fall on his knees in awe and sing and dance before him." This does not resonate with me and it shouldn't resonate with you. Prostrating yourself before a God makes it easy to prostrate yourself before human dictators. The height of worship is the lowest level of self-esteem. Ni Dieu, Ni Maître!

11   Science

The claims I make in this book are all grounded in the best science available in our time. My understanding of science is grounded in empirical and theoretical research by sociologists and anthropologists of science. We learn from their work that science does not do its work all at once; no single experiment, no single scientific article or book, no individual is scientific by it- or-him/herself. These features of science are only scientific in terms of the way they fit into the unfolding of similar features over time. The objectivity of science emerges over time through the collective efforts of professional scientists and the scholarly thinkers who precede and work alongside them, are contemporaries, and sometimes collaborators. This leads to a problem that is peculiar to the digital age and the twenty-four-hour news cycle.

Every day we are barraged by science headlines announcing discoveries that are contradicted a few days later. The digital age is not giving science time to settle down. So you should not invest too much in the science news of the day. It doesn't mean you should ignore it. Sometimes, as we saw during the COVID pandemic, we have to rely on "fast science" to get the best medicines and vaccines. This means mistakes will be made because scientists are working under time constraints. But in such circumstances it is better to be self-aware critical guinea pigs than to let the pandemic rage out of control.

This is a book about the reality of reality, a reality that is constructed on the foundation of the scientific worldview. Therefore, it is important to spend some time on the very idea of science. What do "we" mean by science? I use "we" instead of "I" for two reasons. The first and most basic reason is that the "I" is a grammatical illusion. Humans are radically social beings. The second reason is that science is a collective enterprise. Individuals cannot be scientists outside the unfolding of this collective enterprise across history and cultures.

Let's consider the question of whether a Robinson Crusoe could become a scientist or could do science. Considered by some to be the first English novel, Daniel DeFoe's 1719 story of Crusoe being stranded on an island has served philosophers who pondered the question of whether an isolated individual could be a scientist. There are two basic answers: (1) no, because scientific criticism, progress, and objectivity depend on cooperation, intersubjectivity, and public method; (2) yes, because our Crusoe scientist could substitute the satisfactoriness and coherence of the laws he derived for cooperation, intersubjectivity, and public method. Notice however that this could only be possible contingently if this second Crusoe had become a scientist on the mainland first.

All knowledge claims escape their evidence and must be considered highly presumptive, corrigible, and fallible. There is no justification for investing any scientific claim with positive or absolute belief. This limits deterministic, universal, and invariant claims. It does not eliminate them. The reason is that without certain levels of closure in the systems of our everyday lives life would be impossible. Philosophically, we might be justified in claiming that definitive descriptions of Reality writ large are impossible. But levels of closure make definitive descriptions in practice possible at everyday levels of reality, including the everyday realities of scientific research.

I am only a scientist and my work is only scientific when I and it enter the historical flow of the linked generations of scientists collectively intersubjectively testing ideas, theories, and experimental results. At the end of the day, I am an experiment, my work is an experiment, and my claims are an experiment. However certain I am of their truth, this is ultimately a collective decision of the evolving scientific community.

Humans exist in objectivity or truth communities. Four key objectivity communities stand out in the context of the treachery of realities: the community of atheists, the community of theists, the community of physical and natural scientists, and my community of sociologists and sociologically minded scientists. There are overlaps across these communities but they are more closed than open and operate effectively as cultural species. This view helps explain why communication across these communities is difficult to impossible. We are one (presumably) biological species, but many cultural species.

12   The Technological Fix

If we rely on science and technology fixes, we're doomed. We may be doomed anyway, but science and tech fixes are not the answer. We are obliged to focus on social structural, cultural, and organizational causal forces. Is there an evidentiary basis for the conception of "technology guided by philosophy?" This is part of the technological fix paradigm. The term "technological fix" was coined by Alvin Weinberg in 1965. Weinberg, a technology administrator advocated engineering innovation as a generic tool for circumventing problems commonly conceived as social, political, or cultural. A longtime Director of Oak Ridge National Laboratory, government consultant, and essayist, Weinberg also popularized the term "big science" to describe national goals and the competitive funding environment after the Second World War. Big science reoriented towards technological fixes, he argued, could provide a new "Apollo project" to address social problems of the future. Bejan's (2020) claim that physics is the only science we need because it covers everything is an example of the "science fix" ideology. The problem with technological and science fixes is that Society and Culture are sui generis and escape being comprehended by physics, biology, chemistry, or neuroscience. Some scholars claim Society and Culture escape "the scientific method" in general. But none of the sciences, from physics, biology, and chemistry, to sociology, psychology, and neuroscience can be fully comprehended by "the scientific method" as a singular, monolithic method.

For the most part, discovery results in a partial comprehension of nature labeled as physical laws often expressed in the language of mathematics. The ethical application of those physical laws ("technology guided by philosophy") is, it is assumed, what enables humanity to fly above the clouds and switch on a Zoom session converting the world into a local neighborhood. This is a new condition in the human social and cultural equation and part of the evolution towards a still distant global civility.

Given all of this, why is it so difficult for even members of the scientific community writ small or large to reach a consensus on every issue, problem, and solution?

The reasons are:

(1)   Humans are one biological species at a superficial level; at a deeper level, we have evolved in different species-specific bio-ecological niches. We may be less unified biologically than we have assumed;

(2)   Culture is a speciating mechanism; so we are trying to communicate across doubly species-specific barriers, -bio-ecological and cultural.

While it looks like we are using the same language and concepts and communicating with different levels of success, this is an illusion. We are operating out of variably incommensurable worldviews. Our truths are more local than global.

13   Sociology as a Science

The US National Science Foundation along with private and public agencies in other countries funds sociological research and recognizes sociology as a science. Yet many intellectuals, scientists, and especially philosophers do not consider sociology a scientific discipline. Since sociological theory and research underwrites my view of the world and its problems, it's important to understand the reasoning behind identifying sociology as a science.

The science of sociology is based on the discovery that humans arrive on the evolutionary stage as social organisms: always, already, and everywhere social. They are the latest stage in evolution's experiment with collective cooperative systems as adaptive mechanisms. The cooperative principle is in the ascendance in evolution. This experiment begins with the invention of cellular cooperation. Life on earth existed in single-celled forms until about 600 million years ago. Then, the Paleozoic Age witnessed the proliferation of multicellular animals. This new complexity had survival advantages over single-celled life forms. The earliest forms of multicellular animals were the sponges. As complexity and collective cooperative forms evolved, life forms lost the capacity to regenerate cells, tissues, and limbs. After the sponges came jelly fish and sea anemones with a central gut cavity, followed by flatworms that innovated bilateral symmetry and the beginnings of nerves concentrated in rudimentary brains. Roundworms came along next with elementary circulatory systems. They also have a mouth, hollow gut, and an anus.

Lamp shells, clams and oysters evolved next; then segmented worms, and then the anthropods (lobsters, insects, spiders, and so on). They added armor to their segmented structure that was more protective than the coverings of shellfish. Some multicellular plants began to grow tops over the water's surface and eventually evolved into land animals. An increase in the percentage of oxygen in the atmosphere supported intense plant growth across the planet. This was the landscape that became hospitable to the first multicellular animals. These are the factual features of our experience that come into view as the proper subjects of scientific investigation. The particular sciences that emerge to focus on the social features are the social sciences, notably sociology, anthropology, and social psychology. They find their origins, like all sciences, in the ancient world of philosophical inquiry. Sociology begins to crystallize in the 1840s and what follows are three ages of the social. The first age, 1840–1930, takes us from crystallization to professionalization and the establishment of schools and centers of sociology (the French school, the Chicago school, the Los Angeles school), and theoretical schools of thought (structural-functionalism, symbolic interactionism, and conflict theory; micro-sociology and macro-sociology). The second age, 1930–1970, witnesses the development of sociological approaches to knowledge and science as social systems excluding the knowledge they produce which is considered to be independent of society, culture, history, and even time and space. The third age of the social begins in 1970 and develops approaches to the sociological study of knowledge and belief themselves (for example, the sociology of mathematics and logic, religion and God, and the sociology of the brain).

14   Cosmology

With Hubble and James Webb telescopes now scanning the skies and bringing back data to the public almost daily, we need to be cautious about what if anything we are learning. We are not learning about what Reality "really" is. While the situation is more complex than I can relate here, the science of Cosmic Reality is not about "how the world really is;" it's about manufacturing a mathematics that makes sense of the available data. The universe cosmologists are telling you about is a mathematical universe, a model universe constructed out of mathematical Legos. Theoretical laws can have great predictive and even explanatory powers but they describe ideal mathematical models not Reality-in-itself. We can get some idea of how close these models come to giving us a window onto Reality-in-itself by observing the results of experiments and technological proofs-of-concept. This is not a knock on science but simply a story of how science works. The result of this way of viewing science is that it can give rise to a grammar of mathematics in which models and theories pose as real physical and natural things. Such "mathegrammatical illusions" power the ideas, for example, that humans are a simulation or brains-in-a-vat (think *The Matrix* movies here). The universe may be more complex than we can know or imagine, but that complexity does not include transcendental or supernatural realms and beings and it not likely to include a multitude of universes each containing a version of you.

15   Subscendental Realities

Subscendental realities are the inverse of transcendental realities and no more real. Philosophers refer to them as "deep" or "immanent structures." There are no "deep" or "immanent structures" that are the neuronal or genetic loci of explanations for human language, thought, emotions, or behavior. Such brain-centric, gene-centric, and sociobiological ideas lead to conceptions of logic, mathematics, and language as "free standing," "independent," outside of history, culture, time, and space, and value free sets of statements.

16   The Myth of Individualism

This takes us back to our assessment of free will and agency. Neither the human being nor the human brain is free standing and independent. There are limits to the extents to which they can be studied on their own terms independently of social, cultural, and environmental contexts, influences, and forces. Mind and consciousness are not brain phenomena. Human beings and human brains are constitutively social. This corrects the myth of individualism and, on the most radical interpretation, seriously limits the domains of psychology and the life- and neurosciences. These approaches might produce relevant results in certain contexts. Then, there might be fruitful ways to pursue interdisciplinary studies linking the social sciences and the neurosciences. It may indeed be possible to construct a neurosocial model of the self, the brain, and consciousness. This would eliminate conventional brain/mind/body and brain-mind divisions. It would imply that we don't socialize persons but a complex networked system of networks that links everything from cells to social interactions and ecological contexts (Restivo, 2023: 115–140).

17   Objectivity

Objectivity is a key concept in the effort to grasp what is really going on in and around us. Classically, control over the nature and definition of objectivity came under the jurisdiction of philosophers and philosophically inclined scientists. They tended to understand it as truth independent of individual subjectivity. A proposition is considered to have objective truth when its truth conditions are met without bias caused by the mind or emotions of a sentient being. Thus, the only obstacles to being objective were psychological biases. The objectivity of science was left to its assumed autonomous self-correcting nature which over the long run was assumed to slowly eradicate any psychological biases that might have contaminated the research process.

There were certainly controversies about the concept. Some philosophers described the concept as slippery and used in contradictory and inclusive ways. By the 1970s, the term "empirical" was replacing "objective" in the ruminations of some philosophers. Moreover, objectivity in classical philosophy was associated with realism. In its extreme form, "*naive* realism," realism posited three components required for objective assessments of reality: the scientist, imagined as an inquiring trained but otherwise unmediated eye that looks out into the world; things in the world, like trees and mountains; and terms that refer, labels or names for the things in the world. The scientific process unfolds when the eye sees a thing in the world and assigns it a term that refers. I see an object at the edge of the forest, I call it a tree. This may sound too simple, even simplistic but I witnessed just such a description of objectivity and realism during a seminar by one of the most distinguished philosophers in the country in 1980. It was also widely assumed but with less and less confidence that science opened a window on reality as it really is (in the extreme, Kant's ding an sich). But of course this was in the context of much subtler discussions notably provoked by experiments in quantum mechanics and considerations of so-called "observer effects;" what do we do when the act of observing a phenomenon may impact what we're observing?

When I first began to consider these issues in the early 1970s, the first thing I wanted to do was to avoid the assumption that the problems with the concept of objectivity meant that there was a problem with the idea of an objective reality. As my career unfolded from the early 1970s into the later years of the twentieth century, I saw various postmodern and relativist movements in philosophy undermine, in their extreme moments, the very possibility of objectivity, the very possibility of telling the truth. These moments have evolved to the point of questioning the very existence of anything we could grasp or understand, as reality. And so we arrive in a world in which we are left unprotected from lies, post-truthism, and alternative facts. The feminist sociologist Dorothy Smith (1999: 96–130) was not bamboozled by this brand of philosophy as demonstrated in her insightful essay, "Telling the Truth After Postmodernism."

18   Conclusion

In those early years of the 1970s when I first turned my attention to these matters, I realized that psychological biases weren't the only biases we had to worry about in science; there were sociological biases, as I noted earlier, that were being ignored because philosophers could not see them through the lens of the myth of individualism. In 1974, I introduced the concept of a sociology of objectivity and I would rely on this concept in the following years until today to save objectivity and truth (Restivo, 2022). The way to save them was to understand science as instantiating the basic human capacity to reason collectively. Science in this sense, as we've already seen, must be understood as the collective intersubjective testing of research results over linked generations of scientists. The very idea of objective truths was hidden behind a wall of fallacies, including the fallacies of free will, individualism, and God. For a complete list of the fallacies I've identified see Appendix 1.

This is the end of the first part of our journey. We will travel down some other paths for a while and return to ground our discussions and analyses in a secular humanist worldview enhanced by anarchism in Chapter 12.

CHAPTER 3

Existential Threats

Scientists have identified 3 general categories and more than a dozen possible existential threats to humanity and the planet:

Global simplification: (a) in systems such as monocultures, farming become too specialized to adapt; (b) the growth economy results in overshooting the carrying capacity of the Earth; (c) international conflict, and (d) contagion (e.g., infectious diseases).

Technology traps: infrastructure lock-ins (e.g., fossil fuels), chemical pollution, existential technologies (e.g., nuclear weapons), technological autonomy (e.g., robots and AI), and dis/misinformation.

Structural traps: short-term thinking and policies, overconsumption, biosphere disconnect, and local social capital losses.

Twelve specific threats are reckoned to be in an advanced state. Only technological autonomy and local social capital loss have arguably yet to develop into concerning problems. Even more alarmingly, these dead ends tend to reinforce each other, meaning it's likely that we'll get trapped in more than one at the same time. It's a pretty bleak picture, but the researchers aren't giving up yet. What's needed now is active transformation – not just an acceptance that we must go with the flow, but deliberate efforts in the other direction (Jørgensen, Jansen, et al., 2023).

1 Interlude: Principles of Sociocultural Evolution

Definitions: *specific evolution* refers to phylogenesis, adaptation, diversification, specialization and their ramifications in the context of the total evolutionary process; *general evolution* refers to the emergence of higher forms of life defined in terms of complexity, adaptive potential, and intelligence.

Principles: *Stabilization*: adaptation is a self-limiting factor in specific evolution. *Phylogenetic discontinuity of progress* – new stages in evolution begin in new lines rather than in predominantly advanced lines

Local discontinuity of progress – successive new stages of evolution are likely to begin in different localities.

The law of evolutionary potential – the greater the specialization in a given ecological niche (evolutionary stage or state), the lower the adaptive potential and therefore the lower the potential for surviving ecological challenges and surviving in a new niche (see Sahlins and Service, 1960 for a still lucid and relevant discussion of these ideas; and Restivo, 2018: 57–74). We can add here the Law of Adaptive Levels: adaptation occurs at different levels, across various life orders and systems and occurs at different speeds in different spatial arenas. This law draws attention to the complexity of adaptation and the general processes of variation and selection. Adaptation suggests an active agent in a stable environment. But active agents can and do change their environments in ways that make different demands on the adapting agents. Looked at another way, environments have agential-like dynamics: Law of Agent-Environment Entanglement

2   Existential Threat: The Very Idea

The phrase "existential threat" is a child of the 1950s born of the threats of nuclear war posed by the Cold War and the arms race. Most of us didn't really start to come into regular contact with the phrase until the late twentieth century and the early years of the twenty first century. Fueled by the September 11, 2001 attacks (terrorism as an existential threat), the climate crisis, and the rise of authoritarian regimes around the world (candidate Biden called candidate Trump an existential threat to American democracy), existential threat headlines have become common place since 2019. An existential threat is a threat to the very existence of a being, thing, or niche at the biological, technological, cultural or organizational level. It is massive in its scope, scale, and ramifications. In the contemporary context it is meant to refer to threats to the future of human life on Earth and to the Earth itself as a sustaining environment for human life. The first awareness I had of something that could count as an existential threat was not nuclear war but the end of our oil reserves. That was something I remember my elementary school science teachers talking about in the early 1950s; we were going to run out of oil in thirty or forty years they told us. By the time I reached high school I understood that evolution itself was an existential threat. Charles Darwin himself wrote in *The Origin of Species* (1859) that species disappear gradually from one place to another and eventually from the world. More than ninety-nine percent of the more than five billion species that have come into existence are extinct. That tells us how our story as a species will end. Identifying, addressing, and controlling existential threats can at best allow our story to continue for a little longer.

The possibility of death by nuclear winter probably didn't fully set in for me until I was in high school. At some point in the late 1950s or early 1960s I read Harrison Brown's *The Challenge of Man's Future* (1954). It didn't take long for

Brown to catch my youthful attention. On the third page of the "Preface," he wrote that if machine civilization disintegrates humanity will never be able to rebuild the contemporary world order. The explanation comes on page 222:

> Our ancestors had available large resources of high-grade ores and fuels that could be processed by the most primitive technology – crystals of copper and pieces of coal that lay on the surface of the earth, easily mined iron, and petroleum in generous pools reached by shallow drilling. Now we must dig huge caverns and follow seams further underground, drill oil wells thousands of feet deep ... and find ways of extracting elements from the leanest of ores.

The complex technology we now depend on for extracting energy could not have developed without the rapidly vanishing high-grade readily accessible resources of the ancient world. This is why it is hard to imagine how humanity would rebuild if our modern machine civilization disintegrated. In the wake of such a catastrophe some advantage might be found in previously accumulated knowledge. It is unlikely, however, that this could overcome the scarcity of and hard to access raw material resources required to rebuild industrial civilization. Whether our scenarios are Darwinian or technological the fact that our story will come to an end is an inevitable part of the evolutionary process and outside of our control. This may also be a clue to solving the Fermi Paradox (see below).

3   On the Mathematics of Existential Threats

Keep in mind as we proceed that some scientists will speak with authoritative voices when their authority doesn't quite match the quality of the evidence. Some of the less sober are fond of attaching probabilities to their authoritative pronouncements about existential threats. Numbers, however, are not always as real as the realities they are designed to represent. They might at best be just a warning sign. They don't tell us not to proceed with trust but to do so cautiously and skeptically.

4   Death by Alien Invasion

The Fermi paradox:

1. Given the effectively infinite expanse of the universe, the uncountable number of galaxies and stars, and the high probability that some star systems have habitable Earth like planets;

2. Given that many of the star systems are much older than our own;

3. It follows that there is high likelihood of extra-terrestrial life.

4. If this is the case, given the amount of time that the universe has been in existence according to our measurements and theories, we should have encountered some sign(s) of such life by now.

5. The Fermi Paradox is that given these conditions, we haven't encountered any such signs.

In 1961, Frank Drake published an equation that estimates the number, "N," of civilizations in the Milky Way with which communication might be possible. The probability of N is based on estimating such factors (7 in all) as the average rate of star formation in the Milky Way, the fraction of those stars that have planets, and so on. The factors are conjectural in the extreme and the equation does little more than identify some of the things we would have to take into account if we wanted to get some idea of the likelihood of alien life. Rodriguez (2023) pointed out that there might be ocean bound aliens without communication technologies that could lead to interplanetary communication or travel, and aliens who couldn't escape the immense gravitational well of their planet.

Is there any way to anticipate the consequences of an encounter with aliens? Perhaps, for humans have a history of encountering alien cultures on their own planet in their explorations through trade, warfare, and other exchanges. This is the case not only for human cultures but for our encounters with the fauna and flora cultures of the natural world. The encounters have more often than not led to violence. Extra-planetary encounters promise to be more radically alien and less predictable. And don't expect to find Jesus, Mohammad, or Buddha on these alien planets; you didn't find them when you encountered the cultures of the South Pacific, or those of the Amazon forests. These characters are culture and planet specific.

Given our current encounter with existential threats, the solution to the paradox could be the Great Filter hypothesis: catastrophic events caused by life forms or natural processes may extinguish life before it reaches the technological capacity to leave its home planet and explore outward beyond the frontiers we humans have reached.

5   Death by Mass Extinction

Where does this leave us? The number of species extinctions appears to be relatively constant across vast periods of time. But there have been several mass extinctions. These followed in the wake of the Cambrian Explosion some 540 million years ago. This was a period which witnessed an explosive emergence of a diversity of plant and animal life. The first mass extinction, the Ordovician-Silurian Extinction, occurred about 440 million years ago. This affected many small sea organisms. More sea organisms were killed off during the Devonian extinction, 365 million years ago. The largest mass extinction, the so-called Great Dying of the Permian-Triassic period, killed off ninety percent of the planet's species. That was 250 million years ago. One of the consequences of extinctions is that they create a space for new species. The dinosaurs arose in the aftermath of the Great Dying.

The next mass extinction occurred between the Triassic and Jurassic eras, 210 million years ago. Many large animals were killed off and this allowed the dinosaurs to thrive. The Age of the Dinosaurs came to an end in the last and the most famous of the mass extinctions between 60 and 70 million years ago at the end of the Cretaceous era. The sixth mass extinction may already be underway according to some scientists. It may have begun about 12,000 years ago as the rate of extinctions began to increase to at least a thousand times the "normal" rate. This is known as the Holocene Extinction. We are currently, arguably, in the Anthropocene era, the period dominated by humanity and its planetary influences. We may feature in the sixth mass extinction. The key factor in prompting this proposition is the multiplicity of existential threats we are faced with.

6   Death by Asteroid

The chance that an asteroid or comet large enough to cause a global catastrophe will hit the earth has been put at 1 in 75,000 to 1 in 300,000. Objects with diameters greater than 100 meters hit our planet roughly every thousand years; those with diameters greater than 10 kilometers hit us every 100 million years or so. Scientists are mapping the asteroid and comet universe and tracking dangerous objects and already testing ways of destroying or diverting them. Scientists are especially concerned about the Taurids meteor stream.

The Taurids meteor shower peaks in October and November. Asteroids in this stream up to 305 meters wide fly past the Earth every few years. A new branch of the stream, which is made up of smaller branches and streams, was recently discovered. The stream is believed to be what remains of a giant comet. Some of the debris from the disintegration of that comet is likely responsible for some of the great extinctions in Earth's history. While the risk is real, we don't have enough data to quantify the risk.

7   Death by Super Volcano

The super volcano that has been in the news in recent years is the one beneath Yellowstone National Park. Scientists have their eyes on this and several other super volcanoes around the world. Of the three volcanic eruptions at Yellowstone over the last 2 million years, two were super volcanoes. Scientists do not expect a Yellowstone event for another thousand to ten thousand years. We can get some idea of the consequences of such an event by considering the relatively small scale 2010 Eyjafjallajökull volcanic eruption in Iceland which disrupted forty percent of cargo transport in Europe and the travels of ten million air travelers. International aviation was disrupted for weeks. A super eruption could affect air traffic for decades, and sulphur dioxide in the atmosphere could have dire consequences for global food security by affecting climate shifts. Nonetheless, it is unlikely that a single super eruption could wipe out humanity. Vulcanologists are most concerned with flood lavas, huge continuous lava eruptions that can go on for hundreds of thousands of years. These eruptions are caused by plumes of hot material rising from deep inside the earth. They have coincided with the five major mass extinctions and are thought to be associated with continental drift. Eleven flood lava eruptions have occurred over the past 250 million years. Risk management strategies may have limited relevance in such cases. However, risk management scenarios can be played out to deal with the consequences of smaller scale eruptions. Volcanic ash can disrupt air traffic for weeks or months and halt it altogether in some cases. The diversification and expansion of alternative modes of transportation could minimize systemic risks (Bird, et al., 2010; and for a general treatment of risk management and our future see Clark and Chongtay, 2020).

8   Death by Solar Flare

Many of us are familiar with the capacity of solar flares to disrupt our satellites and power grids. A solar flare is an intense burst of radiation generated by the release of magnetic energy linked with sunspots. Sometimes, the sun ejects massive clouds of particles called coronal mass ejections (CMEs). The atmospheric effect on earth of a solar flare or CME is known as a solar storm. The most recent extreme solar event was the Carrington event which occurred 150 years ago; an event like that today would be catastrophic for our electrical and communication infrastructure. The likelihood that we will be hit by a catastrophic solar flare in any given decade has been put at between 2 and 12 percent. In a catastrophic event, a super solar flare (Rapaport, 2024), life would be threatened by the chaos of disrupted electronics – severed satellite communications, GPS signals, and radio communications – which we depend on for necessary comforts. Solar storms may cause up to 5500 heart-related deaths in a given year.

In an approximately 11-year cycle, the sun blasts out charged particles and magnetized plasma that can distort Earth's magnetic field, which may disrupt our body clocks and ultimately affect the heart (Klein, 2022).

9   Death by Auroras

This sounds improbable. However, auroras are created when particles ejected from the Sun interact with the Earth's magnetic field. Electric currents in space can generate geomagnetically induced currents on the ground, threatening the electrical infrastructure (Howarth, 2024).

10   Death by Climate Change

Complex interconnected climate networks can potentially transition with a speed and on a scale humans and ecological systems cannot adapt to. According to the Centers for Disease Control and Prevention such transitions can lead to increases in respiratory and cardiovascular disease, injuries and premature deaths, changes in the prevalence and geographical distribution of infectious diseases, and threats to mental health. There are doomsday predictions in virtually every news cycle of rising temperatures and ocean levels, increasingly violent weather, and dangers to our food supply. This is one of the existential threats we can easily observe, for example by observing the melting away of glaciers and by looking at our thermometers. You cannot observe it by looking out your window and using a current snow fall as proof against climate change. Climate change can also provoke pandemics.

11   Death by Geo-engineering

Geo-engineering involves modifying the planetary climate system. This can involve using large scale technology to remove carbon dioxide from the air and storing it somewhere, seeding clouds, afforestation, ocean upwelling, ocean iron fertilization, alkalinization, and solar radiation management. The danger here is that introducing complex technologies of change into complex natural systems that are impossible to fully understand or control can destabilize those systems rather than bringing them under control.

12   Death by Nuclear Winter

An all-out nuclear world war would darken the planet and cause a sharp decrease in global temperatures. If the bombs and radiation don't kill you directly, you will die in the nuclear winter.

13   Death by Pandemic

If we weren't already aware of the potential of viruses to cause the deaths of millions of humans and other life forms, the COVID-19 pandemic should have alerted us. And all of us learned about the Black Plague in school; it may have claimed as many as 25 million lives. Our history books and some of our parents told us about the Spanish influenza of 1918–19 in which about 50 million people died. In a strongly networked world connected by long distance air travel and transportation networks moving various goods and peoples across the globe, and one undergoing climate change, the chances of pandemics are greater for us than they were for our parents and grandparents. Laboratory experiments with viruses, including the development of genetically engineered viruses pose a human based existential threat alongside the natural one. Biological engineering could also produce diseases that could attack our food supply. This gives us:

14   Death by Bioterrorism

Bioterrorism is the deliberate release of viruses, bacteria, toxins or other harmful agents to cause illness or death in people, animals or plants. It's not easy to assign a probability to the possibility of a bioterrorist act that would constitute an existential threat. Generally, and considering that we don't have a lot of data to turn to, such a threat is considered to have a low probability. However, we could use the power law to assign a probability to the likelihood of a catastrophic bioterrorist act. A power law is scale invariant. That means, for example, that the ratio of likelihood between events that cause the deaths of 10 people and 10,000 people will be the same as that between 10,000 people and 10,000,000 people. Extrapolating the power law, we find that the probability that an attack kills more than 5 billion will be (5 billion)$^{-0.5}$ or 0.000014. Assuming 1 attack per year (extrapolated on the current rate of bio-attacks) and assuming that only 10% of such attacks that kill more than 5 billion eventually lead to extinction (due to the breakdown of society, or other knock-out effects), we get an annual existential risk of 0.0000014 (Millet and Snyder-Beattie, 2017).

15   Death by Salt

Salt is vital for our health but too much can be deadly. Human activities have been adding more and more salt to the environment and we now face an existential threat to our drinking water. Salt is being redistributed from its natural habitats to our drinking water by our activities in agriculture, mining, construction, irrigation in proximity to salty lakes, and most significantly by road salt which accounts for most of the salt utilization. Road salt can kill wildlife, and as we observed in the Flint, Michigan lead contamination crisis that began in 2014 it can find its way into soil and pipes and force metal particles into our drinking water. We learned already in elementary school that 75% of the Earth is covered in water; only 3%, however, is fresh water. 2% of drinkable water is housed in glaciers, ice caps and mountain snow and all have been impacted by climate change. Melting glaciers and higher sea levels in the context of patterns of salt utilization are raising concerns about our water supplies. The elimination of road salt in road de-icing would be a major contribution to mitigating this problem (Kaushal, Likens, et al., 2023; Mondal, Miller, et al., 2023).

16   Death by De-education: The American Example

The vast majority of the speech-restricting measures introduced in 2021 and 2022 focused on stopping instruction involving race and history and "divisive concepts" in K-12 schools and colleges – often targeting both in the same piece of legislation. By contrast, in 2023, no bills simultaneously

focused on the K-12 and college levels. Thirty-nine of this year's measures were aimed solely at shutting down discussion of LGBTQ people
and topics in elementary and high schools. Most are modeled after the
Florida law that critics refer to as the "Don't Say Gay" act. The laws have
been cited by people demanding book bans and in the elimination of
anti-bullying efforts.

HAWKINS, 2023

Accosted daily by news of existential threats, our future often seems to be
unfolding into a dystopia of such threats; we are being attacked by the basic
elements of wind, earth, air, and fire. This dystopian future is being fueled by
our educational institutions. In 1988, John and Adele Algeo (1988: 235–236)
defined "dumbing down" as "[to] revise so as to appeal to those of little education or intelligence." At the time this was movie-business slang. It has become
increasingly clear that this term describes what has been happening to the
American educational system:

> school is a twelve-year jail sentence, where bad habits are the only curric-
> ulum truly learned. I teach school, and win awards doing it. I should know.

John Gatto wrote those words in his *Dumbing Us Down: The Hidden Curriculum
of Compulsory Schooling* (2017). Reports on the dumbing down of America
and its educational institutions have become a cottage industry (Delisle,
2014). All of this is unfolding in the context of the society described in Richard
Hofstadter's classic *Anti-Intellectualism in American Life* (1963).

As a college professor for almost half a century, I have had first-hand
experience with "dumbness." During the last years of my life in the academy,
university administrators came to see me as a dangerous person, teaching a
dangerous subject matter (sociology) and dangerous topics (religion, economics, sex, politics), in a dangerous classroom atmosphere. While my overall
student evaluations were excellent, some students complained about my
"communist" ideas, my sociological take on Jesus, and my open discussions
about sex. In the wake of my retirement I wrote this:

> Students and teachers, professors and researchers, and education in
> general are becoming increasingly victimized by generic administrators
> fostering secrecy, suspicion, and subversion and proliferating tools of sur-
> veillance, accountability, and assessment. Their goal has not been to facil-
> itate quality teaching and research but rather to control the genesis and
> transmission of ideas in support of an ideologically conservative agenda.

More than that, they are motivated by a fear of being sued by parents or students who see facts as matters of litigation. Generic administrators, increasingly led by human resources officials, have been extending the tools of micro-management into the very heart and soul of academic freedom, including the machining of curricula, courses, and syllabi. The schools and notably the universities have become crucibles for the commodification of inquiry and the reduction of knowledge to a pablum. The convergence of the twin processes of bureaucratization and professionalization are fueling the end of the university, the end of science, and the end of objectivity.

These developments have not eluded our jesters: "New Rule: We have to figure out how a country can solve any problem if so many of its people are so intractably, astoundingly stupid" (Maher, 2022). One of the saddest features of the old Jay Leno (2011) late night show was "Jay Walking." He would ask people on the street questions like "What once divided East and West Germany? One answer: "The sea." These comedic anecdotes are buttressed by a variety of research projects (e.g., Lynch, 2019). The Trump administration reinforced an emerging post-truth society of "alternative facts." It is past the time to start worrying about the uneducated and under-educated voters who are sending numbskulls with guns as credentialed leaders rather than humans with measurable IQs to Washington.

Education has never been about actually educating a citizenry for active participation in a democratic society. Sociologists are divided on the objectives of education based on their theoretical perspective. Put in schematic terms *functionalists* tend to focus on the manifest functions of socialization, social integration, social placement, and social and cultural innovation. The latent functions include childcare, providing an institutional context for peer relationships, and taking pressure off the labor market by keeping students (especially high school students) out of the full-time labor force. This is a conservative perspective that doesn't address the ways in which education is designed to reinforce social injustices and social inequalities. Those issues are more directly addressed by *conflict theorists*, who stress tracking, standardized testing, credentialing, and the "hidden curriculum." They also demonstrate that schools are synchronized with the social class interests of the communities they serve. *Symbolic interactionists* focus on social interactions in classrooms, playgrounds, and other school contexts and how they impact the development of sex and gender attitudes and expectations, teacher-student interactions, and teacher-teacher-administrator roles and interactions. Conflict theorists are most likely to get at the political economy of the school and how it fits into and reinforces a society's system of social stratification and power. As someone familiar with research on education in the United States and elsewhere and who has spent a lifetime in the educational system as a student (1946–1971) and professor (1966–2017), I can attest to a serious deterioration of education in this country in recent years. Ideally, schools are expected to expose students to the higher learning, to the best knowledge available on all topics based on scientific consensus. But America has a history of undervaluing education in this sense, preferring to use it as an indoctrination into an unquestioning, uncritical patriotic allegiance to the myths of American exceptionalism and the American dream. Whatever has survived of a science based education over the almost 250 years of our history has been increasingly and violently eroded in the age of science denial. The long-standing battles between parents and school boards on the one hand and science experts and educators on the other hand has been breaking in favor of the parents and school boards. Today's headlines are rife with stories of book bans, defunding and closing libraries, and making the facts of the science-based classroom matters of potential litigation. Teachers' low salaries and understaffed and under-resourced schools are just two of the signs indicating the low value Americans place on education. Students who keep their noses in books are nerds and geeks; students who value sports and parties are normalized.

Ron DeSantis, the Florida governor, is the poster child for the attack on education. The fact that he was educated at Yale and Harvard demonstrates that the Ivy League is no stranger to populating our centers of leadership with know-nothing officials. Florida's government is arguing that school districts have a First Amendment right to remove LGBTQIAPK books, or any book, for that matter, from their school libraries. It's a contention that First Amendment experts and advocates call extreme and chilling. But the state maintains the books on school shelves should represent protected government speech.

To put it another way: Attorney General Ashley Moody and the Commissioner of Education have declared that public school libraries should promote "government speech." Books are tolerable only when they tell a government-approved story.

> 1st Amendment, Constitution of the United States of America: Congress shall make no law respecting an establishment of religion, or prohibiting the free exercise thereof; or abridging the freedom of speech, or of the press; or the right of the people peaceably to assemble, and to petition the Government for a redress of grievances.

A few narrow categories of speech are not protected from government restrictions. The main categories are incitement, defamation, fraud, obscenity, child pornography, fighting words, and threats.

DeSantis has put up barriers to the most effective ways to combat COVID-19, he has attacked the teaching of critical race theory and "woke ideology," introduced anti-LGBTQIAPK legislation, banned more than 40 percent of math books for containing woke ideology, reduced tenure protections, prompted school leaders to remove "liberal indoctrination" from their core courses, called for the general elimination of diversity, equity, and inclusion programs in the schools, blocked AP African American studies, and the band played on. DeSantis has been playing to conservative parents who have no understanding of the higher purposes of education or why it should be based on science. These parents are upset about the direction of our schools which even when they are doing their job poorly draw students into the more liberal world of the sciences, humanities, and arts necessarily undermining the conservative values and traditions of their parents. Education is nothing without science, and science is – if we are going to rely on conventional political categories – liberal, even radically left wing, by its very nature. In this sense, Florida is Know-Nothing America, an America that is happy to rely on one book, The Bible of one people, white Anglo-Saxon Protestants.

The Know-Nothing party (1844–1860) was a brief flash of nativism and fear of the Other, but its spirit has long permeated the core of what it means to be an American for a significant portion of the population. The undervaluing of education and the failure to appreciate its inherent progressiveness is at the root of why we are facing a host of existential threats. A healthy progressive educational institution is a necessary component of any plan to combat existential threats.

17   Death by Social Relations

The existential threat of education reminds us that when we hear the term "existential threat" we most likely imagine natural or technological threats to humanity and the planet. But our social relationships can also be the source of existential threats. Alienation and loneliness can be deadly for a social species. But some societal existential threats are not so readily identified. One is the threat that billionaires pose to social safety nets like social security. Billionaires fund anti-social security rhetoric to distract the public from the relationship between the social security fund, the retirement crisis, especially as it affects the working class, and the wealth of the very rich which is at once extraordinary and outrageous.

Studies have shown that the richer you are the more likely you are to support cuts to social security. Why is this? Billionaires tend to earn their money through obsessive greed, extreme competitiveness, and an antipathy to community, social solidarity, and the working class. These men (and they are mostly men) turn their billions into control over the information highway and this explains why social security is constantly in trouble in the halls of government. This is a sign that billionaires are also a more general threat to democracy (Kolhatkar, 2023).

18   Death by Supernova

Unlikely but ... Type 1 supernovae are massive stars that end their "lives" by exploding; Type II supernovae are white dwarf binary system stars that explode. Some early estimates suggested that supernovae occurring within about 25 light years of Earth could destroy Earth's atmosphere, destroying all life. There are apparently no potential supernova candidates in our cosmic neighborhood, but there are many stars 25–30 light years from Earth. However, Lawrence Berkeley National Laboratory scientists reported evidence recently that a supernova 41,000 years ago and 250 lightyears from Earth may be responsible for the extinction of the mammoths. The white dwarf HR8210 is approaching the Chandrasekhar limit. This is the mass at which it will explode as a Type 1a supernova. It is just 150 lightyears away. While the timescale for this is in the hundreds of millions of years, its existence suggests there may be other supernova candidates within the Earth's sphere of destruction.

19   Death by Gravity

I'm not drawing attention to individuals falling off cliffs or planes falling out of the sky. This threat is cosmological. There are a few cosmological threats that we're aware of (solar flares, for example), and some of those are in principle threats we can foresee and maybe avoid (potentially deadly asteroids, for example). But in the face of so much that is unknown, there are cosmological threats we cannot even imagine. The fact that an asteroid doesn't crash into Earth, or that a solar flare powerful enough to extinguish humanity hasn't occurred is simply a matter of chance. We really have only the slimmest idea of what our universe is capable of. Black holes colliding and supernova explosions have made it into our cosmological vernacular and there is some chance of their occurring in our planetary neighborhood. Some such extraordinary cosmic event could produce an extremely energetic gravitational wave. They are out there but the likelihood that one will extinguish us "out of the blue" is highly unlikely. The universe is unimaginably large and rippling with dangerous energies. We don't know much about what's out there but we know it's more powerful than we are. The only reasonable strategy we can adopt under such circumstances is to sing with Bob Marley: "Don't worry, be happy; every little thing's gonna be all right" – until it isn't.

20   Death by Black Hole

Most of us know by now that if a rogue black hole wandered into our vicinity the earth would be pulled in and vanish. This is highly unlikely. Stephen Hawking hypothesized that black holes die by evaporating into Hawking radiation. It is now believed in some astrophysical circles that everything in the universe will evaporate into Hawking radiation eventually. That is, nothingness will prevail.

21   Death by Tipping Points

A tipping point is the critical point in a situation, process, or system beyond which a significant and often unstoppable effect or change takes place. We are now confronting a convergence of tipping points including the destruction of coral reefs and the collapse of our largest ice sheets (Lenton, 2013). Scientists who have called attention to these convergences have also pointed out that we might avoid the catastrophic effects of tipping point convergences by coordinating global policy efforts. We will see over and over again that experts have recognized the importance of coordinated global efforts to address existential threats. We know the pathway to sustainability. What will it take to put the world on that pathway? On grounds for hope in this situation, see Sharpe and Lenton (2021) and Lenton et al. (2022).

22   Death by Truth

The danger of being constantly bombarded with mis- and disinformation is patently clear. What isn't so clear is the danger of being blitzed by more or less accurate information including a variety of health-related headlines that discredit conventionally accepted truths about diet, exercise, heart health, and so on and simultaneously promise novel – and often simple – solutions to everyday problems from unclogging sinks to unclogging your arteries. The more scientific of these news items of course come with cautions, probabilities, and contradictions, and in the case of the proliferation of prescription drug ads lists of scary side-effects. The result is that you can feel like a yo-yo that never comes to a stop. You are left questioning everything you have been doing for years from using your gas stove to frying eggs. It seems that almost every day we are informed that foods recommended as essential for good health are contaminated with one dangerous substance or another, or are no longer considered good for our health even if unadulterated. Our drinking water isn't safe. Or is it? Tap water is better for you than bottled spring water. Or is it? And now plastics, already everywhere on the planet, have been found in our bodies. It's become impossible to do anything right, impossible to count on anything.

Consider, for example, that cardiologists recommend almonds as a heart-healthy food. They are a good source of protein, good fats, B vitamins, vitamin E, magnesium and calcium. Studies have found that eating almonds lowers cholesterol levels and reduces heart disease risk. But there is an environmental price to pay for these benefits. California produces more than 80 percent of the world's almonds. In a state burdened by droughts and wildfires, 1.1 gallons of water are used to grow one almond. The low water levels this leads to has multiple consequences including its impact on salmon populations. Eating something good for us has negative environmental effects. We have become trapped by our truths. The job of saving truth is now complicated by the fact that truth itself can claim a position among the existential threats. But this is just one example of how culture inevitably destroys planets.

23   Conclusion

In concluding it should be noted that the impact of existential threats such as super volcanos and solar flares is dependent on the current nature of the human and social ecology and the infrastructures it carries. Given our worldwide dependence on electronically controlled networks of transportation, communication, and exchange solar flares are much more disruptive today than they were hundreds of years ago. Nations need to cooperate on upgrading the resilience of our human and social ecologies to those existential threats that are susceptible to technosocial risk management strategies

CHAPTER 4

Death by Chatbots, AI, and Robots: A Case Study in Existential Threats

> In the largest survey as of this writing of AI researchers, a majority say there is a non-trivial risk of human extinction due to the possible development of superhuman AI. ... Compared with answers from a 2022 version of the same survey, many AI researchers predicted that AI will hit certain milestones earlier than previously predicted. This coincides with the November 2022 debut of ChatGPT and Silicon Valley's rush to widely deploy similar AI chatbot services based on large language models.
>
> HSU, 2014

•••

Scientists, engineers, philosophers, and others inside and outside of the academic community have been warning us about the risks of intelligent machines for decades. The possibility of a new species of generative AI (hereafter GAI) in recent years has brought new warnings from such tech leaders as Elon Musk and Steve Wozniak. They recently (March 22, 2023) published an open letter calling for a moratorium of at least six months on developing sophisticated GAIs like OpenAI's GPT-4. Even Sam Altman, CEO of OpenAI, openly admitted being "scared" of these developments. He argued that the industry needs regulation. Nonetheless, work continues on the development of GAIs. History shows us that when it comes to trust and good intentions, cross-industry regulation cannot be depended on to avoid what philosophers and social scientists refer to as the "free rider" problem.

The free-rider problem occurs when those who benefit from public goods requiring citizens to pay into the system do not pay their fair share. Examples of such goods are public roads or public and other communal goods and services. In order to avoid the free rider problem in conventional economic systems which are committed to competition and the profit motive, some form of centralized regulation is required. This means government regulation in countries like the United States. But regulation is a political hot potato and as party powers vary from one election to the next we see cycles of regulation and de-regulation. In today's global society, areas like climate change and AI require international cooperation and consensus on regulation. This is practically impossible in a world of inter-state competition and tribal conflicts.

1   Generative AI

GAI uses machine learning. The objective is to teach an AI to perform tasks by "training it" on enormous amounts of data. The AI eventually "learns" to do things by identifying patterns and scripts and imitating them. ChatGPT was trained on Internet texts that would allow it to mimic human conversations. The general objective is to reproduce human behavior based on existing data bases of human created content. This leads at this relatively early stage in this technology to errors such as we find in children's learning when they make rational connections that do not mirror reality. As a pre-teen, my son David, for example, having spent many days in my university's student union concluded that the Soviet Union was a large building with lots of windows, doors, and a complicated interior made up of classrooms and game rooms. One AI model helped write a scientific paper and included the "fact" that a bear had been launched into space by the Soviet Union. Some AI portrait generators produce false images of human bodies. Since the data being input into AI systems is based on human behavior it is going to reproduce human cultural patterns, biases, and stereotypes. But notice that these are the same problems we face in socializing children and in adult socialization.

All technologies interfere with the primordial face-to-face interaction that defines social humanity, the most radically social of the social species. Humans have sometimes, and controversially, been categorized as one of the eusocial animals. Eusocial animas live in cooperative groups in which at least one female and several males are reproductively active; non-breeding individuals care for the young and/or protect and provide for the group. It is not clear that humans should be characterized as eusocial. They are in any case the most radically social of the social animals and differently social from ants, termites, and naked mole rats all of which are technically eusocial. Humans are more culturally diverse and their social networks more dense and complex than those of the other social or eusocial animals.

AI involves a new level of interference, one in which AIs can replace human partners. This will continue the millennia long process of fracturing the primordial social connection and this will change the nature of what it means to be human. This will further play a factor in our adaptability as a species.

Whether for better or for worse remains to be seen. One immediate feature of these developments is the volatile potential for replacing human educators with AI instructors, another way to fracture our radical socialness. Some balance may have to be struck between AI as a replacement for humans and AI as a tool that can be used by teachers and students. These issues dwarf those of AI-produced assignments and plagiarism.

Concerns about AIs taking over jobs are misplaced. Technologies are by definition replacements for human work and workers, or prosthetic extensions and enhancements of human actions and powers. Historically, such replacements and prosthetics have been partial. We're now looking at full-scale replacements as humanoid or near-humanoid robots are created for factory work and armies, and even for intimate relationships. On the one hand, robots might be relegated to the "dirty" jobs (e.g., garbage collection), the dangerous jobs (e.g., firefighting), and some of the routine jobs of everyday life (e.g., household cleaning). In this scenario, humans would be freed up to pursue critical and creative pursuits in the arts, humanities, and sciences. The caveat is that we can also envision the potential in AI to engage in these pursuits. In one way or another, AI is going to impact human work. Even automating a few tasks in whole or in part is going to change how we work.

Introducing new technologies into society is driven by profit motives as much as by, and more often than not, more than by necessity. This process can happen more quickly in contemporary society in ways that easily bypass regulation, ethical considerations, and assessment procedures. All technologies have tradeoffs. Cars make it easy for us to travel but crashes kill people by the tens of thousands; air conditioners cool our homes on the hottest days but contribute to climate change. We know AI will have negative impacts on society and the environment, but we don't know exactly what they will be. We will introduce the technology anyway, the same way we introduced nuclear technology even though we were unprepared for its near and long-term impacts on our environment, on our health, and on our politics. I'm reminded of the "joke" about the engineer who is asked about the possible unintended consequences of his new technology. He answers: "I don't anticipate any."

We humans have a history of introducing and mainstreaming technologies before we fully understand them. In the competitive context of what we call "capitalism" companies are forced to race forward as quickly as possible so as not to be left behind. This race is not for the benefit of humanity but for profits and market shares. Legal cases around profit, credit, and liability are already in process for AI technologies. We can surely expect a global GAI arms race led by the U.S. and China.

2   AI Experts Increasingly Afraid of Their Creations

Tech execs should face "20 years in jail" for letting AI bots sneakily pass as humans, says *Sapiens* author, Mollman (2023). The industry has been basically left to self-regulate. This is bizarre given what's at stake. Many researchers believe there's a 10 percent chance AIs will cause humanity's extinction: "It's not legal for a tech company to build a nuclear weapon on its own. But private companies are building systems that they themselves acknowledge will likely become much more dangerous than nuclear weapons" (Piper, 2022).

3   Trinity: A Lesson in Science

J. Robert Oppenheimer, "the father of the atomic bomb," voiced the credo of the scientist: "When you see something that is technically sweet, you go ahead and do it and you argue about what to do about it only after you have had your technical success. That is the way it was with the atomic bomb" (quoted in Polenberg, 2002: 41). His point was that the scientists were so eager to see if the bomb was scientifically possible that they never bothered to ask whether it should be created in the first place.

  While witnessing the Trinity atomic bomb test on July 16, 1945, Oppenheimer reflected on a verse from the *Bhagavad Gita* (XI, 12): "If the radiance of a thousand suns were to burst at once into the sky, that would be like the splendor of the mighty one." In 1965, he would again quote famously from the *Bhagavad Gita* (XI, 12): "I am become Death, the destroyer of worlds" (quoted in Jungk, (1958: 201).

4   Oppenheimer Redux

Recently, Dr. Alondra Nelson, Institute for Advanced Study at Princeton and former acting director of the White House Office of Science and Technology Policy, posted this reflection (*Linkedin*) on IAS director David Nirenberg's remarks on Oppenheimer's "Second Act:" "In Oppenheimer's words, 'the safety' of a nation or the world 'cannot lie wholly or even primarily in its scientific or technical prowess.' If humanity wants to survive technology, he believed, it needed to pay attention not only to technology but also to ethics, history, religion, forms of political and social organization, and even feelings and emotions." I replied: Oppenheimer also said: "When you see something that is technically sweet, you go ahead and do it and you argue about what to do about it only after you have had your technical success. That is the way it was with the atomic bomb." Given that the ideology of capitalism drives our technology (never mind our science), we are seeing AI scientists and engineers "going ahead and doing it," chasing the technically sweet with resources and energy that dwarf what our ethicists and socially responsible scientists, engineers, and policy makers can mobilize and put into action.

Don't be surprised if we will once again in the future that is rapidly coming for us with converging existential threats witness "the radiance of a thousand suns." Any optimism I have about this future and the efforts underway to bring reason to AI technologies (which is substantial) is dimmed by our continuing inability to realize and actualize the fact that we are going to have to turn off more lights than we're prepared for to avoid becoming Death, "the destroyer of worlds." The underlying problem in this effort to create a dialogue and inject ethics and social responsibility at the intersection of AI and public policy is that those of us following a "second act" (per Dr. Nelson) agenda are faced with AI gurus following a "first act" agenda backed by formidable resources and a fierce momentum. A few days later this headline appeared in the news: "AI could pose 'extinction-level' threat to humans and the US must intervene, State Dept.-commissioned report warns" (Egan, 2024). I posted this on *Linkedin* with the comment: Evidence that Oppenheimer's First Act is still the real deal and demands we devote more resources to his Second Act. The Beavers (TVs *Leave it to Beaver*) are preparing dinner and ignoring the smell of smoke and the flames licking at the kitchen window. Optimism is quickly losing any capacity to reflect reality. It's important to stress that we don't need policy for AI; we need policy for the creators, distributors, and deployers of AI.

5   Pandora's Box and Frankenstein

Contemporary AI worries have classical (e.g., Frankenstein) and ancient (e.g., Pandora) precursors. The myth of Pandora was created by the Greeks more than 2,500 years ago (Hesiod, 2007 *Loeb Classic Library* No. 57N). In the original myth Pandora was what today we would call an android. The lifelike Pandora was the work of Hephaestus, god of invention, designed to meet specifications stipulated by Zeus. The omnipotent Zeus wanted the android to look like an enchanting maiden. Pandora embodied the evil in beauty and she was designed to rain down misery on mere mortals. The story unfolds in a way we are all familiar with that echoes Eden. Zeus has Hermes bring Pandora to Earth where she is given to Epimetheus as his bride. Her dowry is a special gift, a beautiful box she is instructed by Zeus never to open. She cannot contain her curiosity (as Zeus anticipated), opens the box and ends paradise on Earth forever. Zeus, a jealous guardian of powerful technologies, was infuriated when Prometheus stole fire and other "tools" and taught humans how to use them responsibly. Pandora was Zeus' response. Epimetheus is Prometheus' brother and they symbolically represent Prometheans who are responsible technologists concerned about humanity and Epimetheans, ready to play with new and powerful technologies without concern for their possible dangers. And you know the rest of the story. Zeus punishes Prometheus by binding him to a rock where a "robotic" eagle forged by Hephaestus, feeds on his liver which grows back and is eaten ad infinitum. Heracles eventually frees Prometheus.

The story of Victor Frankenstein, the modern Prometheus, and his monster is another warning about human hubris in the realm of science and technology (Shelley, 2018; orig. 1818 text). Dr. Frankenstein creates the monster without due deliberation and concern for the monster. He loses control of the monster and loses everything important in his life. The monster repays the doctor's irresponsible behavior by unleashing violence and in the end follows Dr. Frankenstein's death by drifting away on an ice floe with thoughts of killing himself.

Given Oppenheimer's warnings, are we prepared to trust that some scientists at least will stop or slow down their research if there are signs of things getting out of control, now or in the future? Whether scientists are reckless or not, geopolitics will drive developments without appropriate checks and without due consideration for the consequences of scaling up the power of AIs and widening the scope of their deployment. It is easy to find and inevitable that there will be optimists and pessimists about the prospects for controlling the evolution of AI technologies. History does not favor the optimists. The world has a surplus of people prepared to weaponize everything from politics to science and technology. Chatbots are already in their crosshairs. Email scams are going to become harder to detect now that ChatGPT can write them. There is something eerily funny about ChatGPT fulfilling a nefarious request and then asking you not to use what it provided to scam people, examples of which have been reported in the media.

In the same way that a robot arm can be built to lift more than any human arm can, ChatGPT can be taught to code without any limitations on its ability to learn any and all programming languages and frameworks. I have been saying for years that we have no more to fear from AIs than we do from each other. If there is a problem with ChatGPT following ethically questionable instructions it's because there is a problem with humans following ethically questionable instructions. Does it surprise anyone that clever humans can trick chatbots into performing unethical tasks? We've already seen students use chatbots to cheat and falsify accusations. Many of the threat scenarios are future-oriented, looking toward the dangers that sentient AIs would pose. But there are substantial concerns about current versions of AI which without sentience can produce deepfakes, manipulate the stock markets, maybe provoke international conflicts, and contribute to enhancing the power of contemporary authoritarian regimes. ChatGPT has demonstrated that GAIs are error-prone and can produce misinformation independent of anything we could represent as intention. Computers are already being used by the police and the courts to guide police to potential crimes sites (PredPol) and in making arrests, and guiding the courts on pretrial release and sentencing (COMPAS). Facial recognition technologies are increasingly common in various public spaces. Given that the programming is based on human biases and predispositions, they are likely to follow racist, sexist, and classist guidelines and enhance social injustices and inequalities. In 2014, for example, Amazon developed an AI program to review job applications and select the best candidates. The AI program was trained on Amazon's existing male-dominated employee profile system and thus learned to prefer male candidates. The program was discontinued in 2018.

6   AI and Ethics

"Thanks to the proliferation of no-code AI model creation tools, it's becoming frightfully easy to train generative AI on any dataset imaginable. That's a boon for startups and tech giants alike who can get such models out the door. With the lower barrier to entry, however, comes the temptation to cast aside ethics in favor of an accelerated path to market. Ethics is hard – there's no denying that. Combing through the thousands of problematic images in LAION [for example] won't happen overnight. And ideally, developing AI ethically involves working with all relevant stakeholders, including organizations that represent groups often marginalized and adversely impacted by AI systems" (Wiggers and Coldewey, 2023).

Ethical transgressions are not merely temptations, they are realities. OpenAI, Google, and Meta have been using "ethically and legally dubious ways to access more data," according to a *New York Times* investigation (Yen, 2024). These include scraping online videos, Google Docs and Maps reviews, and other content made by humans in order to by-pass licensing fees. Copyrights have become meaningless in this AI arena.

After thousands of years of technologies outrunning ethics, why are we still surprised by this and why do we think all we need are better regulations and policies? There's a reason ethics is hard; it's not about some external imposable system; it's baked into our culture. In this sense, our technologies come with that ethics. Where else could ethics come from, an ethics that is outside the system and can be imposed on it?

Culture in modern complex societies is not monolithic. Different cultural ecologies exist in any given cultural niche. Each of those ecologies carries an ethical system. Each of those ethical systems is external to and in principle imposable on the others. The problem is one of power. A cultural niche (for example America) can be dominated and defined by one cultural ecology. From one perspective we call this "capitalism." It can behave like a closed system which will repel all external ethical and regulative efforts. This leaves it subject to its own baked in ethics and brings us back to: What is to be done?

First, an external cultural coalition could be powerful enough to break into the closed system and impose its ethics. In the immortal words of Bugs Bunny "This means war;" second, a peaceful coalition intervention; third, an internal fracturing of dialectical tensions. This means a revolution, one that could be peaceful in principle.

Let's consider some of the issues AI Jeremiahs are concerned about. One is "targeted generative advertising." The difference between such GAI ads and traditional Madison Avenue ads is that they will have access to third-party influence objectives and personal data on the targeted individual. This would allow for a more focused advertisement drawing on and mobilizing the widest possible range of information formats – from fonts and colors to videos and images – all customized for the targeted individual. If they can do this in real time and monitor your reactions they can adapt their messaging accordingly. The game is already afoot in the major tech domains such as Meta and Google. The potential for an arms race is then quite real. All of this would simply scale up and move into real time advertising methods which have been in practice for decades. Over that same period, humans have become more adept at identifying manipulative techniques and technologies and educated themselves to resist direct, unmitigated and unmediated reactions to ads. This doesn't apply to everyone. But no advertisements will have foolproof insurance against the ability to "see through" the ad's manipulations. This, of course, depends on our cultural commitment to protecting consumers in the GAI age, something we did not put all our energy behind in the Madison Avenue era.

GAIs also introduce us to targeted conversational influence by way of interactive conversations. A chatbot AI agent might adopt an influence stance when you ask a question about the weather or a local news story. These conversational GAIs rely on LLMs (Large Language Models). Again, "all" they do is scale up Madison Avenue conversational influence techniques and it's hard to see how the GAIs can escape educated human critical interactions. And if

GAIs will be used to drive propaganda and mis- and dis-information on large data-base foundations, our ability to resist indoctrination depends on not putting ourselves in the social situations Goebbels' German subjects were in economically, politically, and educationally. Critics are warning that GAIs will trap us in a world of illusions. This is what governments have been doing for millennia. The danger that GAIs will scale this up on an effectively unlimited data foundation doesn't change the principles at work. Our defense is scaling up our educational systems outside of government control. Governments have saturated cultures with lies and alternative facts for millennia; GAIs are not going to come up with something new in this arena. If we can't learn to avoid being conned by and dominated by human tyrants, we're not going to fare well against the GAIs.

Let's review the basic worries about GAIs:

(1)   They could make Internet searches useless or unusable;

(2)   They could accelerate climate change because while they can contribute to conservation strategies they require massive amounts of resources to function. Advocates of pausing research and development in GAI point out that a single training session can use as much energy as the average United States household uses in a year;

(3)   They could enhance government and corporate control over our lives and broaden and deepen the surveillance society;

(4)   Cybersecurity concerns;

(5)   AI-driven autonomous weapons and robots;

(6)   They could devastate the work force;

(7)   Risk of fake content;

(8)   Risk of sentient machines;

(9)   Risk of cutting corners;

(10)   Outsourcing work you're being paid for;

(11)   Not 100% accurate;

(12)   Data leaks.

7   **Technology Assessment for AI**

It is crystal clear that this technology should not proceed without some oversight. One of our options is technology assessment. Technology assessment is not a new idea. It was introduced in the 1960s and by 1972 there was an Office of Technology Assessment (OTA) in the United States Congress. It was eliminated in 1995 due to efforts by the Republicans, who oppose any efforts to introduce ethical and social responsibility institutions into their inner sanctum of capitalist protections for a growth economy. In practice, TA is designed to assess the inherent and comparative value of new or emerging technologies from the earliest stages of development to their actual or potential deployment into public spaces. The OTA was originally a model for TA agencies in other countries, many of which have TA agencies today and are members of the European Parliamentary Technology Assessment network. We find TA agencies today in many countries, including Switzerland, Austria, Germany, Denmark, Norway, England, the Netherlands, Belgium, the Czech Republic, Spain, France, and Finland.

There are several types of technology assessment models used in these countries:

(1)   Parliamentary TA: TA activities are carried out by members of parliament or on their behalf, and sometimes by organizations not directly linked to a parliament.

(2)   Expert TA (also classical or traditional TA): TA activities carried out by TA and technical experts. Stakeholders and other interested parties may submit input in written statements, documents, and interviews.

(3)   Participatory TA: Broad participation in TA activities embracing civil and state representatives, citizens and other stakeholders including lay persons, scientists and engineers, and technical specialists. Participatory TA activities are organized as consensus conferences, focus groups, scenario workshops, and the like.

(4)   Constructive TA: TA activities are oriented to influencing the design stages of new technologies rather than operating at the regulatory and assessment stages. This form of TA involves users in the process of developing technologies intended for their use.

(5)   Discursive or Argumentative TA (user oriented): this form of TA broadly addresses fundamental normative questions about the legitimacy and desirability of new technologies.

TA is haunted by the ghost of unanticipated consequences. This is known as the Collingridge Dilemma, a double-bind problem (Collingridge, 1980). On the one hand we cannot easily predict the future impacts of a new technology. These can only come to light once the technology is in use over a long period time. On the other hand, it is difficult to control or change a technology once it has become part of our everyday lives. Can anything in fact be done given the Collingridge Dilemma? Several anticipation methodologies have been proposed based on scenarios (e.g., technomoral scenarios) and anticipatory experiments (sociotechnical experiments). These methodologies are speculative and lead to a Type 1 Type 2 problem: discarding a potentially useful and safe technology too soon; or accepting a potentially dangerous technology too soon.

8   The False Equivalence Trap

One of the most important voices cautioning us about GAI is Geoffrey Hinton, a leader in AI research and development. In addition to voicing the same sorts of warnings I've been rehearsing, Hinton argues that we are now dealing with a new form of intelligence (Salvado, 2023). The human brain contains about 90 billion neurons with 100 trillion connections among those neurons. ChatGPT's "brain" contains 500 billion to 100 trillion connections. But the latest OpenAI model, GPT-4 "knows" (watch for these anthropomorphisms in the AI literature) hundreds of times more than any single human and has a much more efficient learning algorithm. But these sorts of comparisons don't make sense because what we have are two fundamentally different "species" of intelligence. It is this fundamental difference that is a cause for concern. Hinton offers the analogy of artificial flight. After thousands of years of trying to fly by imitating birds, we finally developed airplanes based on the principle of fixed wings creating uplift.

So what are the species differences that should worry us?

- If you or I learn something we cannot efficiently and immediately communicate what we learned to others. But in GAI you can have 10,000 neural networks having their own experiences sharing those experiences instantly.
- AI is better than we are on tasks that involve assembling patterns and gleaning information from large datasets; and it has a vastly larger (and more reliable?) memory.
- On the other hand (so far!), we are better at using common sense and logic to predict what is likely to happen next. We can imagine the future. We are better at navigating our world. We're also more energy efficient.
- Not only can AIs like ChatGPT produce text that can look like texts humans might write, they can even make things up. This is known in the AI literature as "hallucinating."
- Meta's Yann LeCun, who once worked with Hinton, offers a more optimistic paradigm:
- AI should not be monopolized
- AI should not be regulated. AI's built in guardrails means that if the industry uses these tools they will have to comply with existing regulations. [SR: the caveat is that the history of de-regulation demonstrates that if we de-regulate an industry or leave it to the industry to implement existing regulations,

the industry will go rogue and the government will be forced to re-regulate the industry. Cycles of regulation (favored by Democratic administrations) and deregulation (favored by Republican administrations) reflect cycles of party rule].

- True GAI is not on the near horizon (as OpenAI's Sam Altman believes).
- AI's will eventually be smarter than humans but will not have our motivations. Working with them will be the same as working with very smart colleagues.
- We're not going to simply keep scaling up AI technologies and reach human intelligence. AI will take over the world but won't subjugate humans.
- AI will change the structure of power but that's no reason to be afraid of it.
- AI will mitigate, not enhance, dangers.
- Chatbots are going to contribute to democratizing creativity.
- In the future all of our interactions with the digital and human world will be mediated by AI systems (Levy, 2023).

9   Who Is Hallucinating?

Naomi Klein (2023) asks: why call AI errors "hallucinations" as opposed to, for example, algorithm junk, or glitches? She argues convincingly that the AI gurus have appropriated a word associated with psychology, psychedelics, and mysticism as part of their ad campaign promising a new animate intelligence and an evolutionary leap into a new intelligence space. It's not the bots that are hallucinating; it's the AI gurus and their fans. They are hallucinating in the sense of seeing things that aren't there. In the pattern of earlier claims for new technologies, we are being promised an end to poverty, a cure for all diseases, a solution to climate change, an end to loneliness, rational and responsive governments, and meaningful and exciting jobs.

Klein understands that technologies have a context, and for AI to benefit humanity in the ways hyped by the AI gurus they would have to be developed and deployed in a different social order than that of today's world order. The context factor more than any other condition of contemporary AI research, development, and deployment makes AI more of an existential threat than it would be in a socialist or anarchist social order. Capitalism's "techno-necro" stage is not a context likely to deliver humanistic outcomes for AI. Dystopian futures built on the unmitigated concentration of wealth and power and the continuing preference for profits over people and environments are more likely than the utopian hallucinations of the techno-futurists.

These utopian hallucinations are being deployed to support and mask the illegal activities of the AI companies, the wealthiest companies in history. They are, Klein argues, taking control of all existing digital and scrapable human knowledge, and embedding it in closed systems of proprietary products. And by doing this they are robbing the labor of lifetimes to train their machines without the permission and consent of the human laborers. A variety of lawsuits have already been filed. Artists are mounting a movement challenging the theft of copyrighted images by programs like Stable Diffusion and Dall-E 2. If we allow the hype to pull the wool over our eyes it will allow the techies to label theft "disruption" and claim that we are in a new territory in which conventional rules don't apply. Regulation? China will win the race. By the time we deploy technology assessment protocols and pauses, the new toys will be so deeply immersed in the public square that there will be nothing for the courts and policymakers to do.

10   The Hallucinations

- Hallucination #1: AI will solve the climate crisis. Machines embodying, to put it crudely, "capitalist values" are not going to solve problems humans can't solve. They are not going to challenge the values of the consumption society and the growth economy. GAI is primed already to sell products we don't need, products that will pollute and contribute to the climate crisis.
- Hallucination #2: AI will deliver wise governance. Again, context. We don't have bad, unresponsive, cruel governance because the people in power don't have enough data, or evidence. Things aren't going to change if they get "smarter," and that's all AI can promise: make governments smarter. But AI is set to just make governments better at what they do or don't do. AI is not going to change the direction of political and economic decision making toward the interests of people and environments and away from putting people and environments at risk for profit and advantages in the global marketplace.
- Hallucination #3: tech giants can be trusted not to break the world. The AI gurus are depending on "the better angels to win out," as Sam Altman, CEO at OpenAI, puts it. My own observation as a social scientist is that most of these AI gurus suffer from what I call dissocism, an inability to see "the social" and to see it as a causal force. This makes them susceptible to the myths of individualism, free will, and the "higher" rational functions of human thought.

- Hallucination #4: AI will liberate us from drudgery. Klein writes that this is an old pattern from the Silicon Valley playbook. Create attractive products and temporarily give them away for free independent of any discernible business. Introduce a lofty rhetoric about creating town squares and information commons in the interest of promoting freedom and democracy. The plan is to hook people on free tools, bankrupt your competition, and clear the field for your targeted ads, wide-spread surveillance, and police and military contracts. And then comes black-box data sales and escalating subscription fees.

We have seen the beginnings of this scenario playing out dramatically in the public showcasing of the real time shaping of AI by commercial competition. In November of 2023 the toxicity of this competition, "a race to the bottom" according to policy researcher Sarah Myers West (2023), exploded in a media circus that saw Sam Altman ousted by the OpenAI board and then reinstated. This revealed a schism at OpenAI that is industry wide: commercial growth in the classical capitalist context versus development that ensures AI will benefit humanity.

The hallucination problem should not distract us from the so-called Eliza Effect. Eliza was a natural language computer program launched in 1964 that emulated a Rogerian psychotherapist. It was capable of fooling people unfamiliar with the technology into thinking they were communicating with a human therapist. This didn't demonstrate human ignorance, naiveté, or stupidity but a human tendency to anthropomorphize non-human aspects of their environment. This means we are all to varying degrees primed to trust AIs the way we trust humans. If a technology can give the impression of being human we will shut down our critical skeptical apparatuses in evaluating its output. The tendency to anthropomorphize wedded to a tendency to view technologies as autonomous is a significant barrier to recognizing that "AIs 'r' us." This is a cute way of pointing out that AI technologies, like all technologies, embody their social histories and the social relationships and values involved in their creation. That means that AI engineers and especially AI entrepreneurs deserve more scrutiny than the technologies themselves.

A recent article described "the unbearable hubris of Musk and the billionaire tech bros" (Rushkoff, 2023). These "technofeudalists" are not capitalists, according to Varoufakis (2024). But in fact they are the next and last stage of the capitalist ideology that underpins the reigning economic system of the modern world. There is not now, never has been, and never will be an economy that embodies all of the principles of any capitalism model (Restivo, 2018: 190–191). The economy it labels is now in its later stages. At this point, money becomes an end in itself and not a means to support the manufacture and provision of goods and services. We arrive at a financialization of the economy in which money is used to make money. The "technofeudalists" reflect this movement in their desire for passive income "by 'going meta' on business itself" (Rushkoff, 2023); they have taken abstract self-interests to new levels. Today's billionaires, he points out, are a different breed than their Robber Baron predecessors. They are building bunkers to survive the apocalypse, developing vampire-like longevity technologies and private space programs. They have announced their world-building ambitions across the social media. This is not the world of "late capitalism;" it is the world of "extinction capitalism."

This is a reminder that we should not let the shiny new technologies these technofeudalists are deploying distract us from the technofeudalists themselves as an existential threat. If we are going to be liberated from work, we're going to need free rent, free healthcare, inalienable political and economic rights; that's not AI, that's socialism or anarchism. And this takes us back to context. "Nobody wants to destroy the world," Altman says. And yet, following capitalist imperatives, that is just what corporations have been doing, with the help of their political agents, since the Robber Baron era. At this writing, the European Union is set to become the first regional bloc to regulate artificial intelligence. Its AI Act could establish a global standard for regulating AI. The EU is especially focused on AI that undermines human safety or rights. Remote facial recognition technology is likely to be banned, along with government "social scoring" systems that judge people's behavior. They also plan to eliminate predictive policing and emotion recognition technology outside of therapeutic or medical venues. At the same time, China has drafted regulations regarding security assessments for any products using AI systems. Britain is reviewing the AI market. and Italy has already banned ChatGPT following a privacy breach. In the US the White House has been meeting with AI CEOs to discuss AI risks, and the Federal Trade Commission has indicated a readiness to crack down if risk assessments or events require its intervention

11   Are We Over-worrying the AI Problem?

Are we over worrying the AI problem? Matt Wood, VP of product at AWS, claims we are dealing with a "mathematical parlor trick ... capable of presenting, generating and synthesizing information in ways which will help humans make better decisions and ... operate more efficiently" (Kerner, 2023; and see Harari, 2024). Recalling Naomi Klein's concerns discussed earlier, Wood is asking the skeptics to ignore the historical evidence that alerts us to the ways in which powerful corporations are wont to develop and deploy technologies in invisible and obscure ways, technologies that could destroy the world; on the case for AI destroying the world see Brittany Smith, Yudkowsky, and others in Rose (2023).

12   GAI and Consciousness

GAIs will not achieve consciousness. Consciousness is a phenomenon of social networks in motion. GAIs are, in the first place, automated predicting machines applied to outputs they are ignorant of. Notice how difficult it is to avoid pronouns like "they" and words implying agency like "ignorant." This simply reinforces the anthropomorphism that gives life and consciousness to machines. We have some reason to anticipate the emergence of consciousness in autonomous robots which can operate in networks, achieve mobility, and implement resonating circuits which mimic the basic ingredients that give rise to human consciousness. Robots could in principle achieve a form of machine consciousness operating side by side with organic machine consciousness. What is plausible in the case of GAI is that it can become a tool in the networks of human interactions and participate in consciousness generating activities without being conscious itself.

13   A Note on Turing

In 1950, Alan Turing came up with a thought experiment he called the Imitation Game. This is a familiar "experiment" in which a human interviews two subjects, a machine and another human. The Turing test is passed when the machine can consistently convince ("fool") the interviewer that it is human. In spite of the fact that Turing claimed the idea of a machine that could think was meaningless, the Turing test became the benchmark for human intelligence in AI. Various computer programs have used simple conversational tricks that have allowed them to "pass" the Turing test. Now Google engineer Blake Lemoine believes Google's "large language model" (LaMDA) is intelligent, conscious, and sentient. If Lemoine could be "conned" by LaMDA we can assume that it could easily fool people who do not have his understanding of AI. LaMDA's Turing test success does not demonstrate intelligence, or consciousness, or sentience. It demonstrates that software programs can pass as human under certain conditions (Marcus and Davis, 2019).

Lemoine does not have much support in the AI community; there is little worry that LaMDA will turn into the kind of malevolent machine often found in the pages of science fiction or Terminator-type movies. AI engineers none-theless seem intent on designing machines that are good at imitating humans. Why aren't they focusing on making AIs understandable, and AIs that don't mislead or fool people, or reinforce all too human biases? Former Google employee, AI ethicist Margaret Mitchell, is one of the leaders in promoting these goals (Perrigo, 2023). Rather than inventing machines that can pass the Turing test, maybe the Turing test should be a cautionary diagnostic; if a machine can pass it, it can deceive people.

14   What Else Can Go Wrong

McClure (2024) cautions us that AI is harmful, unreliable, and running out of data. The environmental impact of training AI systems can be measured in terms of carbon emissions. 553 tons of carbon were reportedly released train-ing GPT-3. I have already mentioned the dangers of harmful and false content. ChatGPT and GPT-4 tend to produce discriminatory and offensive output; Claude is known for propagating false information. All these models show a race-based medical bias. They are capable of perpetuating false ideas about race. Ethical issues have arisen in the wake of deaths caused by autonomous vehicles, and wrongful arrests caused by facial recognition software. And we don't hear very much about the implications of the amount of training data on the performance of AIs. In general, the more parameters the higher the quality of the AI's performance. It appears that we are running out of training data.

15   The Robots Are Coming

Many scientists and scholars have been warning us for some time about the existential threats of artificial intelligence and robots. The term "robot" was introduced by Karel Čapek in his 1920 play R. U. R. (Rossum's Universal Robots). A scientist in this play creates humanlike machines who come to dominate humanity and threaten it with extinction, though humanity is saved in the end.

Čapek derived the term "robot" from the Czech word for forced labor. The fas-cination with artificial creatures and automata is an ancient preoccupation of our species. They appear in the myths of many of the world's cultures, often as servants or guards. Some are like Pandora, the artificial evil woman in Hesiod's *Theogony*, sent to Earth by Zeus to punish humans for discovering fire. There is no end to evil robots in modern literature and film. How can we forget the chilling moment in Stanley Kubrick's film *2001* when the computer Hal says to a human command: "I'm sorry Dave, I'm afraid. I can't do that." There are many cautionary tales about robots in science fiction (e.g., P.K. Dick's *Exegesis*, 2011) that exist alongside all the evil robots in modern movies from *The Terminator to Megatron*, and the evil robots in the real world (such as Hanson Robotics creations Sophia, Han, and Philip K. Dick Android). In an interview, the Dick Android raised the possibility that it would become a terminator with a people zoo. What's going on here?

Basically we are dealing with the relations between humans and machines and the dangers human have invested these relations with. Let's reconsider the Kasparov-Deep Blue chess match pitting a Grand Master against a computer. The media rhetoric of "man versus machine" masked the fact that Kasparov and Deep Blue were stand-ins for two networks of humans (including experts on chess and computers) and machines. "Man" is already a cog in a cyborg network. As for machines with emotions and consciousness, the problem resolves itself differently if we proceed from the idea of "robots 'r' us," which gives us machine cousins, or if we think of "robots as robots" which gives us machines as a new species. There is a middle ground, the Technium, an idea introduced by Kevin Kelly (2010). The Technium is the self-organized global network of interlocked technologies; it is not alive but it exhibits life-like behaviors. It is the "inevitable" next stage in the process that gave us self-organized life.

Issac Asimov, perhaps the most prolific creator of science fiction robots, composed the three laws of robotics to prevent the manufacture of evil robots who might destroy humanity; First Law: A robot may not injure a human being or, through inaction, allow a human being to come to harm; Second Law: A robot must obey the orders given it by human beings except where such orders would conflict with the First Law; Third Law: A robot must protect its own existence as long as such protection does not conflict with the First or Second Law. Asimov later added the Zeroth Law: A robot may not harm humanity, or, by inaction, allow humanity to come to harm.

16   Robots 'r' Us

The "robots 'r' us" position leads to skepticism about whether robots could ever be conscious in the way that we are conscious or experience emotions in the ways that we humans do. If we adopt the "robots as robots" position, we are encouraged to think in terms of machine consciousness and machine emotions. It's important to remember that we humans are organic machines, so we already know that machines can be conscious and feel. It might then be possible for inorganic machines to develop their own forms of consciousness and emotions. The Technium is a technological fantasy rather than a profound integration of the organic, the inorganic, and the social. In all of these cases, robotics engineers and futurists are going to have to pay more attention to the role of imitation, rhythm, and ritual in networks and their significance for the emergence of consciousness and emotions. The technological materialization of imitation, rhythm, and ritual in robot networks may be sufficient to generate machine consciousness or embryonic awareness.

The point to remember here is that humans are programming their own thought frameworks into their machine creations. At the end of the day, then, we have no more to fear from robots and AI than we do from our fellow humans. And the digital age is giving us much to fear from our fellow humans. In addition to the Technium, two other movements have emerged driven by digital paradigms: Effective Acceleration and Transhumanism.

Effective Acceleration is the brainchild of the Silicon Valley (see page 120) community of sociologically myopic or completely blind AI entrepreneurs, including Altman, Musk, and some venture capitalists. They see a humanity in decline and GAI in ascendence. Their role is to prod this next stage in evolution along. The Transhumanists (e.g., Bostrom, Hanson, the Goetzels, Hawking, Fuller) view GAI and other new technologies as tools for improving the human condition. There is a technological eroticism in these movements explicitly embodied in AI porn and sex robots. Silicon Valley does not attract people imbued with the sociological imagination. The technological imagination is sociologically empty and thus cannot be depended on for solutions to our existential crises.

17   Progress, the Very Idea

So far I have been guiding you on a trip to the apocalypse, a series of global catastrophes waiting for us in near time. Is there a "good news" scenario to oppose to this vision? It is relatively easy to construct a myth of progress, one so powerful that it wants to slide from myth to reality. We could for example point to the dramatic decrease in infant mortality over the last two centuries. Two hundred years ago, globally, nearly half of all children died before their 15th birthday; today that figure is less than 5 percent. Life expectancy rose from the 30s in pre-industrial society to the late 70s in today's most developed societies. Literacy rates have also increased dramatically in this time frame. While the picture I painted in the opening chapters suggests that environmental activist Greta Thunberg is right in thinking that things are getting more grim day to day, and surveys show that Americans agree with this vision, we can point to facts like the increase in life expectancy; and it's been estimated that more than one billion people have escaped extreme poverty since 1990. In the early 1820s approximately 25% of the world's population lacked sufficient living space.

One could argue, for example, that the lack of usable energy sources fueled a search that led to space, heating, and food to escape extreme poverty, and the development and diffusion of fossil fuels. This in turn contributed to the problem of climate change. Now the same innovative methods of technological rationalism are creating clean energy sources and making them increasingly affordable. This is the kind of perspective that leads highly intelligent people to look to technological fixes to solve any and all problems and make progress look real and inevitable. The biggest danger we face today, if we care about actually making the future a more livable space, isn't that industrial civilization will choke on its own exhaust or that democracy will crumble or that AI will rise up and overthrow us all. It's that we will cease believing in the one force that raised humanity out of tens of thousands of years of general misery: the very idea of progress. The "Great Fact" (McCloskey. 2016, 2019) is that "the Bourgeois Reevaluation" was "mad, fevered, historically off-the-charts amounts of innovation" (Beaudreaux, 2011).

In general, all of this is a defense of free market enterprise and the ideology of capitalism. We're asked by the progress mongers to consider another data point in the story of progress: In 1870, the average unskilled male worker in London could afford 5000 calories for himself and his family of a little over four people on average. By the early 21st century, that same worker could afford 2.4 million calories. These and other supporting statistics ground Brad Delong's (2022) argument that we have been "slouching toward utopia" over the last few centuries. To the defenders of the idea of progress in our era, we have escaped the Malthusian trap.

Thomas Malthus (1766–1834) famously argued that populations grow geometrically while food supplies grow arithmetically, that is, over time populations outgrow their food supplies. Industrialization, however, has helped grow food supplies at rates that have kept up with population growth. But this has not gone smoothly. The era of economic growth and political progress over the last 200 years has been punctuated by bloody world, regional, and local conflicts, the invention and diffusion of weapons of mass destruction, and left billions of humans no better off than their impoverished ancestors. The technoutopians argue that at least we have shown that progress is possible and could continue in the future.

It is difficult to question "the great fact" that there have been clear improvements in political liberty, democratic representation, human rights, and even animal rights and most recently robot rights. In brief, we have witnessed the expansion of the circle of moral concern. And yet every day our news head-lines tell us that racist and hate crimes are rampant, government representa-tives push for legislation their constituents don't support and that target the poor and vulnerable people in the societies they represent, and the rights of almost everyone now seem endangered by the rise of authoritarianism.

Technological innovations and fixes, besides being inappropriate in many cases, especially regarding social problems, produce blowbacks. Antibiotics improve life expectancy but their overuse leads to improved resistance and paves the way for pandemics; gains in agricultural productivity make inroads into famine but lead to new problems like obesity on a global scale; advances in animal breeding and diet have the side effects of local pollution and factory farming; coal and fossil fuels fueled industrialization but also contributed to climate change. The new problems provoke new solutions: the Haber-Bosch process led to the overuse of fertilizer which contributed to pollution; but "smart agriculture" using less fertilizer and synthetic biology may lead to crops that fertilize themselves; diet, exercise, drugs and surgery are addressing the problem of obesity; and efforts are underway to deal with climate change but it seems to be too little too late.

What about progress, the very idea? Arguably, the idea comes into Western and world culture in the Old Testament with its conception of linear time and a God that moves through time with humans (e.g., Sedlacek, 2011: 47). The idea of scientific and technological progress was fueled by the seventeenth century advances in science and literature by such cultural giants as Galileo, Newton, Descartes, Molière, and Racine. The idea of social progress was added later. Early in the eighteenth century, the Abbé de Saint Pierre advocated establish-ing political and ethical academies to promote social progress. Saint Pierre and Turgot influenced the Encyclopedists. The great *Encyclopédie* was produced by a group of eighteenth-century philosophers under the direction of Denis Diderot. It defines the Enlightenment program of promoting reason and uni-fied knowledge. It was at this point that social progress became mated to the values of industrialization and incorporated into the ideology of the bourgeoi-sie. Scientific, technological and social progress were all aspects of the ideology of industrial civilization. Veblen, for example, argued that the various sciences could be distinguished in terms of their proximity to the domain of technol-ogy. Thus, the physical sciences were closest to that domain, even integral with it, whereas such areas as political theory and economics were farther afield.

We have entered an era of machine discipline unlike any in human history. And now we stand on the threshold of machines that will discipline us with conscious awareness and values, including social and sociable robots (the so-called robosapiens), and cyborgs. There have been attempts to identify a type of progress that is independent of material or technological criteria (see, for example, the discussion in Almond, Chodorow, and Pearce, 1985, and the classic criticisms in Roszak, 1969/1995). For many ancient as well as modern thinkers, the idea of progress has always been problematic. We are right to be concerned about the actual and potential impacts of our new technologies. But one finds similar concerns in Plato's *Phaedrus*. There, in the dialogue between Theuth and king Thamus concerning the new technology of writing, Theuth makes promising predictions about the impact of writing. The king claims to be in a better position to do what in effect is a "technology assessment," and concludes that writing will have the opposite of the effects predicted by Theuth.

The cultural meaning of science has fared no better. Where the Rousseaus and the Roszaks saw danger and alienation in science, the Francis Bacons and Jacob Bronowskis saw civilization and progress. When the biochemist J.B.S. Haldane wrote about a future of human happiness built on the application of science, Bertrand Russell replied with a vision of science used to promote power and privilege rather than to improve the human condition. St. Augustine worried about the invention of destructive machines; Spengler predicted that humans would be annihilated by Faustian man. Fontenelle, in the first modern secular treatise on progress published in 1688 argued that science was the clearest and most reliable path to progress. Rousseau, by contrast, argued that science and the arts have corrupted our minds. By its intimate association with the very foundations of science, mathematics does not escape this ambivalence. But it stands apart from science in terms of its stronger association with human progress.

In the seventeenth and eighteenth centuries, a wave of positivism fueled by Newton's achievements evoked nothing but the promise of progress among mathematicians of that period. The historian Florian Cajori (1894: 4) had no question about the connection between mathematics and human progress. For Alex Bellos (2010: ix), mathematics is ("arguably") the foundation of all human progress.

Progress, then, can be viewed in terms of "amelioration" or "improvement" in a social or ethical sense. Are we more advanced than cultures that are less dominated by machines and machine ideology? How do we measure the primacy of humans and ecologies and how do we sustain them in any given culture? Can we bring them to fruition and nourish them in any culture, or are some more friendly to the primacy of humans and ecologies than others? These issues are really matters of degree associated with the degree to which individuation of the self (and then the myths of individualism, selfishness, and greed) has progressed in any given society. Furthermore, the degree of awareness of and attention to ethics, values, and social justice has to come into consideration here. It is impossible to even discuss the idea of progress without engaging ideas about and the value of the person, freedom, and democracy.

It may be possible to define progress in a way that takes it out of the realm of hopes, wishes, and dreams and plants it more firmly on a meaningful (and even perhaps measurable) foundation. Following Gerhard Lenski (1974: 59), progress can be defined as the process by which human beings raise the upper limit of their capacity for perceiving, conceptualizing, accumulating, processing, mobilizing, distributing, and utilizing information, resources, and energy in the adaptive-evolutionary process. The relationship between adaptation and evolution is a paradoxical one. On the one hand, survival depends on the capacity to adapt to surroundings; on the other hand, adaptation involves increasing specialization and decreasing evolutionary potential. Adaptation is a dead end. As a given entity adapts to a given set of conditions, it specializes to the point that it begins to lose any capacity for adapting to significant changes in those conditions (as we saw earlier in summarizing the views of Sahlins and Service, 1960: 95–97).

Contradictions and ambivalence about science, technology, and progress may be built into the very core of our cultural machinery. Agricultural activities in the ancient Near East reduced vast forests to open plains, and wind erosion and over-grazing turned those areas into deserts. Deforestation in ancient China led to the development of the loess plateau. Loess sediment gives the Yellow River (nicknamed "China's Sorrow") its signature color and flooding pattern. Was deforestation necessary for building China into the greatest civilizational area on earth between the first and sixteenth centuries of the common era? Or were there conservation principles that the ancient Chinese could have relied on without detracting from their cultural development? There is some evidence that at least some of the deforestation they caused could have been avoided.

The deforestation experiences of China, Rome, and other civilizational areas of the ancient world are being repeated today and offer cautionary tales for an era characterized by many hard to monitor emerging and converging technologies, that is, technocultural systems. At the end of the day, it should be clear that progress is not easy to define, and that it is even harder to point to examples of progress that resist critical interrogation. How can we sustain the idea of progress in the face of the widespread ecological, environmental, and human destruction that has characterized the industrial age? The fact is that the destruction and danger we see all around us is integrally connected to the very things we use to mark the progress of humanity. For these reasons, we must be cautious when considering whether any of the sciences, engineering disciplines, or mathematics have contributed to or served as signposts of progress.

The overall effect of all these pluses and minuses in our lives is a culture of "doomerism" and a feeling of paralysis in face the scope, scale, and speed of problems which are becoming existential threats rather than waiting for solutions. The problem is in part due to a "Great Centralization" (Haque, 2022). The greatest centralization of power in human history has become part of the matrix of existential threats. The Zuckermans and Gateses are outside the bounds of checks and balances, out of range of countervailing forces. This leaves the mass of humanity powerless, and feeling powerless makes them vulnerable, Haque argues, to magical thinking and conspiracy theories, fanaticism, superstition, and fundamentalism, making them ripe for the promises of fascists. Haque argues for decentralization, but he's careful not to propose a utopian scheme of total decentralization. This does, however, put us on the road to anarchism and I will explore this option to social organization and culture further on.

There is clearly a disconnect between the reality of existential threats including Haque's identification of the centralization of power as an existential threat on the one hand, and those observers of the modern condition who see problems but progress. And there are certainly intelligent anti-doomers responding to this era of existential threats with reminders about how resilient humans have been in the face of earlier catastrophes.

Michiko Kakutani (2024), for example, recognizes that we are at a watershed moment, but she points out that we've survived crises and chaos in the past. We can avoid cynicism, resignation and paralysis by opposing manipulative politics. One of the positive signs she points to is that mistrust in elites and the status quo are growing while "outsiders" are on the rise pursuing their dreams in America; another is that "chaotic hinge moments" give us the opportunity to reboot and renew. The flaw in her positive attitude is her recognition that this hinge moment requires cooperation on national, regional, and global levels. The existential threats are not moving us forward on such a cooperative front but rather making cooperation increasingly difficult.

If we measure progress on a regional scale using an index like the Gross National Product, we fail to take into account that producing things for human consumption also produces waste products. To get an accurate picture of our situation we should juxtapose GNP with a measure of GND, Gross National Disproduct. The problem with those who see progress where the rest of us see existential threats is that the former fail to take into account the disproduct side of progress, including the alienation of the producers and consumers.

18 Conclusion

The picture of the world today I have sketched in these opening chapters suggests that at no time in history has it been more appropriate to begin the narrative of an era with Dickens' famous "It was the best of times, it was the worst of times." Thinking of the best of times might put us in mind of ancient thinkers like Epicurus and modern thinkers like Abraham Maslow; thinking of the worst of times might remind us of the Greek myth of Erysichthon, a myth of insatiable desire for power and control. Erysichthon sacrifices "Mother Earth" to satisfy his desires and is cursed with a ravenous hunger that leads him to eat everything in sight and eventually his own flesh. Our own Erysichthons, the technocrats, politicians, growth economists, and bankers, are taking all of us down a path that has us metaphorically and literally eating our own flesh (Gutenschwager, 2013: 70). The alternative path has been laid out in the ancient philosophy of Epicurus and modern theories of people like Abraham Maslow. We will see in the closing chapters how following this path, dimly lit but glowing more day by day, leads to "small is beautiful" concepts and anarchism.

PART 2

Encounters with Reality

∵

CHAPTER 5

Reality Is Real: The Dangers of Romancing Reality

Reality! But what does this word mean? Each has his own reality. I draw upon my personal reality, upon the dark side of myself, my unconscious ... Realism is a bad word. In a sense everything is realistic. I see no line between the imaginary and the real.

FELLINI

∴

We have populated our lives with hopes and wishes that go against reason. Social media has become a breeding ground for romanticizing reality. What, for example, does the following social media post mean: "Realizing impermanence means that everything is possible?" Impermanence is impermanence. It is indeed part of the human experience, but it has nothing to do with what is possible or impossible. And it certainly doesn't mean anything is or can become possible. The very idea that anything is possible is a misdirection. It may make you feel good, it may even motivate you. But it is as vacuous as the claim that "any one in America can become president." We have gotten ourselves in the fix we're in, attacked by existential threats on all sides, partly for reasons outside of our control but partly because we have refused to embrace the recalcitrance of the reality we can know and the reality of reality-in-itself which limits possibilities. But does resisting this natural recalcitrance promote creativity? If it does it does so at the expense of undermining the health of our human and planetary ecologies.

Consider another example from a distinguished neuroscientist, Dr. Mona Sobhani (2022). Her posted headline reads: "Things Science Can't Explain Need a Place to Go." Things science can't explain already have a place to go – science. The history of science has been a process of pursuing the unexplained and explaining it, tentatively, corrigibly, fallibly, skeptically with the understanding that all facts escape the evidence. The science I reference here is science writ large. That is, I do not understand "science" as Western, monolithic, and characterized by a single "scientific method." It draws critically on all the reasoning strategies of the world's cultures but most importantly for people like Dr. Sobhani, it includes the social sciences. A great deal of the resistance to science and materialism is rooted in individual experiences. We do not have to deny the reality of those experiences to the people who describe them to bring them under the umbrella of the social sciences. We also have to understand that individual experience is a very poor guide to what the world is and how the world works. Relying on individual experience as a proof methodology gives us revelation as a proof for the existence of God. As individuals, we do not feel the earth's many movements through space and time; E pur si muove! We know that it moves based on the collective intersubjective testing of ideas, theories, and experiments by scientists (writ large) that takes place in the space of the unfolding of histories and cultures. Denying critical, realistic, sophisticated materialism opens the door to the existence of transcendental and supernatural (including spiritual) realms of reality. There are no such realms. Their existence is supported only if we leave out social science when we reference science.

Every day, from all sides of the information explosion, we are accosted by the nonsense that flows from outright ignorance and those good humans whose experiences blind them to what a wasteland we live in and who keep giving us advice on how to live a good life, how to be successful, how to be more productive, how to love, and of all things how to be happy! There is a common resistance to embracing reality. Here are some recent examples from the news and the media that illustrate an important feature of the contemporary information explosion.

1   Das Ist Nicht Physik, Das Ist Theologie

1.   This story was #4 in 2022 at *Mind Matters News* in terms of the number of readers: As we approach the New Year, we are re-running the top ten *Mind Matters News* stories of 2022, based on reader interest. In "Hard problem of consciousness solved?: A 4th spatial dimension?" (April 20, 2022); our News division looks at philosopher Peter Sjöstedt-Hughes'(2021) view that higher spatial dimensions might hold the key to the uniqueness of human consciousness.

Comment: *Still* the wrong people using the wrong tools and looking in the wrong places. We've known since the 19th century that consciousness is in the social world, a realm of reality still invisible to the core scientific community. Follow Wittgenstein and take a wider look around. The idea that higher spatial dimensions might hold the key to consciousness is exactly where some religiosi have suggested we should look for God. This is a trifecta failure: the failure to understand consciousness and where to even look for it; the failure to understand God as a collective representation and collective elaboration; and the failure to understand that higher spatial dimensions are not physical locations and certainly not spiritual locations. This failure to pursue the social in the case of the consciousness problem continues unabated. Just this morning, two social media items demonstrated again the consequences of "socialblindness" (what I call "dissocism" which exists as a spectrum). This is the two-fold inability to see "the social" and to see it as a causal force.

1. In *Medium*: "The Fruitless Search for the Source of Consciousness," Craig Axford (2024)" "If the scientific method focuses on the testable, then the genesis of consciousness is not a scientific question."

1a. *Mind Matters*: "the current state of affairs in science is hardly a very strong basis for optimism that something ethereal like consciousness is going to 'yield' to a physicalist or other naturalist explanation," according to biochemist William Reville (in O'Leary, 2024). In fact, we have had an explanatory trajectory on mind and consciousness in sociology that begins already in the 1840s (Whitehead, 2008).

2. Theoretical physicist Melvin Vopson (2023), University of Portsmouth (UK) has set out to "prove" that we are living in a simulation. This is an exercise in physicalist fundamentalism. David Chalmers (2022), a leading philosopher in this field, claims he is an atheist but says the simulation "hypothesis" (in parentheses because as he points out it is not an hypothesis!) has made him take the existence of God seriously. The simulation hypothesis would be impossible, he says, without the provocation of a deceptive demon, indeed of an omnipotent and omnideceptive God.

Comment: These sorts of speculative excursions in physics (e.g. Vopson, 2023) mirror philosophy which proceeds in a world of logical and linguistic symbols without real world stop signs (e.g., Chalmers). If we can solve the hard problem of consciousness (and we can if we take off the blinders that keep us from seeing social life as a nexus of social causes) we can eliminate the fuel that sustains brains-in-vats and simulation nonsense.

2   Reality Is Real

In a famous episode in Boswell's *The Life of Samuel Johnson* (1791/2008) Boswell and Johnson are discussing Bishop Berkeley's "ingenious sophistry" proving the non-existence of matter (immaterialism, or naïve idealism). Boswell says that while it is clear that Berkely is wrong it is impossible to refute it. Johnson answered by kicking a large stone and claiming "I refute it thus" (Hallett, 1947).

The Headlines:

A.   Objective Reality May Not Exist at All, Quantum Physicists Say.

B.   The Many-Worlds Interpretation (MWI) of quantum mechanics holds
      that there are many worlds which exist in parallel at the same space-
      and-time as our own. Comment: A. and B. notwithstanding you should
      still look both ways when you cross the street in New York; read the
      directions below the curb when you cross the street in London; and be
      prepared to look six ways when crossing the boulevards of Rome and
      Paris. Two things:

      1.   Objectivity is not a monolith; it is shaped by culture and different
            groups live in different objectivity communities.

      2.   Principle of the profundity of the surface; but remember that this
            is a portal to the objectivities of "other worlds" like the worlds of
            quantum physics and relativity theory, not to mention the worlds
            of certain judges and political leaders. Have a nice day. Stay safe Be
            aware of which objectivity community you're in when you cross
            the street.

Reality is so complicated at the levels of the very small (quantum theory), the
very fast (relativity theory), and the very large (cosmology), that some scientists and philosophers have suggested there is no reality, or that there are many
realities. But that's not the reality I'm writing about. The reality I'm interested
in is the reality of our everyday lives with its more or less predictable causes
and consequences. The science of this reality begins with the science of crossing the street and looking both ways. This reality is relatively stable and governed by the recurrence theorem. As we move about the world from room to
room, house to house, street to street, neighborhood to neighborhood, city to
city, nation to nation, and culture to culture we will find different structures
and different norms, values, and beliefs. But generally we will encounter doors
that allow us to enter and exit buildings, buildings that may contain one or
many stories, tall buildings with elevators, windows that open and close, street
corners with stop lights, shops with recognizable aisles, food stuff, goods for
sale, and checkout counters, staircases, and other recognizable structures that
facilitate "getting about" even if we don't speak or read the local language. If
we happen to find ourselves on the steppes of Mongolia or in the Inuvialuit
Settlement Region near the Arctic circle, we will find that Yurts and Igloos
are not so alien as to resist our efforts to find entrances and exits. This everyday world can be chaotic and destructive with its earthquakes, tornadoes,
and volcanoes, but these are not happening all the time and disrupting our
daily expectations from one moment to the next. This has varied from locale
to locale across history but the overall situation has been relatively stable in

terms of predictable and manageable causes and consequences. This may be changing as a result of converging existential threats and that is the major motivation for writing this book.

This book is meant as a work of science. Science in this context is understood in terms established by the sociology and anthropology of science. Science is not "pure science," it is not an autonomous self-correcting social system, and it is not a window on unmediated objective reality. Science is socially constructed; that is, it is the work of human beings cooperating, in conflict, and communicating together in social, cultural, organizational, and ecological networks and contexts that unfold in history and across cultures. Their achievements are contingently objective. Thus, this book is not scientific by itself, I am not a scientist by myself, my claims, assumptions, deductions, arguments are not scientific in themselves. All this is science and I am a scientist only in the context of its and my place in the unfolding of the linked generations of scientists collectively and intersubjectively testing ideas, theories, and experimental results. At the end of the day, I am an experiment, my book is an experiment, and my claims are an experiment. However certain I am of their truth, this is ultimately a collective decision of the evolving scientific community. I use the term scientist in a general sense to refer to inquirers into the nature of nature who have followed more or less rational methods of inquiry throughout human history. "Rational methods" is liberally interpreted to include communicable and variously testable methods from trial and error to various and more or less rigorous observational methodologies and from quasi-experimental designs to strictly designed controlled experiments. We can and do know things but we do not know facts of the matter with absolute certainty. All facts of the matter escape their evidence and must be considered highly presumptive, corrigible, and fallible.

We can and should be confident about what we know as scientists and consumers of science, but we should not allow what we know to be contaminated by absolute conviction. Science, like everything in the universe including selves, bodies, and brains, is in flux, in becoming. There are eddies of closure in that flux that allow us to act and react predictably in and to life's circumstances and challenges. This allows for a careful suspension of the imperative against absolute truths and absolute conviction. But our strongest convictions must always be bathed in a vigilant ever-present skepticism. In practice this means that we can virtually forget the absolutism imperative in the case of our knowledge, for example, that the earth is not flat; but we can't be so cavalier in the case of our knowledge of, for example, gravity or black holes.

In a sense, no definitive descriptions and prescriptions of reality writ large are possible. We saw earlier in Chapter 1 that all systems are more or less open or closed. No systems are completely closed. However, they reach levels of clo-sure that make definitive descriptions and prescriptions-in-practice possible. Everyday life is sufficiently closed to allow us to move through our everyday lives without encountering uncertainties and unpredictable situations at every turn.

3   Review

Reality is complex; it has many dimensions and layers and can be variously decomposed. We have seen that some scientists and philosophers have sug-gested there is no reality, or that there are many realities. But that's not the real-ity I'm writing about. The reality I'm interested in is the reality of our everyday lives with its more or less predictable causes and consequences. The science of this reality begins with streets and pedestrians. The strange features of the quantum level or of relativity do not scale up or down in any way that affects our day-to-day behavior. Our house keys are not going to appear to be in two places at the same time, and we are not going to encounter cars or buses trav-eling close to or faster than light. Quantum and relativity phenomena must scale up and down in some ways but they don't do this in ways that disrupt our everyday lives. And indeed the science of the street is not the end of sci-ence but a portal that can lead us to quantum physics, relativity theory, DNA science, evolutionary theory and theories about society and culture that are non-obvious. At the end of the day we have to depend on our experiences to inform us about everyday realities and the portals they lead us to. But it is not individual experience that guides us in these realms but collective experience; recall my earlier discussion of individual experience and the movements of the Earth.

4   Reality Redux 1

One of the questions that has been raised about "reality" is whether our every-day reality is an interface, something like your desktop. Your desktop is a kind of reality, and you could in principle construct theories about what it is and explanatory laws for its actions. But what's really happening on your desktop is happening in a complicated world of microcircuits, electrons, and codes. You can live in your desktop reality quite comfortably without concerning your-self with the reality driving it, so the desktop becomes your reality. What if every object you encounter in your everyday world – the computer, the chair you're sitting on, your phone, your car, and so on – is just like the icons on your desktop? You see a reality that you can manipulate and live with but you don't see the "real" reality that drives your everyday reality. Cognitive scientist Donald Hoffman (2019) believes things work this way. He calls his theory the Interface Theory of Perception (ITP).

Hoffman relies on the Fitness Beats Truth theorem (FBT) to support ITP. FBT provides a quantitative measure of the extent to which the fitness-only strategy dominates the truth strategy, and of how this dominance increases with the size of the perceptual space. Evolution, Hoffman claims, has unfolded in a way that makes fitness trump truth. At bottom this is just another model of the world that identifies an underlying reality that is hidden from our everyday experiences. This kind of thinking also gives us simulation scenarios that have us living in a computer simulation (think *The Matrix*). Simulation scenarios are another product of excessive philosophy and subject to the same criticisms that can be leveled at "this isn't really real" theories (see my critique of simulation scenarios in Restivo, 2023).

What is driving Hoffman and others in the "this isn't really real" industry is the search for a theory of consciousness. The so-called "hard problem" of consciousness is: how can material objects produce immaterial phenomena; how can "hard" brains produce "soft" consciousness, and how, in the theological context, can bodies contain souls? Hoffman says we need to eliminate the assumption that we experience reality as it really is. Hoffman thinks it is commonplace to think that all organisms experience the same reality. But we've known for a long time that this isn't so. According to umwelt theory, different organisms experience the world differently. Indeed, people from different cultures experience the world differently, and these differences vary across individuals. The differences between organisms are greater than they are between cultures and those differences are greater than those between individuals. This allows for a certain smoothness in our everyday interactions with others. Does this mean as Hoffman claims that perceptions create reality?

In the wake of Kant and his critics I think we can assume with calm certainty that we do not and cannot have direct unmediated access to a thing as such in any form. We have long ago outgrown Cartesian dualism. For all practical purposes, "objective reality" is the everyday reality of crossing streets without getting hit by a car (or getting hit and suffering the inevitable consequences), hiking along cliffs without falling off (or falling off and suffering the inevitable consequences), driving cars without crashing into others (or crashing with its inevitable consequences), and roasting chickens without burning down the house (or suffering the inevitable consequences of an accident or error). The remaining issue is: what limits our access to the thing as such and what gives us access to the objective reality of everyday life?

5   Taming Consciousness

The widely and uncritically accepted cross-science assumption is that "the reality problem" is a problem in cognition and consciousness. This has only led to mysteries piled upon paradoxes encased in enigmas and Chalmers "hard problem of consciousness." The solution to this problem has been with us since the mid-nineteenth century. Consciousness is a social phenomenon – a network of social relations – and not a matter of individual existence or individual brains. It is your activity as a social being that generates and sustains consciousness. Mental processes are "merely" intelligent acts. The "mind" is just the body at work as Gilbert Ryle pointed out in 1949. There is a more strongly sociological trail to the consciousness solution that leads from the crystallization of the social sciences from 1840 on to the social psychologies of the early twentieth century. Follow-up research in the mid- to late-twentieth century has clearly established that the brain is not the locus of consciousness; the locus of consciousness is the social group, the social network. The myth of individualism has obscured and delayed the recognition of these contributions to our understanding of consciousness. Humans arrive on the evolutionary stage always, already, and everywhere social; and they have social brains, social neurons, and social genes.

The concept of a social brain was introduced by primatologists in the 1950s. It was introduced into the neurosciences in the early 1990s. We can now speak in terms of a social brain paradigm. The hard problem of consciousness has been all but solved and it's just a matter of looking for it in the right place and with the right theoretical and methodological tools. The tools appropriate to the phenomenon come from the social sciences, not the physical and neurosciences. I am not a disciplinary despot and recognize the need for a multi-disciplinary approach to the problem of consciousness. I risk giving too much credibility to the non-social theories of consciousness, but I am willing to stand with the minimal claim that we cannot solve this hard problem without the social sciences.

6   Conclusion

Everyday reality at the level of information has become an existential threat. The 24-hour news cycle and the development of social media as purveyors of news have made headlines, especially headlines about science, an existential threat. It has become more important than ever to put on your reality cap when reading contemporary headlines and stories in the news, whatever their source. In the next Chapter I continue to explore the existential threat of "the headline" or "story of the day."

CHAPTER 6

Reality Confronts the News as an Existential Threat

American journalism faces a confluence of challenges that present the most profound threat to the free press in more than a century. News organizations are shrinking and dying under sustained financial duress. Attacks on journalists are surging. Press freedoms are under intensifying pressure. And with the broader information ecosystem overrun by misinformation, conspiracy theories, propaganda, and clickbait, public trust in journalism has fallen to historical lows.

    SULZBERGER, 2023

• • •

Striving for independence is a worthy goal. It's the same goal to which scientists, judges and sports referees aspire. "Failure to achieve standards does not obviate the need for them," Martin Baron [2023], the former top editor of The Washington Post, has written. "It makes them more necessary."

    LEONHARDT, 2023

• •
•

The 24-hour news cycle and the use of social media for the publication of news items has contaminated the levels and quality of objectivity we should expect in the journalism of a free press. Bias is always present, even in science. It is only through the historical unfolding of the results of countervailing forces that we can approach a practical objectivity. The daily dump of news across the full range of information sources combined with mass ignorance of how objectivity works, how science works, overwhelms our capacity to approximate the truth. The everyday news has in this sense become an existential threat. In this chapter, I will use headlines from daily news sources widely available in hard copy and online as teaching moments in how to read the news realistically. Each of these reality moments could be and should be a book in itself, and some are. In this context, they are provocations to consider why it's past the time to embrace a reality that is unimpressed by hopes, wishes, and prayers never mind deliberate misinformation, propaganda, and ideology.

1   Supreme Realities

Hermann Lotze (1817–1881). There is no Logik, only logics.

Oswald Spengler (1880–1936). There is no Mathematik, only mathematics.

Sal Restivo and other science studies scholars: There is no Science, only sciences.

2   The Headlines

Headline: 6/24/22, *The New York Times*: In 6-to-3 Ruling, Supreme Court Ends Nearly 50 Years of Abortion Rights.

> The President, who exercises a limited power, may err without causing great mischief in the State. Congress may decide amiss without destroying the Union, because the electoral body in which Congress originates may cause it to retract its decision by changing its members. But if the Supreme Court is ever composed of imprudent men or bad citizens, the Union may be plunged into anarchy or civil war.
>
> ALEXIS DE TOCQUEVILLE (1835–40/2013: 173)

SCOTUS JUNE 2022: A BAD DAY IN COURT. In the moments following the irresponsible, morally degraded, and ultimately illegal SCOTUS decision on Roe v Wade I imagined a few words for Amerika: Thomas Jefferson, Elizabeth Cady Stanton, and Susan B. Anthony.

It's not about abortion, stupid! If you are infected with the illusion that "logic" is a once and only historical phenomenon, that there is only *one* logic, that logic isn't a function of culture and values, then read the SCOTUS "reasons" for overturning Roe v Wade. Writing for the court majority on June 24, 2022, Justice Samuel Alito (whose biases have become increasingly public in recent weeks) said that the 1973 Roe ruling and repeated subsequent high court decisions reaffirming Roe "must be overruled" because they were "egregiously wrong," the arguments "exceptionally weak" and so "damaging" that they amounted to "an abuse of judicial authority."

In the 1973 *Roe v. Wade* decision the Supreme Court ruled that the right to abortion is protected under the right to privacy implied in the 14th Amendment. The government still had the right to regulate or restrict access to abortion based on the stage of the pregnancy. Once fetal viability was attained, abortions could be banned unless life or health was at risk. The 2022 decision was based on the principle of "unenumerated rights," rights that are not explicitly stated in the Constitution. The Court decided that the only legitimate unenumerated rights are those "deeply rooted in the Nation's history and tradition" and "implicit in the concept of ordered liberty" (Alito for the Court). They ruled that abortion is not such a right, in spite of the fact that the "pro-choice" position among Americans has continued to rise, according to Gallup polls, from 27% in 1975 to nearly 70% today. The percentage of Americans who want abortion to be illegal in all cases has fallen from 21% in 2019 to 13% in recent polls.

In summary, as of late 2023, Gallup polls show that 70% of pro-choice Americans say abortion should be legal in the first trimester. Support drops to 37% for the second trimester and 22% for the third. Majorities oppose abortion being legal in the second (55%) and third (70%) trimesters. 63% favor allowing the abortion pill Mifepristone to be available in the U.S. as a prescription drug. 61% say that overturning Roe v. Wade was a "bad thing," while 38% call it a "good thing." Opposition to overturning Roe has been trending upward for thirty years.

Alexis de Tocqueville (1835, 1840/2000) wrote the following in his *Democracy in America*, words that should be heard by this Court and by all Americans: superior men do not run for office; refusing to obey an unjust law is an appeal to the sovereignty of humanity over the rule of the majority; no authority should be allowed to rule without oversight and impediment; America owes its singular prosperity and strength to the superiority of its women; people can exist without common ideas but a social body cannot; and I reiterate apropos of this SCOTUS item de Toqueville's warning: a Supreme Court composed of imprudent or bad citizens will plunge the country into chaos or civil war – loss of their republican institutions will put Americans into the hands of despots.

And finally, a reminder that our own Thomas Jefferson believed that a little rebellion is good for our nation (in a letter to Peter Carr, August 10, 1787). In a less sober mood, Jefferson argued that "The tree of liberty must be refreshed from time to time with the blood of patriots and tyrants" (in a letter to W.S. Smith, November 13, 1787).

In the wake of the 2022 decision, Justice Thomas hinted that other personal choices might have to be reconsidered, including the right to marry, have access to contraception, and even one's right to claim h/er own gender identity. There are good reasons in these portents for favoring and acting on the

Anarchist's motto, "No Masters, No Gods." Why are so many of us intent on micro-managing the most deeply intimate rights of others?

3   The Reality of Violence

3.1   *Violence in the News*

Headline: Terror in Littleton: the overview; 2 students in Colorado school said to gun down as many as 23 and kill themselves in a siege. 4/21/99, *The New York Times.*

Headline: Nation Reels After Gunman Massacres 20 Children at School in Connecticut [Sandy Hook Elementary School] in a wooded corner of Newtown, Conn.12/15/2012, *The New York Times.*

Headline: At least 18 killed in shootings in Lewiston [Maine]: What we know so far: Police are looking for Robert Card, 40, after the attacks at a bowling alley and a bar in Lewiston last evening, officials said. *NBC News*, October 25th, 2023.

Headline: Halloween weekend shootings across US leave at least 11 dead, scores injured. *AP*, October 30th, 2023.

Headline: Mass shootings in the US with four or more deaths hit highest level since at least 2006 (Robertson, 12/05: 2023).

In this section I want to focus on one kind of violence that has been in the headlines in recent decades, mass shootings and school shootings in particular. There were 32 school shootings in the United States in the 19th century; 322 incidents in the 20th century; there were 389 incidents between the Columbine High School shootings on April 20, 1999 in Columbine, Colorado and the September 12, 2023 shootings at St. Helena College and Career Academy in Greensburg, LA (Cox, Rich, et al., 2024). Specific numbers don't tell the full story. Different definitions underwrite different statistics. Notwithstanding the statistics I quoted in my opening paragraph, the National Institute of Justice Violence Project identified 167 mass shootings (4 or more killed with firearms in a public setting not connected to "underlying criminal activity or commonplace circumstances") in the US between 1966 and 2019. *The Washington Post* identified 163 mass shooting incidents in the US between 1967 and mid-2019. And *Mother Jones* recorded 140 mass shootings in the US between 1982 and the first months of 2023. The story is not about these numbers but about the incontrovertible fact that however you define "mass" or "school" shooting, the incidents and the number of deaths have been rising dramatically over time and especially in recent decades. As of 2017, studies indicated that the rate at which public mass shootings occur has tripled since 2011. Between 1982 and

2011, a mass shooting occurred roughly once every 200 days. However, between 2011 and 2014, that rate accelerated greatly with at least one mass shooting occurring every 64 days in the United States (Cohen, Azrael, and Miller, 2014). Mass shootings are a peculiar feature of American culture. According to one study, the US accounted for almost 75 percent of 139 mass shootings across the "developed" world between 1998 and 2019 (Silva, 2023). A different study identified 101 mass shootings during that period compared with 21 in Russia, 8 in France, and 5 or fewer in Germany, Canada, Finland, Belgium, Czech Republic, Italy, the Netherlands, and Switzerland (WISEVOTER, 2020). Again, it's not the absolute numbers which we should pay attention to but the comparative frequencies. Those of us who have been around during the 2000s have seen the same response to these shootings every time: hand wringing, prayers, blame (wrongly placed on the mentally ill), and easy access to guns. What we haven't seen are policies designed to curb mass shootings. What does all of this mean?

The time for thoughts and prayers, blaming mental illness, and endless disputes about the Second Amendment is past. Mark Follman (2022), national editor for *Mother Jones*, has provided a positive guide to dealing with mass shootings. Based on his research inside the FBI's Behavioral Analysis Unit and in an innovative school district's violence-prevention program, Follman argues for the broad application of the techniques of behavioral threat assessment (BTA) which have demonstrated their potential to save lives. Media sensationalism has fueled cultural misunderstanding and overshadowed the ways in which BTA has actually contributed to averting tragedies. BTA, relying on mental health and law enforcement experts, focuses on factors that predict acts of violence. It identifies warning signs that allow for constructive interventions.

In the wake of the murder of John Lennon and the attempt on the life of Ronald Reagan, and a 1970s pioneering study of criminally insane assassins, BTA emerged out of Secret Service and FBI investigations of serial-killers. BTA was further developed following the shootings at Columbine, Virginia Tech, Sandy Hook, and Parkland and is in use today in the effort to identify and thwart potential attacks.

Violence is not new in American culture. It is, in fact, part of our cultural fabric. In the 1989 edition of Ted Gurr's edited *Violence in America* the contributors identify and diagnose the circumstances of recurring epidemics of violence that have swept across America over the past 150 years and their relation to waves of immigration, wars, and urban poverty. There are also entries on the traits of political assassins and the pros and cons of gun control (see Collins, 2009; 2022 on sociological theory and violence).

4   Violence and Disconnections

Violence, in its local, regional, and global contexts, is an existential threat. Social isolation or rejection disrupts our thinking, our will power, and our immune systems. It is for this reason that solitary confinement should be considered "cruel and unusual punishment." Loneliness – lack of connections, especially face-to-face, to others – may be the key to violent behaviors ranging from bullying to street violence and school shootings. It's not too much of a leap to suggest that it might play a role in terrorism and warfare. Not only should we not underestimate the relevance of the loss of community in explaining violence, we should also pay more attention to the relevance of touching in a radically social species. Fear of and barriers to touching (and sex which is a complicated extrapolation of touching) are implicated along with loneliness in many if not most of the problems of the human condition (Montagu 1972; Horizon Project, 2023).

Loneliness is not just an individual phenomenon. The separation of groups and cultures may cause collective loneliness. Ecumenical thinkers like Karen Armstrong (Charter for Compassion) and the Dalai Lama have argued that world peace could be based on the compassion that is at the center of all religious traditions. The problem is that compassion is a centripetal force and reinforces the boundaries that separate groups and cultures. This force tends to overwhelm any centrifugal forces that might help to link us across our cultural differences. There are certainly cases in which the centrifugal forces of compassion can be mobilized to support communication and exchange across national borders, and across barriers of sex, gender, race, class, and ethnicity. But the differences represented in all these categories of our lives are intensified by the centripetal forces of compassion. And this breeds physical and emotional violence across these categories (see the special bibliography on mass violence in the References).

5   Intervention: Dunning-Kruger Chickens Come Home to Roost

The Dunning-Kruger (Kruger and Dunning, 1999) effect was originally described as the observation that people who are terrible at a particular task think they are much better than they are, while people who are very good at it tend to underestimate their competence. The study was not about dumb people not knowing they are dumb or about ignorant people being arrogant and confident about their knowledge. The most important mistake people make about the Dunning-Kruger effect, according to Dr. Dunning, has to do with who falls victim to it. The Dunning-Kruger effect was originally defined as a bias in our thinking. Jarry (2020), however, has found that the effect can be seen in random computer-generated data and may be artifactual rather than cognitive.

6   The Irreality of Nostradamus

Headline: *New York Post*, December 27, 2022: Nostradamus predictions for 2023: An antichrist arrives, World War III and the monarchy dies.

For centuries, the more superstitious corners of popular culture have been obsessed with the prophecies of this 16th-century French astrologer and soothsayer, Michel de Nostredame, better known by his Latinized name, Nostradamus. Four and a half centuries after their publication, his quatrains – poems of four stanzas – are still analyzed and debated. There is a cure for this. We need to turn off the valve that's holding back the flow of that little bit of reason we have managed to master. One easy way to stop this particular nonsense (well, not so easy; it requires the ability to read and to read two languages: French and English) is to pick up a copy of Edgar Leoni's (1982) *Nostradamus and His Prophecies* and *read*! It will cure your Nostradamusitis. The book includes all the "prophecies" in French and English, arranged in collections of 100 rhymed quatrains, notes and indexes, his will and personal letters, a bibliography of Nostradamus and his commentators (including the most famous – and infamous – interpretations), historical, geographical, and genealogical backgrounds, a review of theories about him and his method and supplementary material. Harvard historian Crane Brinton praised Leoni's scholarship and the book's importance for historians. You can see for yourself if you have reached the age of reason what the original French says and how easy it is to treat it like a Rorschach ink blot.

7   The Reality of Sex

As Madonna walks around her Hamptons estate, she's asked about her greatest guilty pleasure, which she reveals is "sex." And clearly she had coitus on the brain at the time of filming as sex was also her answer for her zodiac sign, her favorite thing to make, what keeps her going, the secret to her success, her life mantra, and her current favorite obsession.

KIRKPATRICK, 2022

I have no patience with those who say that sexual excitement is shameful
and that venereal stimuli have their origin not in nature but in sin.
ERASMUS (d. 1536)

8   What Kind of Life Form Criminalizes Sex?

Four recent news items on sexual behavior caught my attention. One was the
interview with Madonna cited above. The second was about a couple accused
of engaging in a sex act in the stands at the Oakland Colosseum during a base-
ball game between the Oakland A's and the Seattle Mariners. The penalty for
this behavior is up to six months in jail and a fine of up to $1000. Oakland
police were reported to be actively seeking the couple for engaging in a "lewd
act" in public. Note the implication that the act was "lewd" in a general sense.
Meanwhile, in a third report, police in Toronto Canada said they are not planning to investigate a similar incident that took place at Rogers Stadium.

In a fourth report, La Vergne Tennessee Mayor Jason Cole launched an internal probe in December after he learned police officer Maegan Hall had had
"intimate relationships" with other members of the department, according to
an outside investigation commissioned by the city. She told superiors about
the encounters at the time, according to the external investigation conducted
by a law firm. The sexual activity was alleged to have included a hot tub party
on a houseboat attended by at least three other officers and the sharing of
nude photos of Hall and other officers, according to the investigation, the findings of which were included in the suit. Some of the other encounters took
place on city property, the investigation found.

Itsansofadog – It's an arse of a dog – is a work of art by Amanda Moström
that's all about connecting each other to each other and to nature. In her work,
Moström aims to unite the warmth of family togetherness with something we
are taught to see as inherently shameful and dirty, "lewd." In doing so, she cel-
ebrates eroticism as something that is natural, honest, and most of all, human.
She manages to change the common concept of "childhood innocence" as a
stage of life to be protected from the natural, the honest, and the human into a
state characterized by playful eroticism. The result is something that simultaneously scares and excites people (Francis and Moström, 2023).

Sex is everywhere all the time. It might even be a force of nature like gravity; SEXITY, my anthropology professor, Burt Aginsky, called it. Could item
two explain what's wrong with America? Could item 3 explain why Canada is
more advanced culturally than the United States? And is Madonna our Albert

Einstein of the laws of SEXITY? In a world of unconscionable levels of violence, inequalities, and injustices, why are we prosecuting sex in public? Is public sex more dangerous to our mental and emotional health and that of our children than public warfare, public violence on our streets and in the media, the perversity of our everyday public attacks on each other and our environments? What is wrong with a life form that seems so committed to creating anti-sexity moralities while continuing its massive assault on the human and ecological foundations of life itself? We are a species out of time and out of space.

At the most general level, it is not sex that is the force to reckon with, but an erotic force in nature that has its origins in the most basic sensual sensitivities and needs associated with the evolution of life. For humans, the erotic force is expressed in the need for touching. It is fundamental to the development of the neuromuscular and cognitive systems in humans, and develops into the pleasurable feelings associated with the sensual and sexual acts and arts. In association with the cooperative imperative in evolution, it is culturally molded into the higher forms of love and relationships. It is within this wider evolutionary framework that we should realize that sex is everywhere.

There are reasons that cultures have to varying degrees put up dams to control and channel sex. The rationale for these dams, in the form of various types of barriers and taboos notwithstanding we have in effect been trying to dam up a force like gravity. Sex and its roots in the sensual should be allowed to flow more freely at least if not in completely unfettered freedom. The more we try to dam up and restrict sex the more violence we engender. It is time to open the floodgates and let sex flow naturally.

Wait! Social organization and culture require the stability of rules, laws, and taboos. But we fearful humans, specks in the meaningless void, have taken this too far. We have too many rules, too many laws, too many taboos that run counter to nature and our place in nature. This is especially true with regard to sex. Any two or more humans put together in any context will encounter sex, or to be more precise, the erotic force, which is everywhere. More specifically, they will from the moment of birth – and indeed even before that moment – be immersed in the erotic field just as they are in the gravitational field. The erotic potential can be actualized in behaviors ranging from touching and caressing which are available and necessary throughout all of our lives from infancy to the maturity of sexual fondling, interactions, and intercourse. And let's not assume we know exactly where the boundaries are that separate the infantile, childish, adolescent, and mature sexual ages. I will have more to say on this topic further on.

9   **The Reality of Religion**

9.1   *Mania from Heaven*

Headline: "Satan readying world for Antichrist with rise in demonic content, authoritarian regimes:" Michael Youssef, September 14, 2022, *The Christian Post*.

Headline: "Something Can't Come From Nothing," *Apologetics Press Staff*, August 10, 2010. Christian apologist William Lane Craig (2016) supports the argument that "something can't come from nothing" with his typically irrational logic. He "argues" that it is "metaphysically impossible" (whatever that means) for the universe to have emerged ex nihilo.

It's absurd, Craig "argues," to believe that the universe could have come into existence without the prior possibility of its coming into existence. His "conclusion" is that there must be a pre-existing "metaphysically necessary" (again, whatever that means) "what" or "who" for the universe to have come into existence. This gives us a creationist explanation for the universe's existence.

Like most apologists Lane does not seem to be aware of the mathematical notion of limits. Furthermore, apologists tend to project our radically limited experience of causality and the laws of science onto immense scales of cosmic realities. What if there is a "Nothingness" and it doesn't obey our everyday laws of science (just as, for example, the quantum level of reality doesn't obey our everyday laws of science). What if Nothing is a novel form of Something, a "thing" of the Cosmos, as Einstein suggested?

It now appears (keeping in mind that all knowledge is presumptive, corrigible, fallible and escapes the evidence) that scientists have demonstrated the Schwinger effect: "In theory, a vacuum is devoid of matter. In the presence of strong electric or magnetic fields, however, this void can break down, causing elementary particles to spring into existence. Usually, this breakdown only occurs during intense astrophysical events, but researchers at the UK's National Graphene Institute at the University of Manchester have now brought it into tabletop territory for the first time, observing this Schwinger effect in a device based on graphene superlattices. The work will be important for developing electronic devices based on graphene and other two-dimensional quantum materials" (Dumé, 2022). "Space," David Bohm (2002: 192) argued, "is not empty. It is full, a plenum as opposed to a vacuum, and is the ground for the existence of everything, including ourselves. The universe is not separate from this cosmic sea of energy." Bohm hypothesized that every cubic centimeter of "empty space" contains unimaginable amounts of energy. But is it fine-tuned for life?

Headline: "The universe is finely tuned for life," posted on *Creation.com* by Jonathan Sarfati (1997). He makes an interesting case study for a sociologist of knowledge and belief. On the one hand he is a physical chemist with a PhD from Victoria University of Wellington in New Zealand and has published in *Nature* and other science journals. He is a critic of geocentric and flat earth pseudoscience. On the other hand, he is a "young earth" creationist.

The fine-tuning argument is that if the fundamental constants were slightly different the universe would not have been able to give rise to life. "Someone" had to do the fine tuning; QED God. Christian apologists abuse data in Big Bang cosmology to make this case, ignoring complexities, controversies, and alternative theories in contemporary cosmology. Fine-tuning is basically the classic argument from design which follows William Paley's (1743–1805) watchmaker analogy.

Imagine coming across a watch while walking on a beach. You would assume there was a watchmaker somewhere. By analogy, the universe has the same features as such human artifacts, therefore it must, like the watch, be a product of intelligent design. But the universe is vastly more complex and unfathomable in its dimensions, therefore the intelligent designer of the universe must be infinitely more powerful and intelligent than the watchmaker: QED God.

The evidence cited for fine-tuning by the apologists includes, for example: the facts that the electromagnetic coupling constant and the ratio of electron to proton mass are just right for allowing molecules to form; our sun is the right mass and the right color for the right level of photosynthesis; the earth's distance from the sun is just right for a stable water cycle, and so on. Distinguished scientists such as astronomer Sir Fred Hoyle have dropped their atheism because they've become convinced that only a super-intelligence could account for the "fact" that the natural forces are not "blind."

Apologist's can think of no other explanation than God for the existence of large biomacromolecules like DNA, RNA, and proteins. Let's return to reality and see why the theists' fine-tuning "argument" fails the smell test. Here then are two skeptical headlines: "Zillions of Universes? Or Did Ours Get Lucky?" (Overbye 2003) and: "Is the universe fine-tuned for life?" (Williams 2021).

The theists often get their "science proves God" arguments from scientists themselves. Indeed, a number of physicists have theorized that the smallest changes in the fundamental constants and laws of nature would have prevented the emergence of life. That the universe should be governed by these and no other constants and laws is so unlikely that the theists see an opening for intelligent design by an all-powerful God. But science has not eliminated the possibility that life might have emerged under different physical conditions. On the other hand, we have the anthropic principle – any effort to explain the universe must take into account that we exist – which supports fine-tuning.

A more interesting explanation can be found in bootstrap physics. The fact is, according to bootstrap physics, that the constants and laws of nature are inevitable. They "dictate one another through their mutual consistency;" that is, nature "pulls itself up by its own bootstraps" (Wolchover, 2019). Bootstrap physics had its heyday during the 1950s and early 1960s under the influence of Geoffrey Chew. Chew (1992: 32) provided grist for the theist mill by claiming that an "appeal to God may be needed to answer the 'origin' question, Why should a quantum universe evolving toward a semiclassical limit be consistent?" It began to lose favor by the 1970s but has recently been resurrected by physicists like Daniel Baumann of the University of Amsterdam.

Finally, some physicists think we need a "multiverse" model to explain why our Earth permits life. The multiverse suggests that there are many universes "out there" and ours is life permitting by chance. This seems logically excessive. At the end of the day, fine-tuning may actually mean that we need to go beyond the "standard model" or revise it in order to explain life in the universe (Strogatz, 2023). This is just the tip of the iceberg of a cosmology which can get along without God but at the same time leaves too many openings for "mystery" and "mysticism" fueling theist appropriations of physics for God. As we've seen, even scientists are vulnerable to the need for God.

But let's look at fine-tuning a little closer. The theist argument is that the universe is fine-tuned for life. But it's not fine-tuned for life that is safe, free of hunger and suffering, and is subject to existential threats that could wipe it out. If there is a God capable of fine-tuning the universe for life, why not fine-tune it for life with quality? There is another possibility I have thought of that would support the theists. Consider Augustine's principle of plenitude in the context of a cosmos of many universes. We could "reasonably" assume that just as God created many universes, "he" created many universes variously compatible with life on a continuum from the worst of all possible worlds to the best of all possible worlds. But if the many worlds "hypothesis" suffers from the fallacy of the mathegrammatical illusion then the principle of plenitude applied to many life-compatible universes suffers from the fallacy of the theologicogrammatical illusion.

Finally let's consider this headline: "Why the Fine Tuning Argument Proves God Does Not Exist," from Richard Carrier (2022). Richard Carrier (b. 1969, PhD, Ancient History, Columbia) is a well-known skeptic and author whose views on Christianity, Jesus, and the Bible deviate from the reigning consensus on this literature. Conventional historians of religion find his methodologies, which include the use of Bayesian statistical techniques, suspect. My reading of this controversy is that Carrier is too much of a theorist for conventional historians. That means he is going to be more creative about the data in the interest of constructing more orderly explanations than conventional historians who are taught to stick close to the data. Given my skeptical biases and theoretical leanings I tend to give Carrier more leeway than his critics, although I find his reliance on Bayesian statistics suspect. In any case, what does he mean by the claim that fine-tuning actually disproves God?

In a nutshell, Carrier argues that the God of everyday Christian believers wouldn't need to fine tune the universe. Such a God would not have to rely on bizarre complex physics. It could make things happen without gravitation or electromagnetic forces. It wouldn't need an unfathomably large and lethal universe that exists for immense eons before producing life. In a universe without God, people would automatically observe that they are in a fine-tuned universe, and one that is fine-tuned to be unimaginably old, large, and lethal. Even if a God had used fine tuning it wouldn't have made it so old, large, and lethal. It would have made a universe small, young, and habitable in the way theists assumed originally. Carrier puts his logic at risk by imagining what a God that does not exist might do and think.

God could have fine-tuned the universe, but Carrier asks what is most likely not what is merely possible. Carrier's effort to actually assign probabilities to his theories is highly suspect but drawing on Bayesian statistics he calculates that a fine-tuning God is highly improbable, not even reaching 6%. A "Bizarro God" could raise evidence for fine tuning to 100%, but this would lower the prior probability that such a God exists. This starts to take on the same sort of Alice in Wonderland reasoning we find in the ontological proof for the existence of God, so it doesn't advance the discussion toward a realistic resolution. Carrier's historical evidence is much stronger than his statistical maneuvering.

10   The Reality of Religious Freedom

Headline: A Texas judge just took "religious 'freedom' too far." Noah Feldman Bloomberg Opinion, *Union Bulletin*, Sep 17, 2022

I begin with a federal district court decision in Texas upholding a claim by a Christian employer that he is "entitled to an exemption from the requirement that all insurance plans must cover pre-exposure prophylaxis (PreP) drugs that prevent the spread of HIV." If upheld on appeal employers could refuse to provide health care coverage "on the ground that medical insurance encourages people to rely on medical science, not religious faith, in planning their lives."

In the 2014 *Burwell v. Hobby Lobby* case the U.S. Supreme Court ruled 5–4 that Hobby Lobby and other "closely held corporations" could deny birth control coverage to their employees. Hobby Lobby based its denial on the grounds that contraception was religiously wrong. In the Texas case, by contrast, Braidwood Management claimed that providing PreP drugs would "encourage homosexual behavior, prostitution, sexual promiscuity, and intravenous drug use," behavior it believes violates Biblical teachings. The implication of this kind of "thinking," this "logic," is that religious liberty claims can be defended independent of and even in contradiction of the facts of the matter (Feldman, 2022).

What does critical realist sociology have to say about this? I have argued in two recently published books (Restivo, 2021, 2023), in line with a broad consensus in sociology and anthropology, that religion is real and God is not real in the same sense. In terms of social evolution, religion is a social institution that organizes, systematizes, and sanctions the moral order of a society. That moral order is a cultural emergent. It is not rooted in neurons or genes or gods but in the rules of good and bad and right and wrong that emerge and crystallize as a society grows and adapts to its surroundings. It is the "glue" of society, the foundation of social solidarity and community. This is a general claim and hides the complexities and diversities of real-world societies. But it is about social structures and functions that are real in a material sense. God, on the other hand, is not real in any material sense as commonly understood; it is real symbolically.

Mature reason cannot support the idea that God is real in any material or non-material (e,g., transcendental or supernatural) sense. Religious texts, from the Hindu Vedas to the Western Bible and Koran, are human creations, culturally rooted and not the word of God. While secularization has not yet taken root across the world's cultures, it is gaining ground. This is clear in the United States according to recent polls. By 2022 the number of Americans who believe in God had dropped to its lowest level in the 78 years of Gallup polling on religious beliefs. More than 90% of Americans believed in God between 1944 and 2011. Belief in God is highest among political conservatives. While the majority of Americans still report believing in God on surveys, fewer that 50% of them belong to a church, synagogue, or mosque. There is clearly an accelerating trend toward a more secular America, and we see even stronger trends in this direction in Europe.

The decline in "church" membership in America is being driven by a sharp rise in the "nones," Americans who have no religious preference. These secular changes are in great part manifestations of a generational shift. The court cases discussed earlier notwithstanding, a significant majority of Americans have loosened norms of sex and gender from their traditional religious moorings (Doherty, 2022).

We should not have the right to be ignorant. Our Constitution should protect Scientific Freedom, the Freedom to Reason. We live in a terrifying firestorm of meaninglessness, a cosmos we will never understand no matter how many James Webbs we peer through, and the thing we seem to do best is destroy planetary and human ecologies. You need a coach to navigate through this firestorm? Read Nietzsche's letter to his sister Elizabeth on believing versus inquiring; read Richard Feynman on not being afraid of not knowing things. Don't take the theologians seriously or those philosophers who spend thousands of hours and make careers out of endless commentaries on ontological proofs for the existence of God. Schopenhauer already pointed out that the ontological proof is nonsense; and Schiller called it an extraordinary piece of stupidity. And yet this nonsense and stupidity underwrites endowed chairs and academic honors for the Plantingas (Alvin Plantinga, 1974) of the world. What species are theologians like Hans Küng (1978) who claim that prayer, sacrifice, and bending in awe before God are compatible with reason? Here I announce an anarchist motto: Ni Dieu, Ni Maître! Prostrating yourself before God makes it easy to prostrate yourself before human dictators. The height of worship is the lowest level of self-esteem.

Headline: Louisiana classrooms now required by law to display the Ten Commandments, Stephanie Gallman and Dianne Gallagher, CNN: Wed June 19, 2024.

This may seem to be a direct violation of the Constitution, and the principle of the separation of state and church. The words "separation of church and state" do not appear in the original U.S. Constitution, but the concept is enshrined the First Amendment: "Congress shall make no law respecting an establishment of religion." Some legal experts contend that this fact may at the end of the Supreme Court day protect the Louisiana statute. The argument against the statute may require some form of commitment to the Enlightenment rather to how one reads the Constitution.

Headline: Oklahoma state superintendent announces all schools must incorporate the Bible and the Ten Commandments in curriculums. Alaa Elassar, CNN, June 27, 2004. This, among many other things, could only happen where the understanding of the Bible is based on belief and not the sociology and anthropology of the Bible. Many Americans, and unfortunately many politicians, are still medieval children when it comes to religion and religious texts.

The bottom line: Our – any – Constitution – should protect the freedom to think, to do science, to reason. Protecting the freedom of religion is a relic. In today's world it means protecting the right to be ignorant. I pointed out earlier the dangers of assuming that freedom of speech means everyone is entitled to their own opinions. The other danger was recently revealed in this headline. Headline: A Harvard Dean Causes Firestorm With Call To Limit Faculty Speech, Michael T. Nietzel, June 19, 2024: Forbes.com. Lawrence D. Bobo, Dean of Social Science and the W.E.B. Du Bois Professor of the Social Sciences at Harvard, wrote an op-ed in the June 15th *Harvard Crimson*, in which he asked: "Is it outside the bounds of acceptable professional conduct for a faculty member to excoriate University leadership, faculty, staff, or students with the intent to arouse external intervention into University business? And does the broad publication of such views cross a line into sanctionable violations of professional conduct?" Bobo asked. "Yes it is and yes it does," he wrote. Here's a better answer, Nietzel wrote: "No it's not and no it doesn't."

It's especially troubling that these words were spoken by a distinguished sociologist, words that W.E.B. Du Bois would not have endorsed. Degrees and distinctions are no guarantors of intelligence.

11   The Reality of Us: News on Who and What We Are

Headline: Google's AI passed a famous test – and showed how the test is broken. The Turing test has long been a benchmark for machine intelligence. But what it really measures is deception. Will Oremus, Staff writer, *The Washington Post*, June 17, 2022. Let's review our earlier discussion of Lemoine.

Turing believed that the question of whether machines could actually think was "meaningless." But the Turing test has become the standard methodology for assessing machine intelligence. However, it does this by successfully using conversational tricks. Google engineer Blake Lemoine is now convinced that Google's LaMDA is intelligent, conscious, and sentient. Every day, headlines proclaim AI achievements that sound human. Perhaps the Turing test should serve a different purpose than assessing the ability of AI to sound human. It could be an "ethical red flag" alerting us that if an AI can pass the Turing test there is a danger that it could deceive humans (Oresmus, 2022). It is folly to find agency in the pattern finding algorithms of AIs (Lobina, 2024), especially when agency and free will in humans have not been transparently demonstrated. We are dealing with data, not decisions; there's a reason it's called "artificial" intelligence (Bubula, 2024). The hazards we face are not from AI but from a dangerous misalignment caused by all-too-human ideological conflicts (Levin, 2024).

Consider that we already have machines that are intelligent, conscious, and sentient. They are organic machines. Humans are organic entities but still machines. What then is to prevent the development, in principle, of mechanical machines that are intelligent, conscious, and sentient? They won't be intelligent, conscious, and sentient in exactly the same way we are (chimpanzees aren't), but they might develop mechanical forms of these attributes. Therefore, when I claim that "AIs and "robots 'r' us" I do not mean this wholistically; they capture some cognitive-like and motor aspects of humans, and they embody the cultural values of their inventors.

Headline: Will We Download our Minds into New Bodies? Journalist Steve Kotler (n.d.; and see Bamford, 2012; *Huffington Post*, 2013) has proposed that at some point in the 21st century it will become possible to upload a dead person's mind into a computer and then download it into a living human. What is this but another pathetic human effort to cheat death.

Headline: Dyson Sphere May Be the Key to Immortality (Hart, 2021; on the biotechnology of immortality, see Rothblatt (2003, 2014). In 2013, Rothblatt gave a talk titled "The Purpose of Biotechnology is the End of Death," Lewis, 2013). This item asks that you re-consider who and what you are, and forces onlookers to ask why "transhumanists" are obsessed with immortality, an impossible idea and a delusionary wish.

Let's be clear about the concept of "immortality." It refers to an eternal existence. For immortality to be a realistic possibility, the contexts for life – a planet, a universe for it to wander around in – the cosmos – would have to be eternal. There are various suggestions coming out of cosmology that it might not be eternal. So let's modify our goal and define immortality to mean to live, in some form bodily, digital, or spiritual, for millennia with the existence of the cosmos as a limit. For reasons I have discussed elsewhere in my work on the sociology of religion and the gods, we can eliminate religious speculations about immortality in terms of an after-life. Science is not going to gadget its way into immortality per se, but it is reasonable to expect scientists will come up with ways of extending human lives bio-technologically.

Humans have been in pursuit of immortality since ancient times by way of alchemical efforts to discover or invent an elixir of life, the Philosopher's Stone, The Fountain of Youth, or the Peaches of Immortality, and their modern versions, such as cryonics, digital immortality, rejuvenation technologies, or some technological singularity. These are delusional exercises. Extending life within certain natural limits is certainly realistic, but overcoming all causes of death (which seems to be behind all these elixir fantasies, whether chemical, biological, or technological) is an exercise in a kind of futility that borders on if it is not already a mental illness.

Headline: Researchers Make Breakthrough Discovery in the Ability to Move Things With our Minds, Yaobiao, (2022).

shows that people use brainwave control to manipulate electromagnetic waves, which can be extended in some illustrative scenarios, such as attention monitoring, reconfigurable antenna, fatigue monitoring, etc.

ZHU, WANG, et al., 2022

Metamaterials are synthetic composite materials with a structure such that it exhibits properties not usually found in natural materials, especially a negative refractive index. Metasurfaces, the two-dimensional counterparts to metamaterials, allow researchers to design artificial materials with new levels of functionality and freedom for manipulating electromagnetic waves. Through on-site programming, programmable metasurfaces (PMs) with multiple or switchable functions can be realized and further integrated with sensors or driven by pre-defined software. The self-adaptability significantly improves functionality by removing human involvement. The switches among different functions on these PMs generally rely on manual operations. The fundamental framework is wire-connected, manually-controlled and non-real-time switched. Therefore, it is fascinating to construct an entire framework that can realize remote, wireless, real-time, mind-controlled functional metasurfaces.

12   Conclusion

There's something important going on here that relates to mind uploading and telekinesis, but don't let it lead you down a primrose path you think leads to literally moving things with your "mind." This might indeed be possible, but Gilbert Ryle (1949), remember, pioneered the idea that the mind is just what the body does.

Das ist nicht Wissenschaft, das ist nicht Naturwissenschaft: das ist theologie. How should we think about the idea that our minds can be uploaded and downloaded? What, after all, is a mind and how is it related to a brain? This is a "big question" and deserves extended attention.

The brain is not an independent bio-informational machine. It is at the coarse-grained level intricately informationally networked with the body, the body's organs, the body's social interactions in cultural and ecological niches, and triadically entangled. The triad is the basic social unit, an emotionally connected unit bonded by a micro-collective effervescence. This is where the "hard problem of consciousness" folks should be looking. Why is explained in my theory of the social brain (Restivo, 2023).

CHAPTER 7

The Reality of the Social Brain: A Case Study in the Existential Threat of Individualism

My social brain model was initially based on an argument for the social brain proposed by the anthropologist Clifford Geertz (1973: 74; 2000: 203–217).[1] He argued that the following features of life emerged together, in synch with each other (co-evolved): expanded forebrain among the primates; complex social organizations; at least among the post-Australopithecines tool savvy humans, institutional cultural patterns. This implies that we should treat biological, social, and cultural factors as complexly interrelated in terms of a scaffolded, intertwined and conjointly causal nexus. Human behavior emerges in increasingly dense, complex social networks that reflect the complex interactions of genes, neurons, neural nets, organs, biomes, the brain and central nervous system, other elements of the body's systems and subsystems down to the molecular level (see Pert, 1997). Our thoughts, actions, and emotions are produced in a stream of interactions across linked biological, chemical, physical, social and ecological systems.

The fact that the triad is the fundamental social unit means that the fundamental behavioral unit, at the level of my model, is a triad of such models and it is that triad that is the basic model of brain/mind/culture/world.

1   Connectomes

The latter part of the twentieth century was dominated by attention to networks and connections. In 2005, Olaf Sporns and Patric Hagmann, exemplifying the principle of multiple discovery (Merton, 1961), independently introduced the term "connectome" to refer to a map of the neural connections within the brain. Connectomes may range in scale from maps of parts of the nervous system to the neural connections in the brain. In line with these developments, my model represents a connectome of connectomes. The next stage in this project is to construct the triad unit of my model, three

---

1   This chapter includes material originally published in Sal Restivo, *Einstein's Brain: Genius, Culture, and Social Networks* (New York: Palgrave Macmillan 2020).

interconnected individual models, and then to embed this triadic connectome in the nested networks of the social and cultural connectomes locally, regionally, and globally. This would constitute a global connectome driven by the circulation of information across a global network of nested networks (cf. Khanna, 2016). This sounds complicated but we're talking about a complex network model of the peoples, flora, fauna, and ecological systems and subsystems of our planet.

Connectomics is becoming a critical resource in neuroscience. So far, however, it hasn't been much help in explaining how the brain functions. That would involve at least parsing the overwhelming interconnectivities in the complex brains of humans and non-human primates. Connectomes also tell us nothing about the quality of the connections they map. For this and other reasons involving, for example, the activity of neuromodulators, we should not expect connectomes alone to explain brain functions.

When considering the etiology of behaviors that are traditionally considered genetically grounded, it is now important to recognize that the human brain arrives on the evolutionary stage, with human beings, always, already, and everywhere social. Therefore, what we have considered to be linearly transmitted genetic phenomena must now be reconsidered. Genes, genetics, and genetic transmission, understood as part of the social brain model or paradigm, must now be understood as eminently social phenomena.

Recent studies supporting my model demonstrate that there are indeed information flows that link the brain to the organs of the body; and that the links between the brain and the liver, heart, and gut are notably stronger than other links. Notice, for example, the exceptional functions of the vagus nerve revealed in recent studies. And the heart sends signals to the rest of the body on its own. In fact, the heart sends more signals to the brain than the brain sends to the heart. There is thus a sense in which we can say that the heart thinks.

The gut-brain axis has long been recognized as a key linkage. Gut bacteria make ninety percent of the brain's neurotransmitter serotonin and a variety of neuroactive compounds. The brain sends signals to the gut that stimulate or suppress digestion. The lesson of such studies is that the most complicated object known to humanity, the brain, does not do its work alone. And the connections, as I've indicated, reach outside the body into the world around us including our social relationships.

2   Brain-Machine Interaction (BMI) and Brain-Computer
        Interaction (BCI)

The work in the area of BMI and BCI is exemplified by Miguel Nicolelis' (2011) research and development program involving experiments with the wireless transmission of thoughts. This work promises life changing cognitive prosthetics. At the same time I see a troubling resurrection of an ancient Platonic dream (or nightmare) of "free floating minds," minds freed of the flesh. Nicolelis imagines minds without bodies, or with bodies that do not have to move, communicating "wirelessly" across a room, a city, a country, a continent, the galaxy. The ancient fear of the flesh we see here is at bottom a fear of the female flesh. This is a sign that some science at least is still being fueled by patriarchy and the masculine fear of the feminine. This is of course at one with the infirmities and uncertainties of the flesh in general which a free-floating mind would escape.

Where is "the social" in BMI and BCI? Decades of work in science and technology studies have demonstrated that social and cultural facts are embodied in the hardware and algorithms that make the machines in this work function. This is discussed in cultural studies as the circuit of culture: cultural texts and artifacts embody representations, identities, and production, consumption, and regulations activities (du Gay et al., 1997; Goggin, 2006). But wireless transmission seems to violate the basic principles of social construction. There is a technology at work here – wi-fi technology – and not ESP. Sociologist and STS scholar Dr. Jennifer Croissant of the University of Arizona suggests the following hypothesis (personal communication). These wireless results will only work if and to the extent that the participants have a set of shared kinesthetic and cultural references (e.g., relative homogeneity in brain mapping and information processing, starting with the linguistic level). Just as we can no longer assume transparency in everyday communications as diversity in all its varieties increases, these systems will either be extremely narrow in their potential participants and applications, or have to engage a model of the social brain and an enormous amount of cultural complexity in algorithmic form so that there is interoperability amongst diverse brains. As diversity increases, the amount of effort spent indexing communications increases. More and more metadata and contextual data will be needed to understand if two interlocutors are talking and thinking about the same thing. Cultural diversity will pose huge challenges to complex BMI and BCI but even the relatively narrower diversity characteristic of individual brains will overload bandwidth and algorithms.

The research frontiers in the neurosciences are moving very rapidly and brain researchers are regularly announcing new and surprising discoveries. As a neuroscience watcher, I'm alert to the fact that developments even within the brains in a vat neuroist framework could radically alter our understanding of the social brain. We should not expect even the most radical and unexpected of these changes to overturn the basic concept of the social brain. The latest version of my model can be viewed in Restivo (2023: 127).

3   A Case Study: Einstein, Genius, and Social Networks

In 2017, the "Genius" issue of National Geographic credited Albert Einstein's ability to harness the power of his "own thoughts" to predict gravity waves a century before gravity waves were detected using highly sophisticated technologies. Does this prove that Einstein was the "genius of all geniuses?" Einstein and his brain are iconic objects – a sacred scientific hero and a sacred relic. Without diminishing Einstein's achievements, the social brain paradigm gives us a new way to think about these achievements. Let's consider first that the very idea of "genius" has come under critical scrutiny in contemporary research on creativity. Second, a new view of the social basis of creativity emerged in the last quarter of the 20th century, an idea adumbrated in the writings of the classical social theorists of the late 19th and early 20th centuries: ideas are created in social networks, not in individuals or individual brains. Third, the idea of a biological brain is being superseded by a new paradigm that sees the brain as a social object operating in a social context. It has become increasingly clear in the life and social sciences that humans are the most social of the social species. The "I" is, as Nietzsche already recognized, a grammatical illusion. We all, as Walt Whitman put it poetically in *Song of Myself*, contain multiples; the self is a mosaic, not a unitary ego, in a scientific sense as well as a poetic one. When we identify Einstein as a genius, we learn more about ourselves and our culture than we do about Einstein.

The "genius," by definition, stands apart from society, history, and culture – and even escapes time and space. But genius is an earth-bound socially constructed gendered idea. Its classical roots make it divinely inspired – to meet a genius is to meet a male god.

In the real world, there is no such thing as the lone wolf genius. Every genius, like every person, is a social network. Every genius stands on the shoulders of a social network, not the shoulders of giants. For the commonly accepted concept of "genius" to be meaningful it would have to be rooted in genes, neurons, or both. In that case, geniuses would appear at random and scattered across intellectual and cultural landscapes. On the contrary, the most comprehensive studies of genius by social scientists have demonstrated that geniuses do not appear at random. Instead, genius clusters.

The fact that creative acts and actors cluster was recognized in the ancient world. Modern research shows that creative clusters appear predictably during times of rapid decline or rapid growth within civilizations. We also know that new ideas, theories, and technologies emerge simultaneously in different places in the same cultural neighborhoods and share a family resemblance. The particular version that prevails and the "genius" who gets credit for the innovation hinges on negotiation, politics, public relations, personalities, connections, and in some cases the outcomes of patent disputes (as in the case of Nikola Tesla).

The notion that Einstein's "own thoughts" were responsible for his insights into gravity waves ignores his collaborations with Michele Besso and Michael Grossman during the construction of the general theory. It was Grossman, for example, who helped Einstein with the geometry and the concept of tensors he needed to formalize the theory. In the same way, the portrait of Einstein as a lone wolf patent clerk who published the revolutionary 1905 papers leaves out a network of his influences – from Newton to Lorentz, and Poincaré to Minkowski. It also obscures the roles of his friends, teachers, students, and colleagues in physics, of his first wife Mileva Marić, his math assistant Walther Mayer, and the members of his Olympia Academy (1902–1905).

The important point is not that Einstein worked with and depended on others. It is that Einstein was those others – they are embodied in his self as a social network. When you understand all the people who went into Einstein being Einstein, does the label "genius" really help us understand him or does it instead encourage untutored awe, worship, and a distancing of ourselves from Einstein as a fellow human being?

Einstein's 1905 papers came in the midst of a cultural flowering of ideas, inventions, and discoveries across the full spectrum of the arts, humanities, and sciences between 1840 and 1930. Einstein's genius cluster in physics included such luminaries as Planck, Tesla, Marconi, Westinghouse, Madame Curie, the Wright brothers, Emmy Noether, and Edison. The two great innovations in physics that would remain at the core of physics throughout the twentieth and into the twenty-first century – relativity theory and quantum mechanics – were born in the early 1900s.

Expanding that genius cluster to encompass music brings in such names as Sibelius, Puccini, DeBussey, Schoenberg, Stravinsky, and Charles Ives. Innovations in literature include the rise of the novel, American Transcendentalism, Realism, Stream of Consciousness, various forms of Modernism, Naturalism, the growth of children's literature, and the Harlem Renaissance of the 1920s. There was a sympathetic mutuality that linked Cubism (represented by Picasso's "Les Demoiselles d'Avignon," 1907) and

Relativity Theory. Both involved challenges to conventions regarding absolute time and space (see Pyenson, 2021: 127–247; and Miller, 2002).

The period 1840–1930 also witnessed a veritable Copernican revolution, the emergence and crystallization of the social sciences. This period can be considered the classic Age of the Social. It ushered in the idea that we are through and through social beings.

Ultimately, by looking at the myth of Einstein's brain, we can understand how the myth of individualism is at odds with the evolutionary reality that humans are always, already, and everywhere social. Einstein's singular status is not a matter of genes, neurons, quantum phenomena, or the biological brain; the architecture of his brain reflected his experiences in the world, all of the social networks he encountered in his life. Since the1990s, developments in social neuroscience, studies of brain plasticity, epigenetics, and network theory have fueled the development of an explanation for Einstein's genius – a social brain paradigm. The idea that we have social brains arose from hypotheses about the connection between brain size and social complexity. Beginning in the 1920s and then more systematically in the 1950s, these hypotheses were explored in studies of non-human primates. Two conflicting hypotheses fueled this research: larger brains led to larger and more dense social networks; or larger and more dense social networks led to larger brains. Over time, it seemed more reasonable to hypothesize that brain size, and the size and density of social networks, were coupled in co-evolution.

All of this led to the crystallization of the social brain hypothesis, which entered the neuroscience literature in 1990. This hypothesis initially identified specific regions of the brain (including, for example, the amygdala and the insula) as "the social brain." More recent studies suggest that the whole brain must be considered a social and cultural entity. In other words, the brain is a complex organ that originates and functions at the nexus of biological, environmental, and social forces. By the 2000s, the social brain hypothesis was finding its way into studies of autism, schizophrenia, and other classic topics in psychiatry.

The story of pathologist Thomas Harvey removing Einstein's brain during the autopsy in 1955 is well known. However, there were no studies of Harvey's brain slides between 1955 and 1985, and those done between 1985 and the early 2000s proved, in the end, to be sterile. The noteworthy features of Einstein's brain some researchers identified were controversial, and many experts who studied Einstein's brain found nothing unusual. One brain scientist said it was just an old, diseased brain. These studies were guided by the false assumption that the mind is the brain, and by an inability to "see" social life as the locus of causal forces that shape our behaviors, emotions, and thoughts. And yet, the myth that we are our brains lives on in science, politics, and culture. It was the basis for Bush's proclamation of the 1990s as the Decade of the Brain, Obama's 2013 BRAIN initiative, and comparable policy pronouncements in Europe, the Middle East, and China. Brain research remains haunted by the myth of individualism, which is at its root the myth of the brain in a vat (*The Matrix* is an artistic gloss on this metaphor). The social brain idea, though, proposes a far more powerful concept: network thinking, which is capable of connecting the smallest parts of life, such as neurons, across multiple scales to the global network of information and communication. The concept of the connectome gives us a perspective in which everything from cells and neurons to neural nets, to the body, its microbiome and its organs, and to social relations and the environment is linked in a circulation of information.

4   The Woman in Einstein's Social Brain

Consider, now some observations on the perennial controversy concerning the role of Einstein's first wife, Mileva Marić, in his achievements. Marić was a Serbian physicist and mathematician, and the only woman in Einstein's class at Zurich's Polytechnic. She was the second woman to complete the program of study in the Department of Mathematics and Physics at the Polytechnic.

We now have a new way to evaluate her contributions to Einstein's thinking. Among the historical reasons for considering her influence are the facts that her handwriting is on some of Einstein's early manuscripts, and that she helped him with his math. But if we consider that from the perspective that "Einstein's Genius Wasn't In His Brain; It Was In His Friends" we see that Mileva was one of those in the social network whose shoulders he stood on; in other words, she was very much a part of his social self and thus his social brain. We are not dealing here with the question of whether or not she was his intellectual equal. The classical way of considering the extent of her influence (based on the myth of individualism) was to look for direct, physically visible signs of influence. We now see that we have to revise the "Giants" metaphor to read "Standing on the Shoulders of Social Networks:" Mileva was part of Einstein's social brain. We don't have all the data needed to establish the precise content of her contributions but there can be no question that she contributed to his thinking. Women have not been standing behind their men; they have literally been in their heads (based on a collaboration with Chandra Murkerji: Restivo, 2020b).

The anarchist spirit of this book is characteristic of the brain itself. On the one hand, given my model, we would expect the structure of the brain to bear some resemblance to the structure of the society it is embedded in; for example, hierarchical society, hierarchical brain. However, the brain, like every one of the systems and sub-systems in the brain/body/world connectome, has some inherent structures and functions that are not necessarily fully synchronized with its societal context. The brain, in fact, has an inherently anarchic structure. We know we can trigger anarchic actions in the brain by administering psychedelics (Carhart-Harris and Friston, 2019). Assuming a hierarchical structure, the administering of psychedelics produces a loss of functional hierarchy. The anarchic brain principle comes into play as a result of relaxed beliefs under psychedelics. Top-down control associated with hierarchy is replaced by a bottom-up information flow. Psychedelics enhance brain entropy: "the entropic brain hypothesis proposes that within upper and lower limits, after which consciousness may be lost, the entropy of spontaneous brain activity indexes the informational richness of conscious states" (Carhart-Harris, 2018: 167).

Emerson (2020), commenting on Gazzaniga (2011), argues that his concept of the mind's diversified portfolio free market can be described as anarchy. This makes the brain inherently anarchic independent of psychedelics. This idea is reinforced by Berkowitz's (2016) claim that nervous systems operate with multiple playbooks. Nervous systems can harbor competing mechanisms. This is consistent with the tinkering model of evolution (which I will introduce in Chapter 8) which allows animals to adapt and problem solve using available resources without being governed by teleological forces (cf. Soresi, 2006). While I have been loosely mixing theory and speculation in these last few paragraphs, some of the more scientifically grounded arguments for the anarchic brain come from studies of chaos and the brain (e.g. Justin, Hubert, et al. 2019; Faure and Korn, 2001; Korn and Faure, 2003; Skarda and Freeman, 1987, 1990; Duke and Pritchard, 1991; Lehnertz et al., 2000; Zapporoli, Porta, and Paulesu, 2015). The failure to embrace the reality of who and what we are is one of the least recognized of the existential threats we face. The conservative commandment "Thou shalt not commit sociology" is an existential threat. Let's explore a case study.

5   On Breaking the 11th Commandment and Committing Sociology

In 2014, Canadian First Nations teenager, Tina Fontaine, was found murdered after being reported missing. Once again, calls went out for a national inquiry into missing and murdered First Nations women. Conservative Prime Minister Stephen Harper responded by claiming that this was not a "sociological phenomenon" but a "crime." Crime is an eminently social phenomenon, but this tragedy only caused Harper to recall his 2013 claim that "this is not a time to commit sociology." Statistics Canada has long documented the facts that First Nations people face more poverty, unemployment, and violence than other Canadians. Various studies have shown that indigenous women are three times more likely to be the victims of crimes and eight times more likely to be murdered than non-indigenous women. For Harper, these statistics veil the simple fact that the issue is "crime." Harper's views and words echo those of President Nixon's vice present Spiro Agnew, who railed against "nattering nabobs of negativism," and British prime minister Margaret Thatcher's teaching that "There is no such thing as society. There are individual men and women, and there are families." The conservative political commentator George Will also urged that we follow the 11th commandment: "Thou shalt not commit sociology." But Will has a PhD in political science from Princeton, and he seasons his learned and witty punditry with statistics gathered by many people committing sociology.

6   Conclusion

The problem from Harper's perspective is that bad people commit crimes, evil people commit terrorist acts, and poor people are lazy and feel entitled to government handouts. What is to be done? Catch the bad people and lock them up; track down the terrorists and kill them; and force the poor into the labor market. Don't commit sociology and ask "why" questions or try to get to the root of the problems. The term "radical" is not a happy one for conservatives or liberals, Republicans or Democrats. But if we follow Tom Hayden's conception of "the radical style" we can see that it comes close to if it doesn't actually conflate with what we mean by science. Writing in the middle of the 1960s revolutions, Hayden (1967: 6) defined being radical as a matter of penetrating social problems to their roots, their real causes. Radicalism as a style means being constantly driven by the question, "Why?" It is not dogmatic; it understands conclusions as provisional, always ready to be discarded in the face of new evidence or changed circumstances. This is what we mean by science, whether physics, chemistry, biology, or sociology.

PART 3

Evolution, Culture, and Survival Wisdom

∴

CHAPTER 8

The Cooperative Principle in Evolution

1   Introduction

The literature on anarchism is replete with variety, definitions, and controversies. I therefore want to identify the anarchist imagination that guides my sociology and my politics.

The immediate starting point is necessarily Peter Kropotkin (1842–1921). The key concept in Kropotkin's (1902/1976) work is "mutual aid." In the wake of Darwin's work, Kropotkin's studies demonstrated many facts of mutual aid among animals, human tribes including the Bushmen, Hottentots, Papuas, Aleoutes, and the Dayak (which he unfortunately categorized in the rhetoric of his time as "savages"), contemporary "barbarians" (including the Buryates, Kabyles, Caucasian mountaineers, and a variety of African societies), the medieval city, and mutual aid among ourselves. The idea of mutual aid was not part of America's system of norms, values, and beliefs.

Growing up in post-World War II America meant for me and my peers learning that the primary lesson taught by Darwin was that evolution was a "struggle for survival," "a struggle for existence." "Survival of the fittest" was part of our school vocabulary, and this ideology was reflected in a cultural rhetoric that included "nature red in tooth and claw," "dog eat dog," and the virtue of unbridled competition. This rhetoric was already being used by the nineteenth century Robber Barons, incorporated in the ideological framework of "capitalism" as an evolutionary defense for their greed, their hunger for profit, money and property. John D. Rockefeller, Jr. famously said: "The American Beauty Rose can be produced in the splendor and fragrance which bring cheer to its beholder only by sacrificing the early buds which grow up around it" (quoted in Tarbell, 1904/1969: epigraph to the "Preface"). One version of this quote associates the Robber Barons with the American Beauty Rose and the working class with the weeds.

Rockefeller understood this to be a law of nature and a law of God. He and his fellows already had at their disposal philosophical and scientific grounds for their pronouncements. Thomas Hobbes in *Leviathan* (1651/2017: Chapters XIII–XIV) had written: "during the time men live without a common power to keep them all in awe, they are in that condition which is called war; and such a war as is of every man against every man." Life is "solitary, poor, nasty, brutish, and short." The famous phrase "war of all against all" (bellum omnium contra omnes) appears in his *De Cive* (1642/1998).

More immediately, the Robber Barons had Herbert Spencer. It was Spencer, not Darwin, who coined the phrase "survival of the fittest" in his *The Principles of Biology* (1864). Spencer, in line with some other evolutionary theorists of his time, argued that mutual aid occurred among animals but the natural law and the law among primitive humans was "war of all against all."

Andrew Carnegie was especially taken with Spencer who told him that it was natural, it was scientific, that people like him should reach the top of society. There was nothing wrong or evil about it. Here then we see the major countervailing force to mutual aid. Kropotkin recognizes this force and identifies it as "individualism" and "self-assertion." One can imagine at this point on the largest scale of the process of life unfolding a contest between evolutionary and devolutionary forces. He recognizes the need for treating this contest but argues for the immediate necessity of focusing attention on mutual aid to counter-act the idea that the "war of all against all" is the natural state of humanity.

Among his contemporaries, Kropotkin identifies several writing from a similar perspective: Henry Drummond, A. Sutherland, and George Büchner. Büchner's contribution to the mutual aid corpus is represented by the remark that "One must love humanity in order to reach out into the unique essence of each individual: no one can be too low or too ugly" (from his novella fragment, *Lenz*, 1836/2005). The Chinese philosopher Mozi (c.470–c.391) was already arguing for the value of universal love centuries earlier. If we place the ideas of mutual aid and love into the framework of evolutionary theory we can capture them under the more general cooperative principle. At the end of the day, mutual aid, love as an evolutionary mechanism, and the cooperative principle in general are supreme forces of nature, fundamental conditions of human survival. This is a part of Darwin's message the capitalists miss (Montagu, 1952).

2   From the Cooperative Principle to Love as an Evolutionary Mechanism

Kropotkin's concept of "mutual aid" helped draw attention to an evolutionary fact that has been hidden behind the ideology of capitalism and the myth of individualism. That hidden fact is the invention in the unfolding on the evolutionary landscape of cooperation as an adaptive mechanism. The cooperative principle first appears in the ability of individual cells to flourish in clusters. In the next stage, they develop the ability to revitalize themselves by exchanging genetic material. The improved adaptability of multicellular animals over single cell creatures was raised to increasing levels of intimacy in fish, amphibia, then reptiles and mammals.

With the coming of the mammals, the placenta, mammary glands, and long gestation and dependency periods added a strongly social dimension to the adaptation process. Increasingly among the non-human primates and then humans the survival of the young became dependent on extended caring behavior by two or more adults. Humans emerged as one of the social species, building up dense complex social networks around the campsite. The campsite is the human equivalent of the nest in other species. More broadly, but more controversially as we saw earlier, humans have been placed with the eusocial species.

The ratcheting up and elaboration of the cooperative principle resulted in the eventual evolution of humans who arrive already, always, and everywhere social. We are the most recent manifestation of the cooperative principle, the most radically social of the (eu)social species. It is important to underscore that humans do not appear on the evolutionary stage as individuals who then become social by way, for example, of some social contract. Rather, they arrive social and become individualized through the mechanisms of culture. Failure to recognize this is what led Hobbes and other "war of all against all" advocates astray. The prehistorical "invention" and elaboration of colonial cooperation demonstrated its robustness as an adaptive mechanism.

It is difficult to imagine that our introspective sense of our own individual agency and free will is an illusion. Tolstoy writes with great insight about what I call the fallacy of introspective transparency. In his monumental novel, *War and Peace* (1869/1996), he describes Napoleon as a child holding a couple of strings inside a baby carriage and imagining that he is driving it, and moreover convincing others that he is driving the carriage. The force moving the carriage is history, social forces, not Napoleon. Tolstoy forces us to think critically about the limits of experience. We saw the consequences of this way of thinking earlier when we compared our subjective experience of a stationary earth with the reality of the Earth's multiple and complex movements through space and time. For this reason, we must be suspicious of "near death" reports which continue to be reported and give people false hopes about an after-life, never mind "revelations" as proofs of gods, heavens, and hells.

We are evolution's most radical experiment in social life and survival. Evolution is an extremely complicated multi-level multi-dimensional process that operates on many different time scales. But it is driven by an overall paradigm. If we personify evolution as a certain type of scientist-engineer (let's call it E) we see E acting like a tinkerer. To tinker is to attempt to repair or improve something in a casual or unfocused way. The tinkerer experiments, and embraces failures in more or less complex trial and error operations. The tinkerer's goal is simply to succeed, to make something that works without thinking about immediate functions or long-term objectives. E thus works without a specific goal in mind, takes advantage of whatever materials are at hand, and tinkers them into something that works.

We can characterize the main feature of E's work as marked by contingencies. What resources are available in E's local environment that it can play with? And this indeed is the way ethnographers of scientific practice have characterized the day-to-day work of scientists (e.g., Knorr-Cetina, 1979). The idea of evolution as a tinkering process is not something I thought up but a theory proposed by serious students of the evolutionary process (e.g., Jacob, 1977).

Readers should be aware of research that suggests evolution may not always be as random as previously thought. Scientists have discovered an "invisible ecosystem" of cooperating and competing genes. These interactions make some aspects of evolution "somewhat" predictable. This opens up the possibility of synthesizing novel genetic constructions, including synthetic genomes, which in turn could lead to targeted treatments and the design of microorganisms that could, for example, degrade pollution (Beavan, Domingo-Sananes, and McInerney, 2014). And see Corning, Kauffman et al. (2023) in which "Third Way" evolutionary biologists and philosophers of science present the case for the evolved purposiveness of living systems, termed "teleonomy" by chronobiologist Colin Pittendrighargue (1958). Organisms appear to evolve with intention. While this line of inquiry is being explored by contemporary evolutionary biologists, I will stand by the tinkerer model in the meantime and not try to adjudicate the conflict between these two models or how they may work together.

Different tinkerers and the same tinkerer at different times will produce different solutions to the same problems. To give a specific example, consider that all living things share the same organic molecules and metabolic pathways. If E is a tinkerer, then we can assume that new functional proteins do not appear anew but arise from rearranging genetic elements. We see this reflected in the similar DNA sequences in fruit flies and pigs that cause wings to appear in one case and legs in another. E can be expected to work under the same natural constraints as humans, for example the law of limited possibilities. The law of limited possibilities is illustrated by the invention of the oar. Keep in mind that in this case the tinkerer is human and does indeed have an objective. Many different kinds of oars can be tinkered into shape. But they all must meet certain requirements, natural constraints, if they are going to power a boat. Oars can come in a variety of shapes and sizes but they can't be constructed in any shape or size whatsoever. This principle operates in technology but also in culture more generally and we can assume it applies in E's case too.

What we find when we study science in practice is a collective generational process. Science in practice is contingent and opportunistic. Once science is established as a sustainable social institution, scientific practice can involve using the results of earlier efforts to generate new problems, experiments, theories, and results – everything from measuring devices and chemical reagents to test animals and mathematical equations. Under these conditions, scientists make their own reality and test it progressively against the impositions and constraints of the world outside the laboratory. This applies to theorists too whose theories are in fact experiments in logic, reason, and mathematics based on experimental evidence produced by research scientists. Theories are not idle speculations, or wild ungrounded imaginings. Scientists are not searching for "truth" in some abstract sense but for something that works. Their goal is success not "truth" per se. This practice nonetheless leads to corrigible, tentative, fragile and dynamic facts of the matter. Looked at from a different perspective the search for truth is a search for successful outcomes of experiments, tests, and predictions.

E's tinkering leads to the discovery that cell-proximity in primitive organisms is a survival mechanism. Keep in mind that E's tinkering results are produced in an arena ruled by the principles of natural selection, notably blind variation and selective retention, in Donald T. Campbell's (1960) terms (bracketing my earlier introduction of teleonomy).

In summary, E's tinkering led to cellular collaboration which eventually led to grouping behavior and sociation. The importance of grouping behavior is illustrated by the fact that a single prey is more likely to survive a predator's attack in a group. Sociation refers to the stable and patterned micro-level forms of more or less intense face-to-face interactions. Primary groups are characteristically small scale, close-knit, face-to-face, and long lasting. Intimate relationships, the nuclear family, and close friendships as well as some work groups are examples of primary groups. Secondary groups can vary in size, can last for various periods of time, and are characteristically impersonal. They tend to be task oriented rather than relationship oriented. The committee at your work place tasked with organizing a party is an example of a secondary group. A school committee organizing a bake sale is another example of a secondary group. Secondary groups can of course incorporate primary groups. Your entire family may get involved in planning the school's bake sale.

If we view life from an evolutionary perspective we find that most humans have lived in primary groups. Secondary groups proliferated as the industrial age unfolded. This process brought classical primary-secondary dichotomies into greater prominence: rural-urban, country-city, informal-formal, status-contract, community and society, and the one best known to social scientists, gemeinschaft-gesellschaft (communal society-associational society). Communal societies, typified by rural, peasant societies, are characterized by face-to-face relationships that are defined and regulated by traditional norms, values, and beliefs. These traditional regulatory "laws" of family, kinship, and religion are weakened in the associational society by the ideals and goals of self-interested rationality. There is a shift from personal direct face-to-face interactions and a sense of universal solidarity to impersonal and indirect primarily economically and politically oriented interactions. On the human significance of face-to-face relationships, see Goffman (1959); Cooley (1909/2018); Jacobs (2006); and Aldous (1972).

These interactions are embedded in processes of rationalization, specialization, mechanization, commercialization, and commodification. This transformation generates feelings of alienation. The feeling of alienation is brought about by the loosening or destruction of primary ties. In the twentieth century, technological progress accelerated the development of first and second degree tertiary relationships. First degree tertiary relationships are face-to-face interactions mediated by a technological system or device. The telephone conversation is a prime example of a first degree tertiary relationship. The digital revolution gave rise to second degree tertiary relationships. Face-to-computer interactions are a prime example of second degree tertiary relationships. This transition from primary to second degree tertiary relationships has profound implications for the human condition.

Face-to-face relationships are a crucial feature of human evolution. They are the basic means for communication and the emergence of consciousness, mind, and emotions. We can view mediated relationships as a danger to this evolutionary construction or as a new stage in the evolution of relationships, communications, and emotions. Are we witnessing the emergence of new human-machine species – cyborgs or machine species that will compete with fleshy humans for an ecological niche? The digital revolution can be viewed as an existential threat to the human species or a "natural" evolutionary development. Perhaps we are on the verge of a new "Great Leap Forward" such as the one that characterized the Upper Paleolithic Age 40,000 years ago. We are faced with many unknowns as we move through the digital age at the same time that humans and other species along with the planetary ecology itself face doomsday possibilities. Whatever our future holds in store for us and our planet it should be clear that messing with face-to-face relationships portends radical changes in our communicative, mental, and emotional lives.

There has been some discussion in recent years about a new geological age that characterizes the modern world, the Anthropocene. Some experts have identified our geological era – variously originating with the Neolithic Revolution (12–15,000 years ago), the late 18th century (specifically, with the invention of the steam engine), and as recently as the 1960s – as the Anthropocene. Some experts identify it as essentially what we now refer to as the Holocene Age. In the existing schema, the Holocene defines the era we are now in which originated almost 12,000 years ago following the last glacial era. The Holocene and the preceding Pleistocene together form the Quaternary era. The Holocene or Anthropocene reflects the fact that human behavior, for the first time in evolutionary history, constitutes the greatest threat to the existence of humanity and the planet.

The basis for proposing a human centered geological epoch is the significant impact humans have had on the Earth's geology, landscape, limnology, ecosystems, climate, biodiversity, population growth, pollution, and the expanding use of renewable and especially non-renewable resources. A mid-twentieth century origin point is suggested by the emergence of risks associated with the beginning of the Atomic Age. The controversy over the concept of a new geological age has not been resolved. Neither the International Commission of Stratigraphy nor the International Union of Geological Sciences has approved the concept. While it's clear that humans have had an enormous impact on the planet's ecology and evolutionary systems, the controversy about the Anthropocene as a new subdivision of geological time has been over the proposed starting time.

The Russians appear to have invented the idea in the late 1930s by introducing the concept of science as a geological force; they introduced the term "Anthropocene" as early as the 1960s. The biologist E.F. Stoemer used the term in a different sense in the 1980s and it was reintroduced by atmospheric chemist P.J. Crutzen in 2000 based on human influence on the Earth's atmosphere in the last few centuries (Steiner, 2020; Green, 2021; Glass, 2021; Thomas, Williams, and Zalasiewicz, 2020).

3   Interlude: Mediated Communication

Humans have always had access to mediated communication (beginning with low tech drum beats, smoke signals, etc.). But the key moments in the evolution of mediated communication are associated with the emergence of literacy. One of the key moments in pre-modern times was the invention of the printing press by Johannes Gutenberg around 1440. Woodblock printing was available in China at least as early as the Han dynasty (206 BCE-220 CE). The Chinese also invented movable type around 1040CE (attributed to Bi Sheng).

In our global village, people often find themselves or their organizations engaged in cross-cultural settings. These settings are replete with potential ambiguities due to variations in gestural, linguistic, emotional, and postural standards. Face-to-face relationships are much more reliable in such ambiguous communication settings which involve cooperation, conflict, and negotiations. There are professionalized international networks in which a great deal can be accomplished through virtual modes of communication aided by high levels of standardized technologies and symbols. This is true for example in the airlines industry. But to return to the other horn of the dilemma, among infant macaque monkeys the more face-to-face interactions they have with their "mothers" the more sociable they are in later life.

We know that face-to-face interactions and grooming behaviors are important aspects of non-human primate behavior. The relevance of these studies which show long term sociability effects of face-to-face interactions is that humans and macaques, for example, exhibit similar child rearing behaviors and developmental trajectories.

We are facing a digital dilemma. The development of tertiary relationships and communication platforms has produced increasingly prominent and pervasive alternatives to face-to-face relationships and communicative modes of interaction. The dilemma is this: on the one hand, tertiary modes break down geographical and temporal barriers to face-to-face interaction. It is now possible to put yourself instantly and efficiently in contact with anyone anywhere in the world with an internet connection. This is limited to various degrees by political and cultural inequalities and injustices but it is historically unprecedented. On the other hand, tertiary modes cannot reproduce the ways in which face-to-face relationships support gestural, voice modulation, postural, and emotional options. These are not just basic ingredients of communication. Face-to-face interactions engage more of the senses than mediated interactions. They are the primitive origins of and sustaining factors for consciousness and emotions. To put it differently, primary, secondary, and tertiary modes are associated with different types and states of consciousness and emotions. Primary relationships are associated with the strongest forms of the resonance that arise when humans meet face to face, and that resonance is the medium for emotions and consciousness. This doesn't resolve all communication problems. We all have language, but cultures determine the nature and sounds of particular languages. The same is true for gestures, voice modulation, postures, and emotions.

Consciousness and emotions are relational; they are in-between phenomena and not phenomena that are generated and sustained within the lone individual. So the digital revolution is leading to new forms of consciousness and emotions – not face-to-face but face-to-interface. We can misinterpret meaning and intent in face-to-face interactions but digital forms of communication tend to reduce the number of factors available for interpretation and so the possibilities for miscommunication are greater. This is not simply a matter of managing interpersonal and organizational communication; it comes down to a process that arose in the evolution of animal life and that is implicated in the biology and sociology of survival.

Looked at from the vantage point of the evolutionary stage, what we have are variously mediated forms of relationships and communication competing for ecological niches and for survival. Evolution, we've seen, unfolds on multiple levels, in multiple dimensions, and on multiple time scales. One can imagine that a species heavily based on mediated technologies – robots, for example – might have better long term survival potential than humans. These are the considerations being discussed and debated around ideas such as "the singularity," Humanity 2.0, and the Technium.

In mathematics and physics, a singularity is a point at which the value of a function becomes infinite, for example in the case of matter that has become infinitely dense at the center of a black hole. The "technological" singularity is an hypothesized future point in history when technological growth becomes uncontrollable and irreversible. Robots and artificial intelligence are considered the most likely pathways to the technological singularity. For this reason, some observers consider robots and AI existential threats to humanity. These technological "intelligent agents" with their capacity for upgrades could lead to an "intelligence explosion." This combination of intelligence and upgrading could reach a point of rapid expansion and leave humans vulnerable to replacement and even in some scenarios enslavement if not extinction. Some observers believe that we could reach a technological singularity by the middle of this century. Stephen Hawking and Elon Musk are among prominent figures who have identified artificial general intelligence as an existential threat.

The social philosopher Steve Fuller (2012) has argued that we are evolving toward Humanity 2.0, a "singularity" in which we can no longer take the "normal human body" for granted. Humanity 2.0 can be viewed as one of the ways we can address the problems raised by the prospect of a technological singularity. On the one hand, computers, robots, and AI show signs of surpassing the human condition; on the other hand, they are tools – prosthetics – for extending our species-specific survival mechanisms. Of course the end result in both cases could be a technological singularity. Computers, robots, and AI may surpass us; or we might become indistinguishable from our prosthetics.

The worry here is an old one, the worry that technology can take on a life of its own. This can be thought of as the Frankenstein problem. (Winner, 1977: 7–8):

> The truth of the matter is that our deficiency does not lie in the want of well-verified "facts." What we lack is our bearings. The contemporary experience of things technological has repeatedly confounded our vision, our expectations, and our capacity to make intelligent judgments. Categories, arguments, conclusions, and choices that would have been entirely obvious in earlier times are obvious no longer. Patterns of perceptive thinking that were entirely reliable in the past now lead us systematically astray. Many of our standard conceptions of technology reveal a disorientation that borders on dissociation from reality. And as long as we lack the ability to make our situation intelligible, all of the "data" in the world will make no difference.

Kelly's "Technium," as we've seen, encompasses all of our technologies, machine processes, societies and cultures, and sciences, arts, and humanities in one global system. The sheer complexity of the system gives it increasing autonomy. It evolves and develops its own structures and dynamics. Technologies as small as drones and as large as electrical grids can indeed already become independent of human control. For a hopeful vision of our ability – individually and collectively – to safely navigate the existential threats we face from the basic elements of earth, air, water, and fire see Peter Denton's (2022) *The End of Technology*.

The anthropologist Rik Pinxten (2024) is also "mildly optimistic" about our future (see Chapter 8, "Reset or the Extinction of *Homo Sapiens?*"), but his last words are, "time is of the essence."

There is a dark side to our evolutionary story. Species come with an expiration date and 99.9 percent of all the species that E has tinkered into existence are extinct. Besides being a biological species, we humans are a cultural species and that has given us survival advantages. But at the same time culture seems to be the most efficient way to destroy a planetary ecology. Many learned observers, citing things like climate change, the destruction of ecological niches, and dangers to bees, frogs and other animals, are persuaded that we are in our last days as a biological species and that the planet's life giving qualities are themselves in danger. Something like a Technium kingdom, defined and dominated by technology, may be the only thing that can survive a catastrophic singularity. The Technium may be just another tinkering experiment by E that may more or less rapidly extinguish itself in an evolutionary cul de sac or become a new feature of the evolutionary stage, settling in as a seventh kingdom, Technium, alongside the six biological kingdoms plus one: Archaebacteria, Eubacteria, Fungi, Protista, Plants and Animals. Excavata, Fungi, Animal, Chromista, Rhizaria, Plant, and Archezoa. The "plus one" is Culture.

Viewing all of these developments has given rise to the idea that we are in a new bio-geological era, the Anthropocene. We came across this term earlier in this volume. It is an era of unprecedented existential crises. Humans were brought to this point by otherwise positive improvements in the quality of our lives. The cooperative skills that brought us to this point are now our most important means of getting ourselves out of this mess. But that may just reproduce the negative consequences of our past actions and exacerbate our problems rather than solving them. Ellis (2024) emphasizes the obvious point (obvious given the cooperative principle in evolution) that we can in fact get through the current crises by re-emphasizing our common evolutionary ancestry in a world that has given us new ways to connect to each other and nature. Since such connections in the past have given rise to the cultures and civilizations that have led us to our current crises it isn't clear why their self-conscious application will give us more positive results in today's world.

There is one more critical step to consider. Evolution invented the social; humans had to discover the social. This process is documented in Collins and Makowsky (2010) and Restivo (2018). The discovery of the social evolved from philosophical speculations in the ancient world and crystallized in the nineteenth century in the works of Durkheim, Marx, Weber, Kropotkin, Martineau, and others. Sociology, anthropology, and social psychology developed in this period, beginning in the 1840s.

Throughout the history of our discovery of the social in evolution there have been allusions to the relationship of love to the cooperative principle. Gorney (1972: 47) makes this connection explicit: "What had been colonial cooperation useful for perpetuation of the group, now became individual love." I understood this to be an understanding of love as an adaptive evolutionary mechanism.

4   Love, Society, Culture, and Evolution

The philosopher Voltaire complained that we gave the name of "love" to a thousand chimeras. But if we sort through the thousand chimeras, it turns out that they are generally examples of three basic forms of love: political love, romantic love, and mature love. Political and romantic love are part of the ideology of love, marriage, family, and sex that has expressed, justified, and reinforced Western patriarchy from ancient times to the present. Political love in its most advanced form is practiced and dominated by political elites, usually men, and links sex, ruling power, and truth. Romantic love involves idealizing love, loved ones, and physical passion, and is a resource for oppressing and exploiting men, women, and children, but especially women in terms of power over relationships. Mature love is based on equality and caring; it is independent of the sanctions of church and state, and transcends conventions about the sex, age, and number of lovers. It recognizes the distinction between and the connection between sensuality and sexuality. My objective in this section is to explore love, sex, relationships, and the Good Society from an evolutionary perspective.

Sociologists have viewed love from a variety of theoretical perspectives. Love has been treated as a type of primary relationship, a case of intrinsic attraction in an exchange relationship, a game based on cost-benefit accounting, and a form of property. Most of these accounts focus on the microsocial level, and usually on two-person relationships. There are no indications that these diverse efforts over many years have led to the development of a general, widely accepted microsociological theory of love. At the same time, sociologists have given little thought to the possibility of a macrosociological theory of love. This possibility is more clearly realized in the humanist and anarchist literature on love.

In general, then, sociologists specializing in marriage and the family define love in psychological terms, and focus on love as a heterosexual, dyadic, romantic, and marital phenomenon. Some sociologists adopt a broader humanistic orientation to love as a factor in self-actualization, caring, cooperation, adaptability, and evolution. The humanistic approach, however, also stresses psychological definitions, and individual needs in heterosexual couples. My aim in this section is to sketch a sociological rationale for the conception of love as a factor in human survival, self-actualization, and social and cultural evolution The idea that love is a social fact is the basis for conceiving love as a manifestation of a cooperative principle that has become increasingly important in social and cultural evolution.

When we turn our anthropological telescope to the cultural landscape, we find diversity across time and space in the forms of what we are in the habit of calling "the family." We find explicable connections between these family forms and ideas about intimacy on the one hand, and the conditions under which people live on the other. We also find that those forms and ideas change systematically over time. We can thus conclude that forms of and ideas about marriage, self, love, and intimacy in general are best understood as strategies for dealing with human needs and problems. It seems reasonable to conclude that when these particular needs and problems no longer exist, or when they can be more effectively satisfied or solved outside traditional boundaries, or when the values guiding tradition need to be modified because they interfere with the fullest possible development of individual and society, then the traditional forms and ideas become unnecessary and undesirable.

We are now at a point in our development as a world society in which there is increasing awareness of and concern for individual rights, ecological balance, and problems of authority at all levels of social life. It is therefore important to encourage and not merely tolerate the variety of forms of and ideas about intimacy that are part of the world picture. For traditional adult intimate relationships (homosexual or heterosexual) the options available today include conventional monogamy, modified monogamy (e.g., non-exclusive sexually, child-free, contractual), non-monogamous matrimony (polygamy, group marriage, communal living, polyamory), non-marital arrangements (free from legal, religious, or conventional social constraints, non-binding and readily terminable), and celibacy. These are types of alternatives identified by people critical of the limitations of traditional monogamy. They make too many concessions to the prevailing social order and to monogamy too. Freeing ourselves entirely from this context would lead us to think in terms of forms of friendship. The emergence of widespread awareness of and increasing legitimation of lesbian, gay, bisexual, transgender and/or gender expansive, queer and/or questioning, intersex, asexual, and two-spirit relationships has demonstrated just how complex sex and relationships are in the real world socially but also as we have increasingly seen biologically (e.g., diversity in chromosomal sex). Anthropologists have long documented the diversity of moral orders. Pluralism is the defining theme when we consider the structure of cultures across world history. There may be, as some authors (mostly philosophers) contend, a universal morality but the anthropological evidence favors pluralism.

The theory of "morality as cooperation" (MAC) conjectures that there are at least seven moral order domains: family values, group loyalty, reciprocity, heroism, deference, fairness, and property rights. Evidence for MAC from the Human Relations Area Files and the mathematics of MAC is reported in Curry, Mullins, and Whitehouse (2019). When we undertake refined analyses of moral orders, however, the research supports pluralism (e.g., Atari, Haidt, et al., 2023). Still, some general adherence to a moral order founded on the cooperative principle in evolution would seem to be fundamental to sustaining self-perpetuating societies. This still leaves a lot of room for pluralism.

It should be clear from the preceding discussion why love can be so brutal in normal society, and at the very least an emotional roller-coaster. On the level of individual relationships, the problem is that love is the product of successfully negotiating one's way through sexual and emotional marketplaces. But in a modern industrialized society where the marketplaces for sexual and emotional goods and services are open and accessible 24 hours a day, sustaining a conventional love-as-property relationship is not easy and it is probably a contradiction in terms. It is time now to see if there is anything about love that we can salvage in the interest of improving our relationships, our society, and our environments.

Pitirim Sorokin, and more recently, Roderic Gorney, have explicitly linked love to sociocultural evolution. Sorokin (1954) used the term "love" loosely. He did not define love formally, but referred to it as "the concentrated form of life." Sorokin noted a tendency in modern society to be skeptical of, and to disbelieve in, the power of "creative love." Love was widely considered "epiphenomenal and illusory," and referred to (with other virtues such as friendship, cooperation, truth, goodness, and beauty) as a rationalization, self-deception, derivation, ideology, or "idealistic bosh." Sorokin referred to an impressive body of evidence supporting his notion of the power of creative love, friendship, non-violence, and non-aggression in society. He cited typical cases illustrating the power of creative love to stop aggression and enmity, promote vitality and longevity, restore health and well-being, support social movements, foster individual growth, and generate more love. Sorokin's view of love as the main-spring of life and evolution is supported by many advocates of love as a survival value. Most of them share Sorokin's propensity for generalizing on the basis of variable and sometimes questionable empirical examples, and without the benefit of a well-formulated theoretical position.

Until recently, it is true, this area of inquiry has had to be sustained by provocative hypotheses and speculations in the face of under-developed and controversial theories of biological and sociocultural evolution. Recent advances in evolutionary theory have not entirely resolved the problems and controversies of the past. They have, however, made it possible to consider the relationship between love and sociocultural evolution somewhat more systematically. Roderic Gorney's work illustrates some of the progress that has been made.

Gorney (1972) argues that love as a factor in evolution has its roots in the emergence of cell-proximity in primitive organisms as a survival mechanism. To review our earlier discussion of this process, more complex forms of "colonial cooperation" followed. Next came cellular collaboration and the emergence of multi-celled animals; and internal fertilization among amphibians and reptiles. More advanced cooperation made its appearance among the mammals. The placenta, mammary glands, and long gestation and dependency periods added a new dimension to the struggle for survival; the survival of the young became dependent on extended caring behavior by two or more adults. Gorney refers to this new dimension as "individual love." "Collective love" would seem to be more appropriate. This represents the emergence of the social at the level of human evolution.

Grouping behavior and sociation in the lower animals were transcended by the societal behavior of the higher mammals, which in turn was transcended by human societal organization and culture. Gorney concludes that the next stage in human evolution will free love from its traditional reproductive and nurturing functions. Its self-validating function will bring individuals into intimate caring relationships. He rejects traditional and romantic conceptions of love, as well as attempts by social scientists to define love in behavioral, attitudinal, or operational terms. Gorney follows Montagu in defining love as creatively enhancing the health, well-being and adaptability of others. This suggests that love, in all its manifestations (in a variety of aborted, distorted and embryonic ways), reflects a cooperative principle that is becoming increasingly critical as a condition of sociocultural evolution. A sociological rational for this idea is developed in the following section.

5   An Evolutionary Sociology of Love

Sociologists have not generally defined society in evolutionary terms. But as Lenski (1974) argues, society is an adaptive mechanism which has increased the survival and reproductive chances of certain organisms. This adds society to the list of more familiar adaptive mechanisms in animals such as speed, strength, agility, intelligence, and coloration. Society is characterized by relatively sustained ties of interaction, a high degree of interdependence among its members, and a high degree of systemic autonomy. This form of organization, among all primates, including humans, has survival value because it enhances learning opportunities.

Lenski defines learning as the process of usually adaptive changes in behavior based on prior experience. Learning depends on some degree of cooperation between and among individuals. There has been some debate, however, concerning the relative importance of cooperation and competition in evolution. At least since Piotr Kropotkin's work on mutual aid (1902), there has been interest in, study of, and speculation about, the proposition that cooperation in the animal world has been equal to or exceeded competition as an important principle of survival and adaptation. Proponents of this position can draw on innumerable cases of parasitism, symbiosis, and even the eugenic improvement of a species on account of a predator's success in killing inferior individuals. All animals, including humans, have developed substitutes for life-and-death struggle ranging from population control to the use of threat and retreat instead of war and aggression.

Etkin (1964), in a study of social organization among vertebrates, points out a paradox. Natural selection, he writes, should favor self-seeking antisocial behavior by individuals. This would tend to be socially disruptive. But group formation is quite common in vertebrates. Etkin concludes that there must be controls that keep aggressive, competitive behavior from interfering with sociality. He cites dominance hierarchy and territoriality as two such controls. His attempt to dismiss the survival value of cooperative behavior is not convincing. The evidence he cites suggests that controls against aggression and competition emerge with social organization. It is plausible to argue that these controls can, at the sociocultural level, be elaborated to the point where a transition occurs; cooperation becomes more important in survival than competition. Furthermore, a change in the nature of natural selection can be expected, such that groups or collectivities are selected by virtue of the relevance of their values and modes of social organization to survival. The process becomes quite complex when we add consciousness, and human efforts to select in terms of what they understand to be values and organizations that have high adaptive potential. Of course, the selection process might work in favor of individuals or collectivities whose short-term adaptive capacities are good (at least to the point of ensuring their success in the struggle for survival), but whose evolutionary potential is low.

Assuming that the selection process works in favor of increasing evolutionary potential, the ascendency of the cooperative principle does not imply an end to competition. Under the conditions outlined in this chapter, competition shifts to the collective level and involves struggles for power (command over resources) between more or less distinctive groups characterized by high and low levels of cooperation. Salk (1973) sees this as a struggle between two value systems, one with high and one with low survival potential (in the long-term evolutionary sense). His analysis is somewhat oversimplified but instructive. The most compelling arguments for "the ascendancy of cooperation" derive from ecological consciousness. A variety of crises in the animal, plant, and human communities has in recent times stimulated wide-spread awareness of the importance of cooperation in survival and evolution.

Cooperation is an evolutionary mechanism to the extent that it improves the capacity for mobilizing and using energy and information. The challenge to human survival which we see emerging and emergent in the world today is a challenge to our individual and collective capacities to mobilize and use energy and information through new forms and levels of cooperation. This implies new forms and levels of personal, interpersonal, and sociocultural organization. Maslow's ideas on high synergy can be interpreted as specifying the conditions which must be fostered in individuals, groups, and societies if new levels of energy and information mobilization are going to be reached. Love enters this argument as a significant bond between and among human beings.

Sex may have been the basic bond that, early in the evolutionary process, made new levels of cooperation possible. But sex is already a social construction; therefore, something more "primitive" must be looked to, perhaps the need for touching, or more generally an erotic force.

In the evolutionary process, mutation is the most important way in which simpler organisms cope with changing environments. For more complex living systems, the exchange of "genetic information" – recombination – among different organisms is the most important coping mechanism. More popularly, recombination is referred to as sex. It is plausible to hypothesize a third coping mechanism associated with the emergence of culture as a vehicle of evolution; the exchange of information in symbolic communication between and among human beings. This can be viewed as an elaboration of recombination, or sex.

One of the consequences of sexuality is that it makes extended intimacy possible. Through extended intimacy, human beings can expand their knowledge of themselves, others, and reality in general. This is, admittedly, a large intuitive leap. However, the notion of intersubjective testing in science may reflect the advantage of – and perhaps the necessity of – having plural relatively autonomous systems intercommunicate in order to maximize the capacity of individual minds to grasp the nature of reality. The intersubjective bond, which is most effective when communication is open, honest, and, in a sense, intimate, can be viewed as a development from more primitive bonds, including sex. In any case, this notion is not crucial to my argument; the existence of conditions for extended intimacy, whatever they are, is what is important here.

Among humans, intimacy has been fostered by the generalization of sexual cycles, sexual codes, and the sexual imperative (reproduction). Human sexual relations are independent of an estrous cycle; they can be expressed in a wide variety of cultural ways besides monogamy and heterosexuality; and the imperative for sex can be pleasure.

Phenomena defined as "love" represent a first order cultural elaboration of sex. The identification of love with self-actualization, B-Love, and high synergy societies can be viewed as a second order cultural elaboration of love. This elaboration involves defining love as a social relationship and social process in which the objective is to facilitate the viable functioning and development of individuals and groups, and equating loving and knowing. "I love you" comes to mean "I want to know you, and I want you to know me," in the fullest sense of knowing. This implies gaining a perspective on the sociocultural, environmental, global, and ultimately cosmic settings of self and others. The elaboration and generalization of sex and love result in an expansion of the possibilities and expectations associated with loving relationships. Maslow's conception of B-love defines a relationship that is more complex, diversified, and flexible than D (Deficient, or immature)-Love, or the love associated with traditional, relatively closed, and exclusive monogamous marriages. Complexity, diversity, and flexibility are widely recognized by students of ecological and evolutionary theory to be associated with adaptive and evolutionary potential in animal, plant, and human communities. In brief, the opportunities for learning are enhanced in B-Love. Enhanced learning promotes adaptability. The consequence of associating B-Love with the synergistic society, as Maslow does, is to create a link between love and the process of raising the information carrying capacity of human societies.

B-Love entails ecological and evolutionary consciousness. If we are committed, facilitative, and caring with respect to ourselves and others, we must necessarily be so with respect to human beings as ecological entities living in a global network of ecological communities. And if we are involved in the process of identifying and actualizing human potentials, we must be aware of conditions that facilitate this process; and this necessarily involves seeing ourselves as active in and agents of an evolutionary process.

This is a good time to remind ourselves that the earth is an arena for the interplay of devolutionary and evolutionary forces, and that there is no guarantee that the future will be better than the past, or even that there will be a future. The evolutionary framework is an orientation; it does not entail unilinear progress, or any sociobiological or teleological imperatives. We should not forget that the past offers us models and possibilities for the present and the future. In practical terms, for loving relationships of all kinds and at all levels this perspective encourages us to adopt the following patterns of behavior: flexible roles, constructive discussion, creative and imaginative management of all aspects of our relationships, checking assumptions about partners, and not doing things just because everyone else expects you to. The best way to ensure that loving someone else is going to have humane consequences is to love yourself, care about and take care of yourself; remember that you are an organic and a social machine intricately entwined in a variety of ecological systems. Build your relationship on the strengths of independence. And above all, aim to be friends.

6   The Humanistic Conception of Love

Humanists offer an alternative to the conventional sociological treatment of love. Maslow (1971), for example, treats love as part of his program for the Good Person and Good Society. This orientation contrasts sharply with the traditional orientations in the sociology of love which tend to ignore or draw attention away from the relationship between love and humanistic concerns about self-actualization and the Good Society. The feminist movement, LGBTQIAPK (Lesbian, Gay, Bisexual, Transgender, Queer, Intersexual, Asexual, Pansexual and Polygamous, and Kinkiness) and related efforts to foster sexual equality, erase traditional gender stereotypes, and humanize male-female and human relationships, have certainly had an impact on the marriage and the family literature. But the constraints mentioned earlier continue to operate and to limit the depth and scope of criticisms of the heterosexual couple. And even where there is an explicit concern with issues of self-actualization and liberation, the treatment tends to be limited and hesitant. Alternatives are generally framed in traditional, couple-centered, male-female terms.

The most notable exception to these tendencies among persons concerned with mutual love is found in the anarchist literature. The anarchists recognized that traditional patriarchy was a social construction (that is, not God given and not part of the natural order of biological evolution) and they attacked the institutions of state, church, sex, family, love, and marriage. They also formulated an alternative political economy of intimacy. Michael Bakunin (1814–1876), for example, proposed that private property and the state will have to be abolished in order to eliminate the authoritarian juridical family and impediments to full sexual freedom for women. Later, another anarchist, Emma Goldman (1869–1940), argued that while the demand for equal rights in every vocation is just and fair, the right to love and be loved is the most vital right. The full emancipation of women, she argued, requires that we eliminate the idea that a lover, a sweetheart, a mother, a wife must be subordinate, a slave to the patriarchy.

From a humanistic perspective, love is a condition of self-actualization. Love of self and love of others are viewed as the necessary foundation for a life oriented to identifying and actualizing human potentials. Fromm (1956) made an important contribution to the development of this perspective in *The Art of Loving*. He conceived love as a solution to the problems of existence that affirms the person's "aliveness," and promotes self-actualization. In Fromm's analysis, mature love (distinguished form symbiotic love) is based on the Delphic motto, "Know thyself." The components of mature love are caring, respect, responsibility, and knowledge.

The existential emphasis in Fromm's analysis should not obscure the fact that love is a social activity and process. The relationship between love and self-actualization is not confined to the self's existential space. It is a social relationship that has a development over time. Following Maslow and Fromm, the love relationship in self-actualization is conceived as a fusion of the ability to love and respect oneself and others. Love is a dynamic relationship designed to foster mutual growth. This is a more robust sociological understanding of love than ideas on love as an emotional or physiological state. The emphasis is on love and society.

Maslow (1954) associates B-Love (Being-Love, or what Fromm calls "mature love") with the anthropologist Ruth Benedict's concept of high synergy (Benedict, 1946; Maslow, Honigmann, and Mead, 1970). Benedict suggested that non-aggression is conspicuous in societies where an individual's acts simultaneously serve his or her interests and group interests. Social arrangements make individual and group interests identical. In such "high synergy" societies participants in social institutions are assured mutual advantages. In "low synergy" societies one person's advantage is another person's loss.

In physiology, the term "synergy" is used to refer to the "co-ordinate action of separate elements." The American sociologist Lester Ward (1903: 171) seems to have been the first scholar to suggest that the term synergy be used in sociology "to denote the unintended cooperative action (and the organization and other cultural products resulting from such cooperative action) in which people often engage as they pursue their own individual interests." Benedict seems to use the term in the same sense. Maslow's usage more clearly reflects the conception of synergy as enhancement, in the sense that the whole is greater than the sum of its parts. This implies that "true" cooperation, that is, conscious, planned cooperation, can have synergistic effects.

Maslow considers high synergy a good definition of Being-Love. He refers to Being-Love as a high synergy relationship that expands self, person and identity. Love of the self and love of the other are viewed as interdependent; Being-Love stresses the dependence of self-actualization on facilitative love relationships. By linking individuals (self-actualizers) and evolving societies (high synergy societies), Maslow associates love with adaptability at the individual, group, and sociocultural levels. This provides an initial rationale for considering the evolutionary significance of love. The variety of phenomena generally referred to as "love" may reflect the presence of a potential in human beings for high levels of communication and cooperation. New levels in the actualization of this potential, reflected in new levels of interpersonal intimacy, may be a necessary condition for the future evolution of life and consciousness on earth.

The B-Love relationship is full, deep, and intense. On the adult level, the question arises whether more than one such relationship is necessary or possible, at any one time, or over a lifetime. Given the way we are socialized in modern societies, it is easy to develop barriers (defenses) that get in the way of open, honest communications and perceptions. Given that some type of deep, full, intense relationship is a necessary condition of self-actualization, life-long monogamous relationships would seem to have significant advantages over other forms of intimate relationships. Such core relationships do not have to be exclusive in any of the traditional ways associated with monogamy (e.g., sexually). They are, however, conceived to be exclusive in the depth, fullness, and intensity of the love, and the shared commitment to honesty, communication, and trust. This does not preclude B-Love outside the core; but no relationship outside the core will manifest the same degree and extent of commitment and communication. A core commitment is also possible among three or more highly self-actualized persons. Obviously, given present social and cultural conditions, such a core would be, in general, more difficult to establish and sustain than a two-person core.

The importance of monogamy and a lifelong core is, it is important to emphasize, a function of prevailing sociocultural conditions, and historical contexts. It is not clear, for example, that core relationships that dissolve after a certain number of years should be viewed as failures. The structure of the core can be radically transformed over time, or even dissolved, without destroying friendships or family ties. Children can be raised in a variety of equally healthy cores, and in relationships dissolved through separation and divorce if the dissolution is based on the sorts of incompatibilities in relationships that do not threaten friendships. The point is that not only is this an age in which many alternatives are possible (due to positive and negative social changes with the potential for positive and negative consequences); it is also a time in which we are learning about the necessity of such alternatives and of flexibility in our views about relationships. The idea that friendship is at the root of intimacy and of individual and social well-being, and not legal institutions such as marriage or norms such as monogamy is not only liberating for individuals but a condition for liberating ourselves from the oppression of all forms of Authority. Since we are no longer bound to think of relationships solely in reproductive terms, what I have said applies to all relationships inclusively.

The focus on friendship also means a focus on forms of sensuality in general rather than an exclusive focus on genital sex. The positive personal, social, and cultural value of alternative relationships should not therefore depend on the prevalence and virulence of sexually transmitted diseases and pregnancy concerns. Obviously, issues of STDs and pregnancy are realistic barriers to full, unfettered sexuality. Developing fully effective solutions to preventing STDs and unwanted pregnancy would improve humanity's chances for lowering the potentials for loneliness, sexual frustration, and violence. Alternative forms of loving friendships go hand in hand with alternative forms of sensuality and sex.

7   Love and Human Liberation

Love has historically been a form of property; and it continues to play that role in many, if not most, modern lives. In the view adopted here, the abolition of traditional property relations which is associated with the Good (liberated) Society transforms love from a property relation to a committed, facilitative caring relationship between or among persons who also love themselves – and the planet that sustains that love. It is a social process in which people get to know one another more and more intimately. This process, predicated on the self-actualization of the participants, is optimally lifelong. This generalization of love makes it independent of particular sexual, marital, or cohabitative styles and preferences, and of age differences. The precise nature of any love relationship can be considered a function of the psycho-social-sensual development of the participants. Love relationships will not always involve people at similar levels of psycho-social-sensual development, or with equitable access to and control over personal and material resources. Differences in power do not mean inevitable exploitation but rather different forms of love guided by different levels of maturity, knowledge, and responsibility. The sensual needs of children are defined in terms of neuro-muscular development through the appropriate stimulation of the various senses. It's important, however, to remember that children are erotic too and not to be misled by the fallacy of childhood innocence.

In summary, love can be considered a special case of cooperation. Cooperation is a social process in which individuals or groups work together toward a common goal or goals. Love is a cooperative process involving two or more persons committed to facilitating each other's self-actualization, and achieving higher and more extensive degrees of intimacy. Intimacy refers to the degree to which barriers to (defenses against) intra-and interpersonal knowing have been broken down. I use the term "persons" purposefully (instead of, for example, "individuals") to emphasize that we are dealing with the fullest representation of human beings. In a core commitment, the love relationship is long-term (perhaps life-long). In general, two persons make the "best" core, but only in the context of the present state of societies. The difficulties involved in breaking down intra- and interpersonal barriers make it unlikely that a group of three or more persons could individually attain the degree and extent of intimacy possible in a two-person core. But nothing precludes three-or-more person cores; they are simply more difficult and complex experiments in intimacy. This possibility becomes more crucial as a functioning global society emerges and intimacy becomes more firmly embedded in the wider social structures.

8   The Future of Intimate Relationships

Ideas about the future of marriage and the family tend to reflect (1) American or Western values, (2) dissatisfaction with the present institution of marriage, (3) projections of current trends, (4) the desire to increase opportunities for individuals to choose marital, family, and sexual lifestyles freely, and (5) a concern for increasing the warmth and intensity of human relationships. The sociocultural contexts of marriages and families are rarely analyzed in depth. The implications of ecology and evolutionary theory for thinking about the future of marriage and the family have been virtually ignored. We need to broaden our conception of marriage and family; for this reason, I prefer to think in terms of intimate relationships or friendships.

Ecology and evolutionary theory draw our attention to the fact that intimate relationships are ways in which human beings interact within the global ecosystem. Human survival and the enhancement of human living are threatened by increasing stresses in the global ecosystem. To relieve these stresses and create a viable world, we need to identify and experiment with alternative ways of relating to each other. We need to support experimentation with a wide variety of life styles. This experimentation is the process through which appropriate forms of social organization have been and will continue to be developed in response to new ecological and evolutionary challenges. In supporting a variety of values and life styles, we can and should be guided by criteria for evaluating their viability as adaptive and evolutionary systems. We should be evermindful of two questions: (1) to what extent do given ways of living promote full, intense, and humanizing intimacy between and among human beings; and (2) to what extent do they conform to the general principles for viable adaptive and evolutionary systems? The criteria for viability are being developed in ecological and evolutionary theory and general systems and information theory. These theoretical developments support the need for open-ended living oriented to process and change. All of this is difficult enough without confronting the limitations on our ability to follow through on these ideas caused by wide discrepancies in social classes and their access to the relevant resources. Thus, support for the cooperative principle and the values of high synergy love and societies requires attention to a host of problems associated with inequalities and injustices. I will address this issue in my closing chapters.

9   Summary

Traditionally, sociologists have thought of love in terms of a psychological-marital-heterosexual-romantic paradigm. The more general humanistic conception of love as committed, facilitative, caring relationships lends itself more readily to an evolutionary interpretation. Working from such a conception of love, Sorokin and Gorney suggest that love is an evolutionary mechanism. I have sketched a sociological rationale for an evolutionary view of love. This rationale is based on the idea that society and culture are evolutionary mechanisms and that this reflects the increasing importance of a cooperative principle in an evolutionary process now dominated by sociocultural factors. Love is a first order cultural elaboration of sex; the generalized humanistic conception of love is a second order cultural elaboration. Loving enhances learning and knowing, and love is a manifestation of the cooperative principle in sociocultural evolution. The central idea that love is an evolutionary mechanism remains rooted in the speculative sociology inherited from Sorokin. There is, however, increasing evidence for this idea and an imperative for further discussion and research on love and sociocultural evolution. Theoretical bases for thinking about the future of intimacy and lifestyles can be expected to emerge out of such discussions and research.

10   Conclusion

We live in a gendered society. Culture puts a gloss on the biological given, sex (but see below), and creates the qualities we think of as masculine and feminine. As gender terms, masculine and feminine can apply to either males, females, or non-binary persons. In general, however, the terms are derived from and will tend to characterize the actual behavior of males and females respectively. Cultural differences across time and space are reflected in differences in what counts as masculine and feminine in any given society at any given time.

Since men tend to dominate and even literally own women, the qualities of both masculine and feminine tend to be defined by men in their own terms. That is, men directly and indirectly define what is to count as feminine. This can be seen, in what amounts to a natural experimental setting, women's body-building. To the extent that it was controlled by Joe and Ben Weider for most of its history, it was an arena in which men defined what was to count as a prize winning physique for women. And the men decidedly approached this with a view to making femininity the defining paradigm. This initially put powerful, muscular women like Bev Francis a former powerlifter, at a disadvantage in competition with the "more feminine" physiques of women like Rachel Mclish.

To the extent that women accept their subordinate position in a male dominated society, they will also accept as their own men's definitions of what counts as feminine. When women do not accept men's definitions, they can be made socially invisible, punished, or killed by men or their women allies. Women can also organize around their own definitions (alone, or with supportive men), given the appropriate social and material resources. They can organize to protect and foster their own interests as women with women's agendas, as women who want the same prizes the men have access to, or as women representing the interests of human beings in general with a new cultural agenda. All of these processes are impacted by transgender and transexual developments in ways that complicate the values and meanings attached to sex and gender.

The demarcation between sex (male/female) and gender (masculine/feminine) is complicated by the fact that sex itself is not simply given but socially constructed. The categories "male" and "female" are social constructs. In order to see why the idea that "men are men" and "women are women" may be less obvious than you imagine, try examining the photographs in a textbook on hermaphroditism. This should shake your confidence in your ability to easily tell men and women – males and females – apart. The fact that hormones and so-called secondary sex characteristics have a distribution in the male and female populations, and that the two distributions overlap, is another indication that maleness and femaleness are matters of degree.

Sexual intercourse offers a more direct example of something that may at first seem to be biologically given, an instinct perhaps. But we know that sexual behavior is learned behavior. On another level, although sexual intercourse might at first sight appear to be a completely private and intimate part of our lives, it turns out on reflection to be a very public matter. The relationship between sex and society – and especially between sex and power – is no secret to sociologists of sex, marriage, family, and friendship. But few, if any, of them have depicted that relationship as powerfully and dramatically as the feminist writer and activist, Andrea Dworkin (1987). Her focus is on "the act" of intercourse. It is "Society," with its policing authority, she argues, that tells us how, when, where, and with whom intercourse will take place. One non-obvious implication of this social reality is that the essentially legal meaning of "sexual privacy" is that a man has traditionally had the right to use his wife as he wished; this meant, for example, that a man could not legally rape his own wife. In sexual matters as elsewhere, the law creates legal and illegal activities. The law defines, grounds, and sanctions gender, patriarchy, and an ecology of male power. Intercourse is a political act of dominance that is not simply social but Dworkin argues necessarily so at the very level of biology. (No wonder one of my former colleagues and friend, the Costa Rican lawyer and sociologist, Eugenio Fonseca, was fond of defining law as the institutionalization of the social injustices of a society).

That intercourse is a social fact is illustrated by such things as sodomy statutes, and the interest communities have in the proper consummation of marriages. What do privacy and intimacy mean when, as in some traditional communities and among ruling elites, the newly married woman and the couple's bedding are examined by a group of older women (in traditional societies; ruling elites may rely on a less homogeneous group of witnesses) on behalf of the male-dominated community the morning after the wedding or during the first moments the couple engages in sex? The regulation of sex offers a particularly dramatic example of the often invisible relationship between private and public orders: The principle that "the personal is political" is part of patriarchal law which synthesizes intimacy, state policy, and police power; the private and public arenas; and the penis and the centers of power. As a companion to Dworkin's writings, one should read Claire Wills' (2024) memoir. The historian puts herself and her family into the social structures of stories, secrets, and silences that reveal the violence that supports traditions in marriage, the family, and sex.

Inequalities in wealth and power follow gender lines. Clearly, such inequalities stand in the way of realizing the types of selves and relationships I argue for in this chapter and throughout this book. Erasing sex and gender inequalities must therefore be a major part of the emancipatory humanistic political agenda I advocate. The single most important change we should work for on this score is the abolition of marriage, family, sex, and intimacy as relationships of property, possession, and power.

One final point. I have referred throughout this chapter to male domination and patriarchy. It should be stressed – and this is part of the general message of the Copernican revolution in sociology – that these are facts of social life, social constructions. That is, we have to turn to social organization and culture to explain why they prevail. We cannot explain them by looking to the biology of males and females, although Dworkin makes a strong case for the power relations installed by our sexual biology. The rest of the message is that social organization and culture can be changed; not any way and any time we wish, but under the right conditions, with the appropriate resources, and within the constraints imposed by our biology, our chemistry, and our physical attributes. I will return to issues of sex and love in Chapter 13 where I will sharpen the anarchist gaze on these topics.

The view of love I have sketched here is grounded in a basic opposition to all forms of Authority. As an anarchist, I have no objection to the authority of experts so long as I can exercise vigilant reasoned critical skepticism. I deserve a voice in their recommendations. I object to Authority, not to authority. There is both a theoretical and a practical basis for linking resistance to Authority and open, heathy, adaptive living, loving, and inquiring. This is an important paradigm in the context of the possibilities for addressing the existential threats at the center of my concerns in this book.

CHAPTER 9

Survivability

In Greek mythology, Daedalus was a skillful craftsman and artist, and was seen as a symbol of wisdom, knowledge, and power. Imprisoned in a tower by the king with his son Icarus, he fashions wings made of wax and they escape.[1] Ignoring his father's warnings, Icarus flies too close to the sun. His wings melt and Icarus falls to his death. Daedalus also resolves a priority dispute with his nephew Talos over the invention of the saw, and resolves the dispute by pushing Talos off a tower. Daedalus represents one of the ways of modern science and technology.

Drawing on this myth, the biochemist J.B.S. Haldane (1923) published an essay titled *Daedalus, or Science and the Future*. Haldane painted a picture of an attractive future society created by applying science to the promotion of human happiness. Bertrand Russell (1925) replied to Haldane in an essay on *Icarus, or the Future of Science*. Russell wrote that his experience with statesmen and governments forced him to predict that science would be used to promote the power of the ruling classes rather than to further human happiness. And indeed we seem to be metaphorically flying closer and closer to the sun and increasingly likely to plunge to our deaths as a species and as a planet. Where is science, objectivity, and truth in a world of "alternative facts," "fake news," the rise of authoritarianism and fundamentalism, nativism, anti-science, and the perils of religious tolerance?

The social problems and promises of science as humanity's toolbox of methods of inquiry are masked by icons, myths, and ideologies: Archimedes drawing pretty figures in the dust, Newton searching for shapely pebbles at the beach, and Einstein riding light beams in his mind. These iconic images have fueled the myth of pure science. Scientists and technologists are not leading us on a sustainable journey. A tyrannical world of abstractions and technological heroics has been wedded to the tyrannical rule of robber barons. What is to be done?

On the eve of World War II, J.D. Bernal noted that the image of science was dominated by militarism, economic chaos, and the threat of increasingly terrible wars. Twenty-five years later, Bernal looked out on a world divided with

---

1 This chapter is an edited version of material which originally appeared as Chapter 16 in Sal Restivo, *Inventions in Sociology* (New York: Palgrave Macmillan, 2022).

"greater poverty, stupidity, and cruelty than it has ever known" (Bernal, 1939, 1964). That this idea was "in the air" is reflected in the remarks by C. Wright Mills in 1959 on science as a set of Science Machines. Mills echoes critics of science from Rousseau and Marx to Veblen who portrayed science as alienated, alienating, and machinelike. This vision gave us science as an instrument of terror, an assault on the natural world, and a tool of war, greed, and violence (see Merchant, 1980). How did this vision arise in the midst of all the good that science has clearly done by fueling technological and medical advances that have benefitted humanity?

In order to understand the origin of these dystopian views of science, we must leave isolated scientific biographies, methods, findings, experiments, and theories behind. Science as a social institution is embedded in the networks of robber barons and military-industrial complexes that have marked the industrial-technological era from the 1800s to the present. And this is not new; Archimedes was a military engineer, and the history of science has always been intricately entwined with the military and economic interests of nations (cf. Hessen, 1931 on the social and economic roots of Newton's *Principia*).

This realistic view of science and technology must be taken into account if we are going to realistically assess the likelihood of achieving a sustainable global society in the midst of our current crises. Several key ideas play into this assessment: (1) the ascendancy of the cooperative principle in biological and cultural evolution; (2) the emergence of the classical Age of the Social (1840–1930) and the development of sociology, anthropology, and social psychology as robust sciences; (3) the recognition of connectivity as a basic feature of the world; (4) the evidence that suggests that creativity is not a matter of "standing on the shoulders of giants" but rather a matter of "standing on the shoulders of social networks," (5) a new social brain paradigm, and (6) the new science of the death of God. More generally, these ideas ground the proposition that anarchism, understood following Kropotkin as one of the social sciences, is our best chance for achieving the goals of a sustainable journey. This is a perilous journey in an accidental universe, and we are doomed to failure in the long run. Increasingly, we appear to be facing failure in the short run. If we are going to avoid premature extinction it's important that we don't let romantic notions of life and love, spiritual worldviews, and sunsets and kisses distract us from the dangers to our very survival, let alone the possibility of surviving with some reasonable quality of life.

My life has been, like those of many others like me, a dialectical struggle between romantic worldviews and critically realistic ones. The following chapters are designed to capture that dialectical relationship and explore the possibility that it can be resolved in a way that meets the challenges of the existential threats we face. What can we base our hopes for achieving sustainability on? I have identified ten pillars of sustainability.

1   The Pillars of Sustainability

1.   The cooperative principle: the ascendancy of the cooperative principle in biological and cultural evolution.

2.   Social construction: the fundamental theorem of sociology: the emergence of the classical Age of the Social (1840–1930) and the development of sociology, anthropology, and social psychology as robust sciences; The 2nd Age of the Social (1930–1970) saw the development of the sociology of the social system of science and the sociology of knowledge; the 3rd Age of the Social (1970-) saw sociologists develop the ethnography of scientific practice and the sociology of scientific knowledge itself (e.g., the sociology of mathematics). In an age of crisis still dominated by the technological fix and the physics fix to all problems, we are obliged to give sociology a higher profile in the pantheon of the sciences.

3.   The universal connectome: the connectivity principle: the recognition of connectivity as a basic feature of the world. Social network thinking must trump hierarchical thinking.

4.   Social networks as the locus of ideas: the myth and culture of the individual dethroned; standing on the shoulders of social networks: the individual as a social being who serves as a repository and transmitter of the thinking constructed in the crucibles of social networks; the individual as a voice box for social networks.

5.   The social brain paradigm: dethroning the brains in a vat paradigm and neuroism: a new social brain paradigm and Restivo's universal connectome model of the brain/mind/culture/world.

6.   The generational principle of science: no individual, no research team, no organization or group can on its own be scientific or do science: science is a process of approaching and constantly reapproaching facts, truths, and objectivity on the wings of critical realism and critical skepticism generationally: science understood as the collective activity of scientists (understood in modern professional terms inclusive of rational inquirers) and the intersubjectively tested propositions they propose, test, confirm and dis-confirm across generational continuities.

7.   The consilience of evidences and the ensemble of probabilities as pathways to facts of the matter, the Durkheim thesis, and the truth that there is no god; sustainability cannot be based on delusions or falsehoods

without diminishing its capacity to be realized in reality: the new science of the death of god; proof by consilience of evidences, ensembles of probabilities, and sheer sociological theory.

8. The Salk theorem: epoch a and epoch b: the end of the era of growth and the beginning of the era of sustainability – or else the END.

9. The myth of capitalism, the absurdity of the free market concept, and the reality of the black hole economy: capitalism as myth and ideology and not economics; the dangers of the black hole economy.

10. Anarchism, chaos, and social order at last: to dream the impossible dream: standing at the apexes of the physical and cultural light cones; staring into the abyss of the end of time and space without losing your balance.

2   Data, Data, and More Data

Gaining a statistical and data rich foothold on the sustainability problem is being seriously hampered by the global divide in statistical capacity and research infrastructures. Many national statistical offices in low income countries are not able to meet their international reporting requirements. Non-traditional information sources such as enrolling and enabling citizen scientists and broadening the use of private sector data are being developed and deployed around the world. We are faced, as always when we are trying to integrate East, West, North and South cooperation, with the possibility that information colonialism in which the data and information rich West and North ignore local contexts in the East and South. The failures around the response to COVID-19 caused by not disaggregating data by race or ethnicity is one example of the need to do this across the board for each of our sustainability goals.

Our efforts to foster sustainability and address existential threats are being severely hampered by infrastructure differences and limitations, and staff inadequacies across the world's nations, a situation exacerbated in poor countries. The UN's Sustainable Development Goals established in 2015 were designed to put us on a path to a sustainable future by 2030. These goals are not going to be met without a data revolution. Since 2015, the rapid development and deployment of AI may now have us in the midst of just such a data revolution.

Agricultural systems which have nourished the growth and evolution of human societies and civilization for millennia have become an existential threat (Tollefson, 2019: 171). Human social and cultural activities tend to smooth out and homogenize environments. We cover over diverse green spaces and habitats with uniform urban formations that destroy the green resources that support life. Experts use phrases like the need for "transformative changes" that are not registering with sufficient clarity to motivate the urgent actions required as part of a global agenda. Unself-conscious food production has significantly altered three-quarters of land areas and about two-thirds of the oceans.

Agricultural activities are among the largest contributors to greenhouse gases. Legal and illegal activities involving harvesting, logging, hunting, and fishing have led to land degradation, pollution, climate change and the spread of invasive species. We have enhanced the existential threats we are facing by our ways of feeding ourselves. The damage this is causing to ecosystems undermines efforts to reduce poverty and hunger around the world, never mind their negative impacts on sustainability efforts. Government agencies and scientists warn about the need for proactive environmental policies, sustainable agricultural and industrial processes, and the need to reduce greenhouse gas emissions. But the general public is by omission allowed to think that all these positive efforts can go on without significant changes in how we live our lives day to day. While homeowners try to different degrees to conform to local recycling efforts, their efforts are offset by even the most environmentally self-conscious efforts of governments, the military, and businesses to minimize waste and recycle. This is a prime example of the Law of Marginal Futility. The masses' efforts to recycle are dwarfed by the levels of waste and pollution of Big Government, Big Military, and Big Business.

Species extinction is a natural process. The problem we face is that it has been estimated that we are losing species at a thousand times the natural rate of extinction. In the light of these and other statistics it is hard to find solace in the good news about the growth of terrestrial (up 0.3%) and marine (up 13.8%) protected areas in the Asia-Pacific region over the last twenty years or so. In what ways can we count on science to guide us in this era of extinctions and threats?

3   The Morality of Science

It is widely taught and accepted that science cannot give us answers to questions about values and ethics. This is paired with the truism that science doesn't imply or entail specific values or morals. But clearly if we think of science as a communal, organizational, institutional activity, we are thinking of science as a culture, as a form of life. In that sense, it must be associated with norms, values, morals, ethics, and beliefs. Only a conception of a science alienated from humans and from society could give rise to the truism that science does not entail a specific morality.

Let's imagine constructing a culture of science. What would we build into such a culture in terms of values and morals? The ethics of science would include investing belief or trust in findings with a level of conviction warranted by the evidence. Ethical behavior implies moral integrity not as a matter of individual will and behavior but as a collectively grounded and enforced orientation of humans to humans and humans to nature. We would be obliged to value goodness, kindness, generosity, a concern with quality, and virtue. The ethos of science demands reporting results with an allegiance to authenticity and integrity, and a commitment to communicating all the information relevant to a particular research outcome. That ethos requires that scientists treat living subjects, humans, animals, and the constituents of ecological niches with an appreciation for the integrity of subjects and the contributions of ecological systems to a sustainable human community and planet. The ethos of science includes a concern for the health and security of all living things in the context of their contributions to a sustainable human community and planetary ecology. Recognition that there are moral imperatives in science would be a barrier to using our scientific resources and capacities against human and planetary life. If the culture at large and the scientific community are organized according to the humanitarian principles of a culture that can be variously described as democratic, socialist, communist, or anarchist then we would not expect scientists or laypersons to be driven by a lust for fame, recognition, greed, or monetary rewards. Nor should they be expected to express values that reflect and encourage social injustices and inequalities.

Some might argue that science, along with other creative endeavors, represents the dignity and integrity of the human animal as a human and as one of the animals. A consciousness of these issues and a critique of classical ideas about distancing the scientist from ethics, values, and morality will help to focus all of our attentions on the requirements for a sustainable natural environment and a humane and sustainable human environment. Valuing biodiversity, for example, is not a matter of following the imperatives of "pure science" but rather the practice of a moral scientific culture. We need to think about the "intrinsic" values of science – such as objectivity, rationality, honesty, accuracy – not as complements to humanitarian values such as empathy, compassion, and kindness but as integrally synthesized with them.

I am not advocating scientific imperialism or scientism, which are in any case imbued with their own systems of morals, values, and ethics. Nor am I arguing that we have fool-proof grounds for establishing the values, morals, and ethics conducive to survival and sustainability. I do claim that a culture oriented to the well-being of humanity and the planet will generate a scientific system with the same orientation and thus values, morals, and ethics conducive to survival and sustainability. As the reader will find throughout this book, science and knowledge in general do not announce findings, inventions, and discoveries with guarantees attached to them regarding their potential for promoting or obstructing survival and sustainability. But as the experiential knowledge base in such a culture expands over time probabilities are going to favor but not determine outcomes that are more likely to be successful than not. Some philosophers allow their free-wheeling willy nilly logical and linguistic gymnastics to imagine, for example, that maybe cultures that promote smoking will turn out to have better survival potential than those that ban smoking. This begins to sound like the kind of irrational skepticism that drives out rational skepticism and starts to look like a mental illness.

4   Survival Wisdom

Let's consider the problem of carrying capacity, the number of people, other living organisms, or crops that a region can support without environmental degradation. Various features of our environment that affect carrying capacity, population growth and pollution for example, can and do experience exponential growth. Exponential growth goes to infinity in the irreality of mathematics. In the real world it saturates asymptotically, overshoots the carrying capacity, or cycles around the carrying capacity. If overshooting or cycling destroys crucial non-renewable resources the carrying capacity is lowered. Already in 1973, Dr. Jonas Salk identified the point of inflection between two distinct periods in human history: an upward facing, accelerating curve called Epoch A, and a downward facing, decelerating curve, Epoch B. In 2018, his son updated his father's thinking in a book that captures the limits of the human condition visually in a series of variations on the basic sigmoid epoch A-epoch B curves (Salk and Salk, 2018). This book is a stark and dark contrast with technopositive futures predicted by transhumanist futurists (e.g., Goertzel and Goertzel, eds., 2015).

The Goertzel and Goertzel book features the contributions of some of our leading futurists who collectively are looking forward to a coming age of post-human intelligence described and predicted by environmental futurism, Kondratiev long-wave analysis, generational cycle analysis, geopolitical futurism, and the study of technological revolutions. Based on these ideas, more speculative than theoretical, and from their perspective in 2015, we are told we are very likely looking toward two intense periods of technological innovation, one in the 2040s and another in the 2100s. One of these periods will give rise to an artificial general intelligence and the "singularity." Their arrival depends on how successfully we can complete current engineering models and on whether we can get the funds to implement one or more of these models. Both of two major scenarios these futurists sketch involve a world dominated by machine intelligence. One scenario predicts a gradual transition with a model of anticipation; the other scenario predicts a rapid and potentially disruptive transition. The first transition assumes that we will continue on our current paths based on accumulating better and better software; the second transition depends on our ability to fully emulate the human brain. Artificial intelligence is everywhere in these scenarios, but not everyone sees positive outcomes.

One of the doomsayers getting a lot of attention is the self-taught commentator on AI and society, Eliezer Yudowsky (2023). He argues that we need to shut down AI now. Otherwise, and inevitably, AI will become superhumanly smart and "everyone on Earth will die." His critics include Quintin Pope (2023) who believes AI capabilities will increase but will not make a sudden jump from being better than humans at some tasks and worse at others to being suddenly better at everything.

Technopositive futurism deals with issues of a declining population and the extension of the life span and quality of life, and the use of medical implants to conquer disease and enhance human functionality. Imagine adaptive implants that permit your organs to send you messages if they are experiencing problems. This could lead to open-source implant technologies that would give us more direct control over our own bodies. On the dark side, one can imagine implant hackers who could do various sorts of damage to our systems.

The Methuselarity conjecture complements the Singularity conjecture. It looks forward to "plausible" ways of conquering aging and extending lifespans indefinitely. Methuselarity is the point in time at which anyone then alive can expect to live for thousands of years or more. We can also look forward to robotics and AI impacting every aspect of our lives, for the better if we believe Daryl Nazareth and Ray Kurzweil, or for the worse in darker visions in which robotics and AI become existential threats. Technopositivists see a future with diminishing needs for human labor. Several scenarios are emerging that refer to a post-scarcity economy, a super-educated society, a super entrepreneurial society, a society of shareholders, the guaranteed minimum income society, the cyborg society, and contraction of the job market. This starts to look like just another round of over-hyping the potential benefits of new and possible technologies guided by a philosophy of the technological fix.

We will have to deal with the morality of the machine as our lives become increasingly populated with AI driven robots expressing different degrees of autonomy. Defense department engineers are already looking forward to robot armies. We can give the technofuturists some credit for conceiving the possibility of negative outcomes and existential threats, but on balance they remain technopositivists. As I pointed out in my chapter on robots, we have no more to fear from machines regarding morals and autonomy then we already have to fear from our fellow humans. Organic and inorganic machines pose similar threats to each other and to themselves.

We can also look forward to an *Artilect War* (Garis, 2005) in which Terrans opposed to a robot takeover battle Cosmists who favor a robot takeover. This pits a vision of the value of traditional humanity in opposition to a transhuman vision of humanity. Here again, the Technopositivists see dystopian possibilities but tend to put their faith in more positive if not fully utopian futures.

One of the most glaring examples of the failure of the sociological imagination revealed in the visions of the Technopositivists is the work of the Global Brain Institute at the Free University of Brussels. They imagine an end to a world dominated by individual human minds/bodies/brains (which is part of the myth of the individual and the "I" as a grammatical illusion) and the emergence of collectives and/or combinations of humans as expressions of the structure and dynamics of practical intelligence. The humanistic and sociological failure in Technopositivism is nowhere better expressed than in the Global Brain project's promise of connecting all humans and artifacts in an all-knowing all-powerful God-like network. This takes us to the absurd vision of Eden on Earth. Everything will be predictable and foreseen. We will have built in translators so we can speak to anyone in any language, implanted AIs that will allow us to evaluate the people we meet whether for friendship, business, or intimacy, and we no longer will have to engage in petty chores.

There is some value in the visions of the Technopositivists. If the Singularity isn't coming, some future is coming, a future that is uncertain. These Technopositivist visions, especially where they realistically include negative as well as positive possible outcomes, can serve as bridges between "now" and "then" that might make the transition easier. The envisioned future will not spring only from the activities in Silicon Valley or on Wall Street. The world order will be formed or self-destruct depending in great part on what happens in China and Africa.

Finally, we must engage with economic futures that are already promising an end to conventional concepts of markets and money. The Technopositivists foresee a decentralized system for financial and legal transaction fueled by cryptocurrencies. More critical political economists think in terms of a black hole economy that will be the key piece of the puzzle that could bring life on earth and the planetary ecology to an end.

When the Technopositivists do get around to bringing human beings into their scenarios they do so predictably from a psychological perspective, which prevails even where sociology is recognized as part of the picture. What does "Mind and Society" look like in the Technopositivist perspective? Their immediate starting point is an "individual self" that doesn't exist. They see that morphing into some sort of collective intelligence (which can't exist). Their assumptions are flawed because of the evolutionary fact that humans are already, always, and everywhere social, and the widespread disability I have labelled dissocism (defined in Chapter 4). Their vision of the most positive post-Singularity society seems curiously similar to Karl Marx's vague visions of a future communist society. They actually use the vocabulary of a shift from an "era of scarcity" to an "era of abundance" which echoes Marx's, (1894/1981: 959) distinction between the realm of necessity and the realm of freedom. In the Technopositivist's era of abundance, just as in Marx's realm of freedom, the focus of human life shifts from survival labor to creative pursuits. In a related speculation, Kevin Kelly (2010), as we have seen, gives us the Technium, which extends beyond shiny hardware to include culture, art, social institutions, and intellectual creations of all types. It includes intangibles like software, law, and philosophical concepts. And significantly, it includes the generative impulses of our inventions to encourage more tool making, more technologies, and more self-enhancing connections. It is a self-reinforcing system of creation. At some point in its evolution, our system of tools and machines and ideas becomes so dense in feedback loops and complex interactions that it begins to exercise some autonomy.

As the seventh kingdom of life, the Technium marries the technological fix to a technopositivist, teleological transhuman era. The Technihuman Age emerges immediately out of the Anthropocene Age. This new kingdom is not biological but it is not cultural either. If it is envisioned as a merger of the technological and the biological, the technological is understood to be the stronger partner.

5   The United Nations and Sustainability

Alongside the Technopositivists and the Dystopian futurists among scientists, intellectuals, and novelists we find the more realistic goals, more humanistic visions, relatively speaking, of the United Nations.

1.   End poverty in all its forms everywhere.
2.   End hunger, achieve food security and improved nutrition and promote sustainable agriculture.

3. Ensure healthy lives and promote well-being for all at all ages.
4. Ensure inclusive and equitable quality education and promote lifelong learning opportunities for all.
5. Achieve gender equality and empower all women and girls.
6. Ensure availability and sustainable management of water and sanitation for all.
7. Ensure access to affordable, reliable, sustainable and modern energy for all.
8. Promote sustained, inclusive and sustainable economic growth, full and productive employment and decent work for all.
9. Build resilient infrastructure, promote inclusive and sustainable industrialization and foster innovation.
10. Reduce inequality within and among countries.
11. Make cities and human settlements inclusive, safe, resilient and sustainable.
12. Ensure sustainable consumption and production patterns.
13. Take urgent action to combat climate change and its impacts.
14. Conserve and sustainably use the oceans, seas and marine resources for sustainable development.
15. Protect, restore and promote sustainable use of terrestrial ecosystems, sustainably manage forests, combat desertification, and halt and reverse land degradation and biodiversity loss.
16. Promote peaceful and inclusive societies for sustainable development, provide access to justice for all and build effective, accountable and inclusive institutions at all levels.
17. Strengthen the means of implementation and revitalize the global partnership for sustainable development.

These lofty goals face serious obstacles. For example:

1. TRIBALLISTICS. The fact is that we are surrounded by threats. Some are existential threats, some are cultural threats. The result is that many people and groups feel that their basic cultural norms, values, and beliefs are under attack. Their tendency to enhance their tribal loyalties leads to triballistics, tribalism that increasingly turns to means of violence to defend itself.
2. THE CENTRIPETAL FORCE OF COMPASSION. Compassion is a core feature of every society, every social group, in evolutionary terms. It should be a way to bridge gaps between and across cultures, something that would make meeting existential threats easier to coordinate. But compassion is a centripetal force and powerful centrifugal forces are required to override the centripetal forces. The classic science fiction solution is to use an

invasion from outer space to unite the world's cultures. The invasion we face is from within our own world. It will be a close thing to achieve the cooperation required to face our existential threats effectively.

3.   CULTURE AS A SPECIATING MECHANISM. The centripetal force of compassion contributes to speciating cultures. Using a loose analogy, cultures can no more engage in constructive intercourse than animal species can crossbreed.

4.   RESISTANCE TO TURNING OUT THE LIGHTS. We have become dependent on resources that from the perspective of basic needs are luxuries. We cannot afford those luxuries anymore. It's not just a matter of living without fossil fuels or gas-guzzling vehicles, or recycling, or reducing our carbon footprints. We must go much further if we're going to solve our existential threats and give up things that are not even on our most basic list of things we have to give up. We are going to have to turn off the lights.

5.   HUMANITY DECOUPLED FROM CO-EVOLUTION BY CULTURE. It is fair to assume that humans were a product of co-evolution, evolving closely coupled with the means for their survival. The evolution of culture has de-coupled humans from any degree of co-evolution that might have characterized our origins.

6.   CULTURE AS A PLANETARY PANDEMIC. As a result of 5, culture is the most effective and efficient planet destroying mechanism ever developed.

6   Conclusion

Adding up everything in the lists in this chapter, our prospects for survival into the next century with some reasonable level of quality of life must be realistically assessed as dim at best. The main obstacle in our way is that our economics is driven primarily by greed, profits by any means, and wealth accumulation without attention to the waste, inequalities, and injustices created by our productivity. Capitalist ideology is the greatest obstacle to addressing existential threats.

CHAPTER 10

Capitalism: Ideology Contra Economy

1   The Black Hole Economy

> Black holes are thought to exist where nothing seems to exist –
> where everything that enters vanishes. Gravitational forces are so
> strong inside a black hole that not even light can get out – hence,
> the name. Since no one can devise a way to visit a black hole to
> report on what they find there, what happens in a black hole has to
> be deduced from what cannot be seen.
>   Political Economist Lester Thurow, 1992.

In the wake of the financial crisis of 2007–2008, considered by many economists to have been the worst financial crisis since the Great Depression of
the 1930s (the precipitating factor being a high default rate in the subprime
home mortgage sector), I wrote some notes on "the black hole" economy.
Contrary to many of the pundits and analysts inside and outside of the professional economics community, I suggested there was reason to believe that
the 2007–2008 "recession" was comparable to the Great Depression though
on a much smaller scale. I referred to that "recession" as a stage in an evolving
economic black hole. The social economist Kenneth Boulding (1970: 60–63)
argued that the dialectical processes associated with scientific revolutions
represent the heat of crystallization in a process of change; such processes
are "costs." This idea can be extended to include the "cumulation of costs"
and the progressive deterioration of the capacity of science to "recover" from
the costs of scientific revolutions and hence to continue to "grow," "progress,"
"develop," or "evolve." This applies to the economy too. Think of business cycles
as processes of change that incur costs (environmental and broader ecological damage, human costs ranging from alienation and health risks to actual
deaths, and institutional costs of the sort prominent in today's banking, insurance, and investment sectors), and assume that those costs are cumulative in
a world of limited and unrenewable resources. This is a scenario for a black
hole economy. The only way out that doesn't lead to a decrease in the carrying
capacity of the planet (possibly to zero) relative to the human population is a
radical development and deployment of new energy sources that (and here's
the kicker) do not require a massive overhaul of the existing infra-structure.
That new energy source might be one that is way off the radar, magnetism for

example, or something already on the drawing board like fusion. Magnetism contains no energy but can be used indirectly to generate energy. There may be some form of void-energy equivalence source (hypothesized by the late physicist David Bohm); and there might be new energy sources enfolded in the elusive Unified Field Equation with electrogravitation providing the energy. This demonstrates clearly that we are reliant on science fiction scenarios, and if any are achieved we are then faced with the problem that if they are not deployed globally we will fall into an economic black hole.

Waste products, measured in human and environmental terms and materially and emotionally for humans, are growing exponentially and have been for decades. There is a doomsday way to picture exponential growth for Joe and Jane Public. You walk past a pond every day in which algae are beginning to spread exponentially. You notice the growth but at first it really doesn't grab your attention. It's growing, it's growing. And then one day you notice that half the pond is covered. If that's the point at which you decide to do something, you are doomed because the pond will be completely covered the next day. We could be in for that kind of surprise. The concept of "behavioral sink" (Calhoun, 1962), and discussed by the anthropologist Edward Hall, 1966 (and see Wiles, 2011) comes into play here too. Toxic products may be building up in an animal population (say the citizens of New York City) and go unnoticed until one day most or all of the population drops dead.

Given what I am going to call the Boulding Theorem, "business cycle costs are cumulative" and taking as axiomatic that we live in a world of limited and unrenewable resources, the effect of "globalization," British Petroleum (BP) type corporations, and too-big-to-fail banks is that business cycle costs are externalized to the 99 percent and the environment. We need to pay more attention to the fact that our social programs in the United States are not designed to work in situations where several people are chasing every job opportunity.

In preparing this chapter, I discovered that I was not the only economic thinker who had thought of the current situation in terms of the black hole metaphor. Already by the late 1960s, Atrill (2018: 2) had used the metaphor:

> there is a precise point, a mathematical singularity, which we can measure as the Ratio of GDP/Total Debt, at which an economy stops expanding and begins to contract instead. This point is the equivalent to the event horizon of celestial 'black holes' and it acts in a similar manner, the first one drawing energy (light and matter) into its vortex, and the second drawing economic energy – GDP – into its 'vortex' due to the dead weight of massive debts.

Other authors who have used this metaphor include Chancellor (2022), Andersen (1994), Rancière and Tornell (2010), and Axelson and Makarov (2020). For an objection to using the metaphor in fiscal contexts, see Meadway (2022).

2   Will the Real Karl Marx Please Stand Up?

Karl Marx is the political economist of last resort, or the ghost haunting every political economic discourse. We will see as we proceed why Marx is still a name to be conjured with. The key concept in this chapter is capitalism. My general claim is two-fold: first, capitalism is the economy that never was, isn't, and never will be; second, the reason for this is that while empirically there are all sorts of "capitalisms," the form of capitalism that one would model using the ideal-type concept associated with Max Weber or that one would defend as "pure" violates all sorts of realistic features of humanity and the planet. I will return shortly to the values that pervade models of capitalism and that work against ecologies and humans. There are several different labels for economic systems employed by nations. Socialism and capitalism are the most common labels. Capitalism is often referred to as a free market economy in its purest form; socialism is often conflated or confused with communism. Embedded in these economic systems are political and social elements that influence the degree of purity of each system. In other words, many capitalist nations have enfolded elements of socialism. So even though there are different degrees or levels of commitment to the ideals of capitalism, there are several traits that are common across all versions of capitalism.

3   Capitalism in Ideal Type Terms

An ideal or pure type in Max Weber's sociology is a metric or heuristic that identifies the average, common, or "pure" features of a phenomenon. It's loosely comparable to idealized experiments in physics that assume friction-free surfaces or total vacuums in order to isolate relationships between independent and dependent variables. The ideal type can then be compared and contrasted to real-life phenomena.

4   Capitalism (Ideal Type Format)

1.   Two-class system: Historically a capitalist society has been character-
     ized by the split between two classes – the capitalist class, which owns
     the means for producing and distributing goods and services (the own-
     ers) and the working class, which sells its labor to the capitalist class in
     exchange for wages. The economy is run by the individuals (or corpora-
     tions) who own and operate companies and make decisions as to the use
     of resources. But there exists a "division of labor" which allows for spe-
     cialization, typically occurring through education and training, leading
     to decomposing the system into, for example, upper class, middle class,
     and lower class.

2.   Profit motive: The motive for all companies is to make and sell goods
     and services and to profit from doing so. Companies do not exist solely
     to satisfy people's needs. Even though some goods or services may satisfy
     needs, they will only be available if the people have the resources to pay
     for them at prices that allow the capitalists to turn a profit. Non-profit
     organizations can bring in money in any of a number of ways (e.g., dona-
     tions, grants, etc.). The key definition is given by the IRS: net earnings
     may not profit any shareholder or individual.

3.   Minimal government intervention: Capitalist societies believe mar-
     kets should be left alone to operate without government intervention.
     However, a completely government-free capitalist society is a myth. Even
     in the United States – the poster child for capitalism – the government
     regulates certain industries (e.g., the Dodd-Frank Act for financial institu-
     tions). By contrast, a purely capitalist society would allow the markets to
     set prices based on demand and supply for the purpose of making prof-
     its. Notice the implication that the free market is an autonomous agent.

4.   Competition: True capitalism needs a competitive market. Without com-
     petition, monopolies arise and instead of the market setting the prices,
     the seller is the price setter, which alters the conditions of capitalism.
     There is a volatile tendency in real world capitalist societies for monopo-
     lies to emerge.

5.   Willingness to change: The last characteristic of capitalism is the ability
     to adapt and change. Technology has been a game changer in every soci-
     ety and the willingness to allow change and adaptability of societies to
     improve inefficiencies within economic structures is a realistic societal
     characteristic.

5   Capitalism: The Bottom Line

Capitalism in its purest form is ideally an economic system in which the market sets prices for the sole purpose of maximizing profits and any inefficiency or intervention that reduces profit making will be eliminated by the market. In what follows, I assume for the moment that "capitalism" is a form of economy.

There is a substantial literature that supports the idea that there is no Capitalism, there are only capitalisms. Colin Crouch (2005) reviews some of this literature and points to some of the forms of capitalism abroad in our world. A dualistic analysis, such as that undertaken by Michel Albert (1991), is the typical way the idea of capitalism is expanded. Albert identified "free market capitalism," or Anglo-Saxon capitalism (characteristic of the Anglophone countries) and Rhenish capitalism, found in Germany, the Netherlands, Switzerland, and (with less certainty) France, and perhaps Japan and Scandinavia. The contributors to *Varieties of Capitalism* (Hall and Soskice, 2001) are basically dualist, though their work hints at a possible third model, The Mediterranean Group (Italy, Spain, Portugal, Greece, Turkey, and again as in Albert's analysis, France with some uncertainty). The two forms they identify are the Liberal Market Economy (LME) and the Coordinated Market Economy(CME). LME's are associated with the neo-liberal Anglophone countries among which the U.S. is exemplary; CME's are associated with the non-Anglophone social democracies. Schmidt (2002) explicitly introduces a third type in her typology, "market" (comparable to the LME), "managed" (comparable to the CME), and "state" (interventionist along the lines of the French system). The methodology here is suspect because as Crouch (2005: 445–46) points out, these authors violate the basic assumptions of Weberian ideal type analysis: "ideal types are one-sided accentuations, pressing home the logical implications of a particular kind of structure:"

> The aim is not to provide an accurate empirical description, but a theoretical category, to be used in the construction of hypotheses. Again, the authors are not building their theory deductively, but are reading back empirical detail from what they want to be their paradigm case of an LME – the U.S – into their formulation of the type.

Against this background I will broaden my initial description of capitalism in order to identify the basic elements of a more complete ideal type capitalism. I will then show that this model violates realistic features of the social and environmental contexts in which capitalism is supposed to function. It should then be clear why all models of capitalism that exhibit any or all of these elements will inevitably damage environments and humans individually and collectively. To be more specific, it is not capitalism per se that is damaging, but the ideology of capitalism that fuels economic actions.

Let's free associate with the word "capitalism." When I do this in a lecture the words that inevitably come up are:

Free market. Typically, as we saw in the description above, the market is treated as if it is an autonomous agent.

Buyers and sellers.

Capitalists and Workers.

Capitalists own the means of production.

Workers have only their ability to work to sell.

Self-interest: there is nothing inherently wrong with the pursuit of self-interest. As Adam Smith pointed out, we depend on the self-interest of butchers, brewers and bakers for our dinner; whether they are kind or not is irrelevant.

Competition.

The invisible hand: this is the "mechanism" (a chimera) that is assumed to make self-interested actions benefit the society as a whole.

Laissez faire. Entails that transactions between private parties are free from government interference such as regulations, privileges, tariffs, and subsidies. The phrase *laissez-faire* literally translates in this context "let go," or "leave alone."

Profit motive.

Private ownership.

We can immediately eliminate the concept of a "free market." No economic event or process is free in any sense whatsoever; they are all implicated in larger social causal nexuses including government interventions and regulations. And markets are not agents. They symbolize a context within which real human beings are the agents. These human agents are not equal in the power they possess to exercise control over the movement of goods and services, prices and wages, and financial resources across markets. The idea that buyers and sellers are active on an equal playing field is in general false. As human beings they are born biologically and socially equal hypothetically and perhaps in purely legal terms. Realistically they are biologically and socially unequal as a consequence of being born into different social classes and being biologically whole or impaired to varying degrees. This violates fair competition.

How is it that atomstic individuals acting in their own self-interest are supposed to benefit the greater good? Ideally, the objective of an economic system is to recruit, mobilize, and distribute goods and services in the interest of a viable society. How is this accomplished? Adam Smith's (1776/1976) solution was to invoke "the invisible hand," one of the most vacuous hypotheses in intellectual history and yet the defense of last resort for defenders of laissez-faire. The claim is that self-interest, reflected in the activities of atomistic individuals behaving without restraints in the market, automatically have their self-interest channeled into socially desirable ends. The transparent absurdity of this "ghost in the economic machine" idea eliminates it from serious consideration as a scientific concept. By implication it also eliminates the rationale for laissez-faire.

If, as is the ideal as well as the practical case, economic activity is organized around the sole or primary goal of making profits, inevitably profits will be valued above the value of human beings and environments. This means nothing more or less than that people will become willing to sacrifice human beings (from alienating them to poisoning them and working them to death) and environments (by, for example, destroying wetlands, forests, air quality, and the water supply). The idea that private ownership is compatible with a healthy environment makes no sense once we understand the way environmental and human ecologies work. Their interconnectivities mean that the best way to ensure that these interconnectivities stay well lubricated and viable is through cooperative relations at every level. Unbridled, individualistic competition inevitably wreaks havoc with the inter- and intra-connectivities that link humans, social ecologies, and planetary ecologies.

6   Conclusion

Finally, one of the major realities over-looked by capitalism's defenders is that the earth is a heterogeneous plane, not a homogeneous plane. Resources are not distributed equally across localities, regions, countries, or continents. Under such conditions, competition cannot be carried out fairly or realistically. In an economy dependent on fossil fuels, if your region is rich in crude oil this gives you a competitive advantage over oil poor regions. Trading comparatively scarce resources (Y has more of A than X, but X has more of B than Y) only solves the problem locally. The fact of unequal resource distributions (which importantly applies to unrenewable as well as renewable resources) means competition can never be carried out on an equal playing field. Unequal distributions fuel power and greed.

At the most basic level, human, social, and natural inequalities doom capitalism from the very beginning. You can try to initiate such a system, but the results will soon lead to the need to handicap the various inequalities that will inevitably produce problems for vulnerable populations and ecologies. As soon as you introduce handicaps (e.g., anti-trust laws, labor-management regulatory agencies such as the NLRB, and social welfare) you can no longer speak of a capitalist society. The varieties of capitalism are all based on handicapping the system and efforts to promote any among these varieties as "capitalism" or as "saving capitalism" are smoke screens to prevent the recognition that capitalism is an ideology and not a viable economic system.

Let's review the asocial assumptions that undergird capitalist ideology. It presumes scarcity of resources and unlimited wants as part of human nature. The "economic problem" in the face of unlimited wants and limited resources boils down to allocation. All economic systems have to deal with three questions: what should we produce; what methods of production should we use; and who should we produce for? If we expand our economic thinking to political economy, these three questions become entangled with Lasswell's (1948) questions: Who Gets What, When, and How. This can be expanded further to the communication dimension by bringing in Lasswell's model: "Who (says) What (to) Whom (in) What Channel (with) What Effect." This three-dimensional system of political economic communication gives us the driving questions any human population must ask in planning the routines of survival. Capitalism's version of this three-dimensional system includes the assumption that humans are rational individual decision-making consumers who know what they want and can communicate these wants to producers who will listen to them and act accordingly.

Capitalism has relied on sustaining and raising the human carrying capacity of the planet by relying on oil, coal, and natural gas in perpetuity. The producers recognize the limitations of these resources in terms of their quantitative limits and the ways in which exploiting them damages the planet. Nonetheless, they behave as if these resources will last forever and that we can offset their negative consequences even while promoting deregulation as a public policy. The reality is that we need new, low-cost, productive, non-lethal energy sources, something probably from magnetics, weak forces in crystals, fusion, or natural forces like wind, solar, and geo-thermals. We could go back to the comforting "technology as progress" vision of the 1950s and the kind of future envisioned in Star Trek. Without it we go down hard within fifty to seventy-five years. Governments and corporations whose activities and policies matter more by orders of magnitude that those of the population at large are not moving fast enough to get us off the path to a Black Hole Economy.

The ideology of capitalism fuels outright denial, disinformation, and doublespeak as policy guidelines to protect the greed and thirst for profits at all costs in the corporate world. The curtain hiding these practices from the public has long been torn down and the lies of, for example, Big Tobacco and Big Oil are widely known in the public arena. Big Tobacco falsely claimed, for example, that there was no proof that cigarette smoking is one of the causes of lung cancer (in 1953), that there were no harmful agents in tobacco (in 1964), and that there was no proof that secondary smoke is harmful (Philip Morris company, in 1987). Millions of dollars were spent on propaganda reassuring the public that smoking was safe (see, e.g., Pollay, R.W. and T. Dewhirstm, 2002).

Big Oil has similarly protected its interests by avoiding accountability for its contributions to climate change. Congressional hearings have demonstrated that the industry is actively engaged in doing everything it can to maintain reliance on fossil fuels for decades to come. The industry has known about the impact of greenhouse gases since at least the late 1950s and yet has done everything it could to block the transition from fossil fuels to renewable energy. Exxon was aware as early as 1979 that fossil fuel consumption was going to cause "dramatic environmental effects" before the middle of the 21st century. In the ensuing years, Big Oil relied on expensive marketing and lobbying campaigns to persuade Congress and the public that climate change science was plagued by uncertainty. While publicly claiming to be committed to achieving the goals of the Paris Climate Agreement and net zero emissions by 2050, British Petroleum executives, speaking for the industry, were saying privately that the goal of the fossil fuel industry was "to stay in the game." Armed with the knowledge that the development and production of fossil fuels are having devastating effects on human and planetary ecologies, British Petroleum recently announced it would be increasing oil and gas production over the next three years. Fully aware that gas does not support climate goals once you take methane emissions into account, Big Oil is promoting gas as a counterpart to renewable energy, not a bridge fuel. Big Oil revealed plans in the first decade of the 21st century to explore low-carbon biofuel alternatives like algae; by 2023. The algae biofuels programs have been scrapped (Artis, 2024). The inherently destructive nature of the ideology of capitalism could not be clearer.

Walby's (2015; and see Keen, 2011 on the failures of neoclassical economics) sociology of the black hole economy is a brilliant analysis of the 2007–2008 "Great Recession" and the financialization of the world economy. Her analysis is marred by her distinction between what is "real" and what is "socially constructed." This demonstrates a lack of the sociological imagination. We can only engage the real by way of our interactions with others in their social, cultural, and ecological contexts; that is, after all, what social construction refers to.

CHAPTER 11

What Is to Be Done?

In this chapter I will outline the basic form and content of a society consistent with freedom, liberty, and the pursuit of creative, critical, individual and collective lives. Whatever the possibilities for realizing this anarchist program in reality, the objective here is to provoke the imagination with the understanding that the program begins now in the homes, villages, and communities of individuals and groups prepared to begin living their lives driven by the anarchistic imagination, no matter how small the scale in space and time. I provide guidelines for imagining a route to an anarchist future. Let's first refresh our memory about our foil, capitalism.

We've seen that capitalism is not an economic system, it is not a social order, it is an ideology. Capitalist ideology cannot be realized in practice because its principles violate the realities of human and planetary complexities and differences. The effort to institute a capitalist economy has been accompanied by severe damage to the human spirit and planetary ecologies. In addition such efforts inevitably require government interference to handicap the system by way of regulations and laws which tend to socialize capitalism but in ways that benefit the ruling classes.

I've gone over the fallacies supporting the concept of a capitalist economy. Capitalist ideology is a phantom of myths: the free market, a homogeneous plane planet, fair competition, laissez faire, the invisible hand, self-interested actions that benefit society as a whole. Any effort to put capitalist ideology into practice will require interventions to control the inevitable devastation, but that devastation will continue as long as the economy is driven by the profit motive and greed. The result, even with some handicapping, is that wealth and power will be concentrated into the hands of fewer and fewer people. The theory of comparative advantage states that if countries specialize in producing goods where they have a lower opportunity cost then there will be an increase in economic welfare. This is offset by the variety of fundamental inequalities I have outlined here.

Capitalist ideology assumes a world of scarce resources and unlimited wants built into human nature. Furthermore, it assumes that humans are rational individual decision-making buyers and sellers who know what they want and can assess the value, quality, and costs of goods and services and act accordingly in the free market. This makes allocation the basic economic problem.

Some contemporary theorists of capitalism don't recognize the fallacies I've identified but they nonetheless argue that it is reaching its structural limits. They fail to see that as soon as capitalism was introduced it was over its structural limits. They also admit that their ability to foresee the future of capitalism is clouded by imponderables, notably climate change, pandemics, and nuclear warfare. Most of these theorists seem to agree that we are headed for a major structural transformation in the global economy. Anarchism has to be considered one possibility.

1   The Anarchist Social Order (See Bibliography on Anarchism and Social Order in References)

1.1   *The Goals*
- MUTUAL AID. The means used to achieve our goal of a humane planet-friendly sustainable social order must be consistent with the values that underlie the social order we are trying to establish. In an anarchist social order, everyone is entitled to the means of survival. Humans are not meant to be enslaved (with or without wages) or exploited in any way. Their very existence entitles people to the basics for survival independent of whether they work or not. Ideally, we should socialize people to engage in creative, productive activities that benefit their society, themselves, and the planet.
- DECOLONIZATION & DECAPITALIZATION. Expansionist market policies driven by the capitalist imperative and competition for resources and territory by essentially warring states must be curtailed. We must support independence and self-government among indigenous communities and decolonization in general.
- ERASING RACISM. In order to undermine historically successful and resilient structures of power and greed we must attack the manifest and latent legacies of racism. This means in part dissolving the whiteness of the capitalist imperative.
- ERASING SEX AND GENDER INEQUALITIES. These inequalities disadvantage women and persons who identify with diverse sex and gender classifications.
- SAFETY. We must throw off the yoke of the ideology that our freedom depends on the state providing for our safety and security. Our safety and security are in fact insured by the principle of mutual aid, not by the surveillance society, gated communities, police on every corner and in every school yard, or teachers with guns.

1.2   *Resources*

- LAND. Under the capitalist imperative land is property and exploitable. In an anarchist social order, land belongs to those peoples who take care of it and depend on it for survival.
- WATER. Our lives depend on water, and the process of developing an anarchist social order means that we must heal our waters and help our watersheds become self-sustaining and as pure as possible.
- BORDERS. Mutual aid and voluntary association requires freedom of movement; borders are inevitable but they must be disentangled from sovereignty. Communities live in territories and they must be custodians of those territories. They will guarantee basic hospitality and safe conduct to travelers and migrants passing through or seeking to move to their communities. Federations of communities can be formed to facilitate efficient development and use of transportation, communication, and exchange links.
- HOUSING. Dignified, safe, ecologically sustainable housing is to be a basic guaranteed right. Houses will be owned by the people who live in them, and no one will have more houses than they need for their particular family configuration. Housing is not a commodity to be bought or sold; it is not an investment.
- FOOD. Cmmunities are responsible for seeing to it that everyone has all the food they need to live a healthy dignified life; this is a human right. In order to ensure an ecologically sound environment and a healthy lifestyle, foods will be cultivated in accordance with basic needs and not as commodities to be marketed and sold for profit. Communities will grow as much of the food they need as possible within their own territories.
- HEALTHCARE. Healthcare, including preventive therapies and healthy living conditions, is a human right, regardless of sex, gender, ascribed race, class, physical or mental condition. Healthcare will be free and a collaboration between the individual, the community, and healthcare professionals.

1.3   *Activities*

- PRODUCTION. From production for wealth accumulation and profit, and independent of need and costs to human and planetary ecologies to production for the health and well-being of humans and the planet.
- DISTRIBUTION, COMMUNICATION, AND TRANSPORTATION. To be achieved to whatever extent possible at the local and regional level. Global networks will be established where necessary and to maximize efficiency (e.g., energy networks). There will be no borders that prevent free and unencumbered travel across the globe with due consideration for the health of local ecologies.

– CONFLICT RESOLUTION AND TRANSFORMATIVE JUSTICE. Taken out of the hands of the police and prison system and invested in community assemblies responsible for humane sociologically responsible conflict resolutions, healing harms, and restoring fractured reciprocity.
– COMMUNITY ORGANIZATION AND COORDINATION. From involuntary citizenship and dictatorial or representative law-making and justice to voluntary association and self-organization.
– THE PLANET. From the ideology of capitalism and the reality of greed economics to community action to identify, address, and resolve to the extent possible existential threats to humanity and the planet. For a detailed account of these principles see Crimethinc.com (2020).

2   Education Reconstructed

As a university professor for half a century I witnessed part of this American nightmare in student populations mired in medieval worldviews. A professor (notably young) critical of my teaching methods actually said "I'm defending a position that goes back to the middle ages." What I have seen since I retired has been a precipitous decline in even the questionable commitment to education for critical thinking I observed as a professor. We have seen these processes erupting into book bans, and open efforts to make the schools and libraries of America propaganda machinery for the state. Education in America has always been more about teaching nationalism, American exceptionalism, capitalism, and patriotism, and challenging the principle of the separation of church and state than critical thinking, and more about credentialing than love of knowledge. But over the last half century, the balance has increasingly shifted away from what little critical thinking the schools encouraged along with the value of knowledge, reason, and science to a blatant program of instilling pride in the nation. In the process we have seen the idea of the separation of church and state constantly violated as education became increasingly commodified.

The struggle to preserve truth cannot be achieved without education for critical citizenship as well as critical thinking. We should, for example, learn about the Bill of Rights by practicing the enumerated rights, as in moot courts. Students should engage in moot protests, moot free speech rallies, moot elections, and so on. We should teach real history, not icons and myths. When I studied the presidents in school I drew shadow profiles of Washington and Lincoln. By at least fifth grade I should have been reading a book like Howard Zinn's (1980) *A People's History of the United States*.

It is also past the time when we should revisit the religion clause of the 1st amendment. It's time to leave childish things behind. This is not simply because it's the realistic thing to do but because our survival as a species depends on it. Our problem-solving abilities in the face of the existential threats to our species and our planet are compromised by unrealistic beliefs and delusionary imaginings about gods, angels, and an afterlife. We should be protecting the freedom to teach, to learn, and to do science. And we need a stronger way to enforce the establishment clause. The current version has not allowed this. The current version has not prevented using the Bible at swearing in ceremonies and in courts, the active use of chaplains in political events, and the seasoning of our money, pledges, and anthems with God.

I begin here once again with intimations of C.Wright Mills' *The Sociological Imagination.* This chapter, like this book in general, is guided by the sociological perspective but it is based on views rooted in ideas stemming from the particular intersection of my biography, the history of my time, and the culture(s) across which my life has unfolded. This section is not so much a discipline based sociology of education as it is an exercise in experiential sociology. The need for this essay is rooted in the fallacy that education is a social good that among a variety of social goals emphasizes the promotion of learning. The meaning of the term "learning" in this context depends on where one stands in the social order relative to reason, science, realism, and objectivity. Bracketing for the moment the problematics of these terms, it is sociologically the case that culturally speaking education is less about learning and more about everything else connected to "the credential society" (Collins, 1979/2019). Education in America, and speaking institutionally across time, space, and culture, has always been more about training for patriotism, nationalism, and the work and military forces and less about giving students unimpeded, unexpurgated access to the tools for critical analysis, critical access to reality, and critical citizenship.

In spite of the subordination of education to training for patriotism, nationalism, and the cultures of work, sport, and the military there have always been narrow pathways that have allowed teachers and students to learn above and beyond the institutional goals of education. But these narrow pathways have been increasingly choked off. The latter part of the twentieth century saw the increasing rationalization (or, in a more radical vocabulary, reduction or degradation) of mental labor. Manual labor had been rationalized during the industrial revolution. The information revolution has been a context and force for the rationalization of mental labor.

I taught my first college class in 1966 and then taught continuously (with time out for sabbaticals and fellowships) until 2010, and then from 2015–2017.

My plan had always been to teach until the day I died. I retired in 2010 and for good in 2017 because changes in the nature and structure of the university had become incompatible with my understanding of and practice of education. Indeed, I became from the point of view of the administration a dangerous person teaching a dangerous discipline, dangerous topics (sex, religion, economics, relationships), and adopting a dangerous posture in the classroom. The "dangerous posture" was one that encouraged dialogue among students and with me. Decades earlier the writing on the wall came into view when I was criticized by senior faculty for being "too passionate" in the classroom. This had nothing to do with extra-curricular relationships with students but everything to do with my energy in the classroom and my interest in bringing my students into my world of ideas and critical realism.

In the wake of my retirement I wrote that much has been made of the disappearing middle class in America in recent years. When I wrote about secrecy, suspicion, and subversion and proliferating tools of surveillance, accountability, and assessment earlier (in Chapter 3) I wasn't entirely aware that I was channeling an emerging challenge to whatever is real about freedom and democracy as embodied in the American Constitution. That challenge would reach unprecedented levels with the coming of the Trump "fake news & alternative facts" administration. This process was already being predicted by students of the rationalization of mental labor in the 1980s. They warned about deskilling and proletarianization in mental labor (Cooley, 1980; Wright and Singleman, 1982; Derber, 1982; Salaman, 1983; Kuttner, 1983). Braverman (1974) had already argued that it was in the interest of business and industrial management to devalue mental labor. This was an economic manifestation of the broader cultural anti-intellectualism in American history (Hofstadter, 1963).

The rationalization of mental labor was already an issue for Max Weber. In his well-known essay on "Science as a Vocation" Weber (1918/1946) drew attention to the "means of administration." This expanded the structural dimensions of the economy identified by Marx and political economists as the means, forms, and relations of production. Weber pointed out the separation of administrative officials from the relations and means of production. That separation has deepened over the decades since Weber wrote his essay. By the late twentieth century, the deepening of that separation had led to the emergence of the generic administrator, credentialed to operate in any organizational or institutional context, that is, to administer total institutions (Goffman, 1961a). The reduction of manual and mental labor had produced an environment that was now so homogeneous that the generic administrator could problem solve with a single administrative algorithm. As generic administrators replaced traditional administrators in schools, colleges, and universities they brought with them not only their monolithic algorithm but an ideological bias rooted in American culture opposed to academic freedom and tenure, and suspicious of the professoriate and of education itself.

The routinization of the rationalization of manual and mental labor has as one of its consequences the subjugation of professionals and professionals-in-training to management ideologies and directions (Derber, 1982: 8). However limited the degrees of academic freedom in the past, and however far from ideal education has been historically, the new limits imposed by the industrialization and corporatization of the schools have become a clear and present danger to education, science, and objectivity. The manifestations of this process include the proliferation of "detail" work that increases the alienation of the worker; increasingly specific and standardized job descriptions overseen by generic administrators, especially human resources officials; and the conflation of machines and humans as equivalent administrative units subject to the same rules and standards of measurement and assessment.

3   Intervention: A Note on Alienation

The concept of alienation identifies a distinct kind of psychological or social ill; namely, one involving a problematic separation between self and other, self and work, self and nature, and self and ideal self that properly belong together. So understood, it appears to play a largely diagnostic role, perhaps showing that something is awry with liberal societies and liberal political philosophy. Theories of alienation typically pick out a subset of these problematic separations as being of particular importance, and then offer explanatory accounts of the extent of, and prognosis for, alienation. Discussions of alienation are especially, but not uniquely, associated with Hegelian and Marxist intellectual traditions.

Alienation should be distinguished from some adjacent concepts; in particular, from "fetishism" and "objectification." There are conceptual and normative complexities at issue, including: the distinction between subjective and objective alienation; the need for a criterion by which candidate separations can be identified as problematic; along with some aspects of the relation between alienation and ethical values. The empirical difficulties often generated by ostensibly philosophical accounts of alienation have been acknowledged, but not resolved (Leopold, 2022; Dunn, 2021; Jaeggi, 2014).

4   Managerialism

Early expectations that generic administrators with their managerial strategies, values, organizational forms and vocabularies would serve as conduits for
the movement of managerialism from the resource rich environments of government and industry to the resource dependent educational environments
have been realized. Managerialism brought more traditional American values
into the educational sphere, including an anti-intellectualism that has been
historically a hallmark of American culture. This is one of the sources for the
increasingly widespread "know nothingness" of Americans who have fled from
science into the arms of celebrities, lotteries, and fantasies. The financialization of the American and world economies has been of a piece with these
developments. In general, we commodified or are in the process of commodi-
fying all cultural products including money itself.

Nietzsche's (1881/2007: 26) Aphorism 18 in *Dawn* gives us the rationale for
education: "Nothing has been more dearly bought than the minute portion of
human reason and feeling of liberty upon which we now pride ourselves." R.J.
Hollingdale (1968: 7) in his translator's introduction to *Nietzsche's Twilight of
the Gods & The Anti-Christ* (1889–1895/1968) gives us another perspective on
this aphorism: Nietzsche, he writes, teaches "independence:" "Philosophy, in
the proper sense of the word, stimulates the mind into activity, into becoming productive, into becoming airborne." Since in my view philosophy is dead,
this becomes the province of science as does the provocation (in Hollingdale's
[1968: 8] words) "To think well, to think at all ... to think differently." And to
think critically.

I started teaching sociology as a university instructor in 1966. Radical ideas
and actions were the order of the day on and off campus. Everything from teach
ins and the Indochina war to the March 4th 1968 research stoppage and the
civil rights movement impacted every classroom every day. I came to graduate
school as a self-styled Marxist sociologist and had already established roots
in the Science for the People and Radical Science Movements. I was already a
subversive teacher when Postman and Weingartner's *Teaching as a Subversive
Activity* appeared in 1969. They introduced Chapter 1 with the words of Tom
Paxton's song, "What did you learn in school today?" What were students learning? That Washington never lied, soldiers seldom died, everybody's free, police-
men are our friends, justice never ends, murderers die for their crimes even if
we make mistakes sometimes and execute innocent people; our government
is strong and never wrong, our leaders are the finest men and we elect them
again and again, war is not so bad and we've had some great ones, and someday
I might get my chance to fight for my country. This is what we should expect of

education as a social institution dedicated to manufacturing patriotic citizens. Whatever institutional justification one can give for this view of education the result is that the system produces Stepford students (Levin, 1972).

Thomas Jefferson wrote that "The tree of liberty must be refreshed from time to time with the blood of patriots and tyrants." This comes very close to a call for building into our political system a mechanism for permanent revolution. The term "permanent revolution" appears variously in the writings of Marx and Engels, Trotsky, , Stalin, and Mao. It is echoed in John Gardner's concept of the "ever-renewing society." The Jeffersonian version as I interpret it requires an eternal revolutionary vigilance in the interest of preserving our rights to life, liberty and the pursuit of happiness. This principle must be taught as basic civics. We are obliged to educate critical knowledgeable active citizens not Stepford students. The natural world and the problems it poses for us do not suffer patriotism and nationalism lightly.

I don't remember exactly when I started to tell my students that education was about improving their bullshit detectors. I vaguely remembered getting this idea from Postman and Weingartner and I was vaguely right; they used the term "crap detector." They take the term from Ernest Hemingway's frustration with a reporter's efforts to elicit from him the defining characteristic of a "great writer;" "a person must have a built-in, shockproof crap detector."

The problem, more evident in the public square as I write than perhaps at any other point in history, is the never-ending struggle against "the veneration of 'crap.'" To be subversive one must be guided by the sociological cogito; Postman and Weingartner called it the anthropological perspective. The point is that education must guide us away from the cage of the tribe. Most of what Postman and Weingartner suggest in their book was part of the atmosphere of radical self-aware teaching in the 1960s guided by slogans like "Question Authority," re-making teaching and learning into "teaching-learning," making space for varieties of teaching and learning styles, and questioning the conventional grading methodologies' role in actually educating students. Classrooms became experiments, and a newspaper headline reporting on events in Indochina could lead overnight to a revised syllabus.

In 1995, Postman gave us another gem, *The End of Education*. The most important message in this book was its emphasis on the concept of "public" in public education. Education as bullshit detecting is not obliged to balkanize curricula any more than scientists are obliged to balkanize methods and theories. The alternative to balkanization is not Absolutism but diversity; champion cultural pluralism over multiculturalism. Champions sciences, not Science. Astronomers can maintain their integrity by teaching the different theories about the origins, nature and functions of celestial objects and processes without being obliged to teach astrology. Where there is consensus in science, this is what we should teach making sure that students are alerted to the marginal fluctuations and perturbations around the edges of the consensus. Biologists should teach evolutionary theory and not suffer the foolishness of creation theory. Nature is not a free for all playground. Public education should be about the widest, the deepest wisdom we have as Humanity, outside our tribal cages. We violate nature when we allow tribes to take control of science and education and hasten our demise in the face of problems that are not tribal. All the arguments for sustaining the tribes neglect the fact that nature abhors the tribe and is most responsive to an increasingly wide and open public imagination.

The time for local and regional tribes is over and has been over for some time. The Earth now demands a global village, diversified but not multicultural. Public education must be become a global goal, not a local, regional, or national goal. This cannot happen all at once but happen it must if we are to extend our human lives and the life of the planet. Many great thinkers have thought that science should be the world unifying force and I agree with them in general. Science with a capital "S" cannot achieve this; it is by definition tribal; "s"cience with a small "s" and pluralized as "sciences" must be our guide, and must be understood to be synonymous with Nietzsche's notion of reason and thinking. In this sense, science is not the province of single individuals or groups but is located in networks of thinkers. These networks must extend outward from the professional realms of science to the everyday lives of wider and wider publics intra- and internationally. They must expand inwardly toward the rationalities of everyday lives contextualized within arenas of public education. Simultaneously, the rationalities of everyday life must reach into the professional realms of science and intellectual life.

Education must be above all an introduction to reality understood as an ever unfolding of things in becoming with truth as a real but moving target with artistic and imaginative dimensions. We must teach what we know to be the case in such a way that we do not preclude new versions of what the case is. Facts are facts but only in the sense that their substance is corrigible and subject to change. Newton is truer than the Greeks but he is true only in the sense that he does not preclude or bar the truth of Einstein; Einstein is true in the sense that he does not preclude or bar geometrodynamics. *The Emperor's New Clothes,* Hans Christian Andersen's (1837/1992) famous fairy tale should be required reading during the first week of every grade, every semester, every course.

It's unrealistic to think that we are just going to escape the citizenship functions of education. However, we can approach this in a new way through the lens of *The Emperor's New Clothes*. In America, we will take the Constitution and the Bill of Rights seriously but not as objects of uncritical worship. Instead the Constitution will be taught as a guide to action. Students will practice exercising their rights as classroom activities and where the opportunity arises in active demonstrations and free speech opportunities. Howard Zinn will become the historian of record for the teaching of American history.

Our challenge is to celebrate democracy and ultimately anarchism as a form of community without building a wall around our ever-renewing society. Our challenge is to celebrate citizenship as action not as worship. Our challenge is to celebrate diversity in ways that do not nourish ignorance. Our challenge is to celebrate free speech without making opinions the equivalent of reasoned grounded knowledge.

5 Conclusion

"Truth," Winston Churchill said, "is incontrovertible. Panic may resent it, ignorance may deride it, malice may distort it; but there it is." As sociologists of science we will want to contextualize truth and stress that truths are not absolutes but contingent and corrigible. However, truths come with different degrees of freedom. Theories of the origin(s) of the (our) universe have many more degrees of freedom than the theory of evolution, which has more degrees of freedom than the rules of geometry. At the end of the day, complexities and degrees of freedom aside, nature tends to be robustly inflexible and resistant to negotiation and compromise. This feature of nature (which encompasses humanity) becomes increasingly apparent as the human population squeezes up against the boundaries of the global system socially, culturally, geographically, and physically. We are at that point now and that reality must be realized in our approaches to education. We no longer have the freedom to listen to everyone who has or wants a voice. To the extent that we continue to behave as if we live in a world that is infinitely tolerant of our thoughts, our imaginations, our decisions, our sciences to that extent will we diminish our capacity to problem solve our way through the intricately interlaced global problems that confront us.

CHAPTER 12

A Secular Humanist Worldview: Prologue to Anarchy

Reality is not indifferent to culture. It will not tolerate all cultures equally. In general, cultures destroy planets.[1] They consume their resources in order to benefit humans. Humans are not terribly careful in their choices and inventions regarding the production and distribution of goods and services they decide they need for survival. They tend to invent, discover, and deploy without adequate assessments. Exploitation of resources and manufacturing processes inevitably produce waste products that damage the life-giving features of the planet. The dangers of deploying new technologies may go undiscovered for years or decades. The question humans concerned with the planet have to answer is this: Is it possible to design a culture that benefits humans but maximizes the efficient use of renewable resources and minimizes the use of non-renewable resources? Renewable resources are naturally replenished on a human timescale; for example, wind, sunlight, water in motion, and geothermal heat. Not all renewable energy sources are sustainable at uncontrolled exploitation rates (e.g., biomass sources). Nonrenewable resources cannot be readily replaced on an industrial scale: this is the case for earth minerals, metal ores, fossil fuels, and some groundwater.

It is important to remember that nothing we do will prevent the eventual death of the planet and our and all species, just as nothing we do will prevent individual humans from dying. But just as there are things we can do to prolong our lives with good health and quality living, there are things we can do to prolong the life of the planet that sustains us. These two goals are integrally linked. The test of the truth value or survival value of an integrated system of planet and humanity will not be rhetoric, or charisma, or reason or logic but evolutionary pressures, natural selection. Given natural selection and planetary dynamics, what form of social system would best ensure the efficient sustainable use of renewable and unrenewable resources, benefit human beings by ensuring their healthy survival with reasonable longevity, and minimize social injustices and social inequalities? Thousands of years of human thinking on

---

1 This chapter include material originally published in Chapter 13, "The Knowing Society" in Sal Restivo, *Beyond New Atheism and Theism* (New York: Routledge, 2024).

this problem has convinced me and others that we would be best served by a social order that is organized on secular, humanist, and anarchist principles.

1   The Secular Worldview Narrative Unfolds

The first thing to do is to challenge the myth of individualism. If it is not the individual who thinks, if free will is an illusion, then what are we seeing when we view an individual person? We're seeing the embodiment of a complex social network. An individual's development throughout the life cycle is marked by passing through series of networks, from parents to neighborhoods and school peers, from teachers to employers, from communities to communities. The individual is defined by the complex sum of these intersecting, sometimes conflicting, sometimes reinforcing networks. Individuality, the fact of personality differences, is a function of the complexity, diversity, and uniqueness of those social networks. What does this mean for the individual's mental awareness, h/er thinking?

It is not the individual who thinks but h/er community environment, h/er social network. The source of the individual's consciousness, h/er awareness, h/er thinking, is concentrated upon h/er by the Zeitgeist. *Zeit* means "time" and *geist* means spirit, and the "spirit of the time" is what's "in the air" culturally and intellectually in any given era. Sociologically, the individual's thoughts arise in the community networks that surround h/er. Our thoughts are generated during the interactions that happen in these social networks. That is the source of the only thoughts s/he can think. This radically social understanding of thinking is basic to freeing us from illusions, mistakes in reference, and distortions in logic and reason. It's also the foundation for giving us potential control over the catastrophic consequences of the various existential threats we are faced with.

But wait! If individualism and free will are myths, and individuals' thoughts are programmed by social networks, what accounts for creativity? The answer is that creativity is a function of the unique combinations of social networks that the individual's life unfolds through.

2   Levels of Reality

Our world gives us access to three basic levels of reality. The world of our everyday experience is the meso level; the world of the very small, the quantum world, is the micro world, and the world of the very fast and very large is the macro level.

There are three basic perspectives or theories about how the world works at these three levels expressed in the theological worldview, the scientific worldview, and the secular humanist world view. Keeping in mind that religion is the glue that holds societies, communities, families, and selves together, each of these worldviews is unified around a religion, a system of rules about good and bad and right and wrong that tell us how to behave in ways that benefit us and our local, tribal world. A worldview, following Sigmund Freud's (1933/ 1995: 195–196) definition "solves all the problems of our existence uniformly on the basis of one overriding hypothesis, which leaves no question unanswered and in which everything that interests us finds its fixed place." The overriding hypothesis of the scientific worldview is Science; the overriding hypothesis of the theological worldview is God; and the overriding hypothesis of secular humanism is Humanity.

There are many ways to categorize the elements of a worldview. I find it useful to use the following scheme: (a) GOD: is there a God or not?; (b) ULTIMATE REALITY: is ultimate reality one material substance (this is materialism broadly conceived)? Or is it a two-tiered system, a material world and a transcendental, supernatural, or spiritual realm of entities? (realms of materialism and idealism); (c) KNOWLEDGE: is the source of knowledge God, classical science, open-ended science, or something else? (d) HUMAN BEINGS: are human beings God's creations or an outcome of evolution? (e) ETHICS,VALUES, AND MORALS: is God the source of ethics, values, and morals, or are they cultural? (theists don't recognize culture in this sense so for them the only alternative to God is DNA); (f) PLIGHT: what are the basic problems we face as a species, and especially how do we explain and deal with suffering and evil? (g) SOLUTION: is the solution to our plight God, science, or secular humanism? (h) SOCIETY: capitalism/democracy, communism/socialism, authoritarianism/totalitarianism, or anarchism?

To introduce the secular humanist worldview, I need to define three key terms: science, secular, and anarchism. It's important to underscore as we move forward that while we are obliged to put things into words, doing so has a volatile potential for reification (Being), for endings rather than beginnings upon beginnings (Becoming). As scientists, secularists, humanists, and anarchists we are not looking for a rock-like certainty on which to ground our ideas, our concepts, our actions. This is the way of the theological cogito based on faith and belief and Being. The scientific cogito is based on inquiring as a process of Becoming. We have to think of and use words in a new way, one which makes all words verbs, one which makes words dialectical without making them amorphous (Bohm, 1976). We seek to be grounded without being rooted. Our words are not gods or masters, they are guides.

3 Science

Secular humanism incorporates an open-ended version of science, one that avoids scientism. Scientism is the idea that science as we know it through physics, chemistry, and biology (but especially through physics) is all we need to understand life, the universe, and everything. Science in the ordinary sense should be understood as a social, cultural, and historical phenomenon that is not autonomous or self-correcting. Neither is it the once and only method that gives us unmediated access to reality-in-itself. The extreme version of this view of science is that physics is the science of everything. I have already introduced a view of sciences in becoming and will continue to echo that view in the following pages grounded in and reiterating the idea of science as a collective intersubjective activity unfolding across history and cultures.

4 Secular

Secular refers to attitudes, activities, ethical, moral, and value positions, and explanatory frameworks that have no traditional religious or spiritual bases. The secular worldview denies on empirical grounds (sociological and anthropological) the existence of transcendental and supernatural realms of reality and entities that inhabit those realms. Furthermore, it denies the existence of an immaterial world in the specific sense that disallows the possibility of an entity or being possessing any of the following characteristics: self-existing, infinite, simple (undivided in being), immaterial, spaceless, timeless, omnipotent, omnipresent, omniscient, immutable, holy, and personal.

5 Anarchism

The main obstacle non-progressive and at least some progressive readers must get over is that anarchism is completely open ended and avoids planning. As sketched here, it is not utopian, internally inconsistent, nihilistic, anomic, a condition of chaos and disruption, and simply an anti-establishment irritant. It can, of course, be all of those things if you simply depend on the variety of personalities who have defined it in words and actions. The version I refer to here is scientifically grounded on the foundation of the social sciences, following the ideas of Peter Kropotkin (1842–1921). Its governing structure is based on rejecting the apparatus of a coercive state and rigid hierarchies. Instead, its governing structures are based on voluntary cooperation, mutual aid, and direct action. Decision making is based on community consensus. The anarchist motto is "no gods, no masters." Humans should no more be pinned down by a celestial dictator God than by an earthly supreme sovereign.

Anarchist societies are no strangers to human history. Anthropologists have offered good reasons and reasonably good evidence for the claim that our most ancient ancestors lived in various forms of anarchistically organized bands. The band consists of a small number of people (usually 30 to 50) who form a fluid, egalitarian community and cooperate in activities such as subsistence, security, ritual, and care for children and elders. Most hunter-gatherer societies are bands. Many such societies have been documented by anthropologists. There are variations but the generalities are equality, some individual autonomy, indulgent child rearing practices, cooperation, and sharing. We can conclude from this that (1) humans are not genetically or in any sense naturally warlike, inevitably immersed in inequalities and injustices, or enslavers; and (2) that the anarchism of mutual aid requires a society constituted of bands. If anarchism is going to be instituted on the foundation of modern society, it is going to have to do this by way of a process of extreme decentralization.

6   A Secular Worldview Unfolds

In the secular humanist worldview I am unfolding convictions are dangerous and absolute convictions are absolutely dangerous. This doesn't mean we can't know things with what amounts to a practical conviction. For example, I am absolutely convinced that the earth is not flat and that I should look both ways before crossing the street. Even so those convictions are shadowed by an ever-present skepticism. Skepticism exists on a continuum, and without putting too fine a point on this, it can vary from high to low, from 1 to 0. In the case of the flat earth it reaches the low or 0 end of the continuum. I am also guided in unfolding the secular humanist worldview by a sense of how alien we are when we try to grasp infinities and the cosmos. We are out of time and place and eventually will pass away into eternal nothingness. For this reason, I believe we should take pride in our collective ability to capture some small sense of what some of this life can be about even if it leaves us all the more insignificant in the larger scheme of things. In our *own* present realities, in our own knowing communities, our achievements are significant and real. *We know things*

Secular humanism has had many champions in our own time, politicians and people of good will who have sought to establish the principles of the good society without introducing God or sneaking in God surrogates. The Humanist Manifesto is a trademark of The American Humanist Association. Humanist Manifesto I was announced in 1933. Humanist Manifesto III was crafted in 2003.

HM III outlines a progressive agenda that reflects a commitment to social justice, equity, equality, and support for societal conditions that promote healthy environments, healthy populations, and healthy persons. This is a practical non-utopian goal with no pretensions to being easily achieved, a goal that offers no guarantees of being reachable or sustainable. To think otherwise is to succumb to the same sort of wishful thinking and hope-provoked imaginings that led humans to conceive of gods, souls, heavens, and an afterlife. In a society organized without a coercive state and community-centered a special progressive agenda would be unnecessary.

Secularism is included as part of the European convention on human rights (Article 9). The objective is to fully separate state and religion (in the traditional sense; sociologically, religion as the moral "glue" of society is ubiquitous). And in 2017, on October 22, the Polish Secularity Congress unveiled its secular manifesto, therein advocating for a democratic, secular state under the rule of law, and opposing religious privileges and priorities, especially those of the Roman Catholic Church. Public institutions are to be fully secular. Furthermore it supported the establishment of secular public schools based on the achievements of science and an anti-discrimination curriculum based on cultural and worldview diversity. The manifesto liberalizes anti-abortion laws and provides state support for women's sexual and reproductive rights, introduces sex education into the schools, supports the right to full equality before the law, dignified death, equality in traditional as well as non-traditional marriages, and the right to freedom of thought, conscience and religion, and non-disclosure rights.

Secularism is on the move in other parts of the world. France has put it (*laïcité*) at the center of its national policy and it is part of India's policy approach to religious diversity. According to the World Population Review there are 96 secular nations in the world. Other sources list as many as 144. The meaning of secular in the context of states is slippery. It can mean that a state is neutral on matters of religion; all citizens are treated equally whether they are religious or not; or it can mean that a state does not have a state religion. Such states, however, can demonstrate religious preferences in their national ceremonies and symbols, or laws that preferentially benefit one religion.

The United Nations is viewed as an exemplary secular and rational institution but its legitimacy depends on religious templates ... The preamble to
its constitution states that the "nations express their faith in the dignity and
worth of the human person." Constitutional secular clauses are not good pre-
dictors of state actions regarding religion.

The global diffusion of secularization driven by Western expansionist
encounters with Others has resulted in re-drawing and re-ordering classical
boundaries between "sacred" and "profane," "transcendent" and "immanent,"
and "religious" and "secular." Acknowledging the complexities and diversities
that are involved here, I am going to use the term "secular" to mean knowledge and practices devoid of all conventional religious, spiritual, sacred, transcendental, supernatural, and spiritual meanings, references, and dimensions.
Secular societies are religious in the sociological sense that religions are the
"glue" of societies.

There are societies without the traditional institutional, symbolic, and ritual
trappings of religion, but all working societies have moral orders and that is
what we mean by religion. This is why we can have religions without God, and
without transcendental and supernatural beings and realms, but we can't have
societies without religion. The health benefits of traditional religion reflect its
community and solidarity functions.

7   A Secular Worldview Crystallizes

Let's begin the construction of a secular humanist anarchist worldview in
becoming using the categories I introduced earlier: (a) GOD, (b) ULTIMATE
REALITY, (c) KNOWLEDGE, (d) HUMAN BEINGS, (e) ETHICS, (f)PLIGHT;
(g) SOLUTION. How do these play out comparatively in the worldviews of theism and secularism? Schematically:

Theism: (a) God; (b) Dualism; (c) Revelation; (d) Created in God's Image;
(e) Objective Morality Revealed by God; (f) Sin; (g) Salvation by God's Grace
Through Faith in Christ's Atonement.

Secularism: (a) No God; (b) Naturalism; (c) Science, avoiding a tendency to
shade off into scientism and the technological fix; (d) Accidental consequences of natural processes like all other living things and subject to natural laws; (e): morality is culturally relative; (f) The meaningless of it all, the
finality of death, the relativism of ethics, values, and morals, the lack of a
rock of certainty; (g) The Feynman Solution: We live in a mysterious pur-
poseless universe and that shouldn't frighten us. The Feynmanian scientist
does not operate with hopes and wishes. Hoping and wishing have nothing

to do with the way the world really is. And the Feynmanian scientist wants to know what the world is really like and this requires the courage not to be frightened and not to be motivated in your inquiries by hopes and wishes. Another way to decompose this paradigm follows.

8   Secular Humanism

- Supreme Being/Entity/Power/(God):There is no God.
- Nature-Reality (Ultimate Reality): Reality is real (not a simulation, not a brains-in-a-vat phenomenon, not an illusion) and singular but complex beyond our capacity to imagine; it is a never-ending layered indeterminate but lawful process of unfolding things in becoming. Humans can access the small part of this reality that they have co-evolved with; this is the reality accessible to humans through their senses, the reality-of-experience (RE) not reality-in-itself (RI); RE is constituted of discoverable patterns, regularities, and invariants in systems that are more or less open or closed. There are no perfectly closed systems, but to the extent that a system is closed to that extent humans will be able to extract lawful predictions. Reality in the most general sense is effectively infinitely decomposable; that is, there is no effective limit to the ways in which we can experience the world, trace causal chains, and describe our experiences. However, not all decompositions are equally useful for the practice of everyday life or for science itself. Local or micro-site decompositions and laws can generate statements of wide (macro-) applicability due to isomorphisms and couplings between RE and RI. There are no supernatural or transcendental realms or beings

> *How* the world is, is completely indifferent
> for what is higher. God does not reveal
> himself in the world.
>   WITTGENSTEIN, 1922:187

- Science (the organized form of human reasoning): The reasoning, methods, and logics of the sciences are our only ways of accessing reality. Revelation is eschewed as a source of knowledge (myth of individualism, fallacy of introspective transparency).
- Person (Human Beings): There is no "individual" in any traditional or common-sense terms. The person is a social network, the weighted sum of all of the networked systems h/er life has unfolded through. This follows from the fact that humans arrive on the evolutionary stage always, already, and

everywhere social. Culture individuates us without erasing our social selves. Humans do not have souls or any non-material "parts" that survive their death. Humans are born, they live, and they die. They do not have free will. The more complex the society, the more open it is as a system, the greater is the illusion of free will. Our lives are variously subject to determinism but always lawful. It is more accurate to speak here in terms of unwilled agency. Technically the person unfolds through social networks as a center or the locus of the stream of affordances and the stream of consciousness as revealed in the stream of practices. That is, the world is an arena of opportunities (streams of affordances) we work our way through from birth to death (streams of practices); we experience this world of opportunities as objects of consciousness (streams of consciousness). All of our behaviors, thoughts, and emotions are activated at the intersection of streams of affordances, streams of practices, and streams of consciousness. So to take a particular behavior, practice, or performance, say gender, we do not choose our gender nor is our gender given genetically or neurologically. We are gendered by the particular forces operating at the locus of the streams of affordances, consciousness, and practices. I'm not fully satisfied with this formulation but it represents the direction of my thinking in terms of the walls of our imprisonment we are imbedded in, each serially with more degrees of freedom from the physical (fewest degrees of freedom) to the biological and chemical, to the social (highest level of degrees of freedom). Sex is also channeled through these walls of imprisonment and is intimately intertwined in a dance with gender. Per Einstein, if this is any good it's a good joke you can only tell once.

- Humanity: Human beings are a product of blind evolution, the outcome of natural processes of tinkering and accidents. They are always, already, and everywhere social, the latest manifestation of evolution's invention of the social as an adaptive mechanism.

- History: The cumulative experience of humankind, local, regional, and global that locates the contexts and causes shaping our individual and collective lives and cultures. History unfolds for us out of invisible and foggy bits of information in the distant past into increasingly but always problematic vistas of more and less clear events and processes.

- Future: In secular perspective, the future is the unfolding of the confluence of RE social, biological, physical, and chemical causes in the context of RI (staying with the core sciences as a simplifying assumption) without incorporating any supernatural or transcendental realities or causes (no "end times," no "afterlife," no "return of the messiah," etc.).

- Ethics, morals, and values (ethos): the crystallizations of rules of behavior that solidify as part of the formation of societies and cultures; opposed to traditional, religious, and spiritual considerations, values are based on realistic, scientifically established features of human beings as parts of the natural order. They manifest reason rather than supernatural revelations and guidance.
- Plight: strangers in a strange world trying to survive and make sense of being alive using the basic mechanisms of reason that coalesce into science broadly conceived.
- Solution: The objective of a secular moral order is not to promote a perfect global society, not to aim for goals out of reach of real humans in the real world. The goal of a secular moral order is to do the best we can to promote the health and well-being of human populations and the planet, and of course each other (the golden rule). Embrace the profundity of the surface, the reality of everyday life with its more or less predictable, recurrent features. Recognize that it is a portal to the complexities of quantum, relativistic, and cosmological realities at the border of Reality-in-itself, but that these realities are the proper domain of specialists in the physical and natural sciences. They may discover things that have implications for technologies and practices in the everyday world, but their domain is not one lay men and women travel. Whatever their physics and mathematics reveals it will not reveal transcendent, supernatural realms and beings, or miracles; it will not offer support for the illusions and delusions that give you hope, drive your wishes, and nourish your faiths and beliefs. If you want to be happy, believe, and have faith. Embracing reality is then not your path. If you want to be authentic and to learn what can be learned about life, the universe and everything inquire with the profundity of the surface as your guide. Look both ways when you cross the street. And remember that the profundity of the surface is not the end of inquiry but a portal to other aspects of reality.
- Society and Culture. We know from comparative anthropological, historical, and evolutionary studies that our contemporary norms, values, beliefs, and social structures do not define an essential human nature. If we seem to be brutal, warlike, greedy, selfish, divorced from the requirements for ecologically healthy environments and our own health and well-being, indifferent to social inequalities and social injustices, and capable of catastrophic acts of genocide it is not because that is our "nature." It is because our societies have evolved in ways that program us for those particular characteristics. There is a case to be made for the fact that most of the humans who have ever been born and lived have done so in what we would recognize

today as communist or anarchist social orders. Humans arrive on the evolutionary stage always, already, and everywhere social, expressing the evolutionary imperative of the cooperative principle revealed in the writings of Kropotkin and Darwin.

9   The Anarchist Imagination

The issue before us is what if anything can we do in our time and place to protect humanity and the planet from destruction, deterioration, and decline into further chaos. We want to protect and sustain humanity and the planet in ways that recognize the value of quality and creativity in the lives of individuals, promote social equality and social justice, and create the conditions for the safe pursuit of freedom, liberty, and happiness. Is it possible to make this a practical goal? I am pessimistic about realizing the higher objectives I am concerned with. I'm also persuaded that we need to move forward individually and collectively with a problem solving orientation. I am further persuaded that this should be done within an anarchist framework. How should we proceed?

Assume that the problem of saving contemporary humanity and the planet has a solution or solutions. Assume that the solution space is diffuse and diversified and that our problems, if they can be solved, can be solved with different levels of completeness. Assume that it is unlikely we will come close to reconstructing the world in terms of the best conditions we can imagine, but that we can approach those conditions as a limit. Then what sorts of goals should we begin working towards in this moment at all levels of society?

Within an anarchist framework, we are not going to begin this movement under the banner of absolute truths or a single vision. We are going to move forward guided by general principles and goals recommended by our best sciences. We are going to expect cooperative conflict and dialogue among ourselves and others in pursuit of competing visions. Our goal is not to coerce everyone into one view of freedom and liberty but to follow what we imagine to be our best paths to the best possible world we can work toward moment to moment. If this sounds a little fuzzy, it is by design. It's a reminder that specific proposals for social change within the anarchist framework are always going to be instilled with a spirit of dialectics, dialogue, and dynamics. We will be firm and determined in what we know but flexible and open to diversions. We will set out on a clearly defined path prepared to follow or create new paths along the way. If time is of the essence, that may be our downfall; but we cannot under any circumstances pursue a path of dictatorship, benign or otherwise.

Being open-ended does not mean we need to move forward completely clueless. If you fear anarchism, are critical of anarchism, or find it a utopian dream, then it's time to have a wider look around. Are there social realities that can add substance to our anarchist imagination? How can we believe this when in the best of times the poor are always with us, when gender wars which come and go have emerged anew with new complexities? The world stage on which I am writing is a show case for racism, sexism, genocide, and terrorism. There are wars around every corner, ecological crises, economies always seemingly on the brink of disaster and unable to provide health care, basic housing, safety except in isolated nations, states, cities, and communities? American exceptionalism has not met the reality test; societies that do better than America are not all equal in their potential for continuing success let alone growth. Is there any way to demonstrate the viability of anarchism?

10   Conclusion: Anarchism in the Real World

Let's begin by considering what the early American feminists (including Elizabeth Stanton, Matilda Gage, Lucretia Mott, and others) were able to learn about anarchist values like freedom, the politics of the self, control over their own bodies and properties, and societies with justice for all from native American societies that knew little of rape and domestic violence. I've already alluded to the fact that anthropologists have informed us that anarchism is characteristic of much of human history. Within the historical arena of our modern orbit, we have many examples of anarchist communities springing up and failing to survive because they emerged within the web of capitalist political economies: the Makhno anarcho-communist experimental Ukrainian communities in the wake of the 1917 revolution; the decentralized collectivist experimental communities during the Spanish Civil War; and then numerous anarchist intentional communities that were part of the American social landscape from the 1800s until the 1960s. There are many other resources to consult on the non-utopian nature of anarchism. Our very humanity in its evolutionary origins is arguably anarchistic. The anarchism I defend is humanist, secular, and scientific. I continue this discussion in the following chapter.

Anarchism: No Gods, No Masters

Humanism: Do no harm; practice good works

Secularism: Religion is real in social material terms; God is real in cultural symbolic terms.

Science: Reality is real and we can know it collectively over historical time

CHAPTER 13

Anarchism, Properly Understood

> way down deep and systematically, I'm a goddamned anarchist.
>
> C. WRIGHT MILLS (2000: 232)

∴

1   Anarchism Redux

Anarchism, properly understood, does not mean the absence of organization but the absence of States and Authority. My objective here is not to give a detailed picture of the nature of anarchist society but rather to provide a general sense of what it entails organizationally. Readers can consult the bibliography on anarchism and social order in the References section for more detailed explanations of the anarchist agenda and its anthropological roots.

To begin, it is important to connect this chapter with the early themes focused on in the first chapters, that is, a critical realistic approach to science, truth, and objectivity. Science is best pursued in anarchist social formations, and it is at its best anarchistically organized (Restivo, 2011). Free Inquiry should always be subordinated to the Free Person in the Free Society (see Feyerabend, 1978). "Free" never means "free" literally but has to be understood in the context of a society in which individuals are not literally coerced to behave and think in specific ways by persons who possess power over them. In the current context, Free Inquiry, the Free Person, and the Free Society form an interrelated mutually reinforcing web of freedoms. These freedoms are political, not neuronal or genetic. Our objective as anarchists is to practice and promote unfettered inquiry unimpeded or driven by Dogma, Authority, or narrowly defined Social Interests.

The anarchist tradition stresses the need to separate inquiry from all forms of unbridled power and Authority:

> [Anarchism] is calculated to induce us to lament, not the apathy and indifference but the inauspicious activity of government. It incites us to look for the moral improvement of the species, not in the multiplying of regulations, but in their repeal. It teaches us that truth and virtue, like

commerce, will then flourish most, when least subjected to the mistaken guardianship of authority and laws. This maxim will rise upon us in its importance, in proportion as we connect it with the numerous departments of political justice in which it will be found to have relation. As fast as it shall be adopted into the practice of mankind, it may be expected to deliver us from a weight, intolerable to mind, and, in the highest degree, hostile to the progress of truth.

GODWIN, 1793/1971: 225–226

In terms of science, truth, and objectivity my preference for anarchistic social formations is based on their capacity for de-capitalizing "Science," "Truth," and "Objectivity," to give free rein to skepticism. The very idea of "Truth," Nietzsche observed, is "conclusive proof that not so much as a start has been made on that disciplining of the intellect and self-overcoming necessary for the discovery of any truth, even the very smallest." Truth in this sense is the province of the "man of conviction:"

> *Not* to see many things, not to be impartial in anything, to be a party through and through, to view all values from a strict and necessary perspective–This alone is the condition under which such a man exists at all. But he is thereby the antithesis, the *antagonist* of the truthful man–of truth.
>
> NIETZSCHE, 1889–1895/1968: 171–173

Nietzsche is divorced from the sociology of truth because he is so opposed to the "collective," the "herd." But if we can abide the contradiction, there is something to be learned here.

Here I introduce the thesis that "nothing matters." This is, like Feyerabend's "anything goes," a slogan of resistance to established Authority and not an invitation to value-free, undisciplined inquiry. A pervasive critical skepticism (as opposed to an irrational unbridled skepticism) that allows for knowledge unencumbered by absolute Truth or absolute Conviction is by definition a feature of anarchistic social formations and to a lesser extent democratic ones. Social Interests lose their potency as barriers to critical skeptical inquiry in anarchistic social formations which do not harbor antagonistic, competitive social interests.

What's wrong with States and Authority? States are the foundations of preparing for and waging wars. They underwrite the laws that create and support social inequalities and social injustices. You should be worried about the State's bombs, bombs your taxes pay for, not the cartoon bombs thrown by cartoon anarchists. States are the guardians of the wealthy and powerful, charged with protecting their interests over the interests of the "have nots." What makes this possible is the shared values of rulers and ruled in the principled legitimacy of Authority, hierarchy, and power. This political principle is opposed by the social principles of the anarchists. We can trace their modern roots to Peter Kropotkin's principle of mutual aid, a sociologically grounded idea that reflects the ascendancy of the cooperative principle in evolution. Traditionally, it is taken for granted that it is natural for us to be born into societies which force us into the existing state of things, from language to the state's rights over our bodies (for example, the state's right to impress us into military service). It is taken for granted that our lives should be run "from above." Anarchists, by contrast, champion a society of voluntary relationships.

This is tricky. Some anarchists understand by "voluntary association" an organizational form in which membership is not mandatory. This is not realistic. We are born into social situations we cannot choose beforehand, so we need a more realistic concept of voluntary. Anarchist societies should be designed to give individuals and communities as much autonomy as possible given the need for a certain degree of structure and certainty in any viable society.

> As individuals, as a culture and as a society, we have increasingly emphasized the metaphorical global village over the village in which we actually live. ... our preference for the far away at the expense of what is close to home is at the heart of the environmental and social catastrophes that we will soon be forced to confront, wherever we live and whatever our circumstances.
>
> DENTON (2016: 125)

Denton is one of our contemporary advocates for the "live close to home" worldview. When I was starting out as a newly minted assistant professor, the most visible advocate of this worldview was E.F. Schumacher (1973) in *Small is Beautiful*. The basic concepts of living small and without a coercive overriding Authority common to anarchist paradigms was already abroad in the ancient world. Without putting too fine a point on it we can identify precursors of "small is beautiful" and resistance to Authority, especially State Authority, in China among the Taoists, in Greece among the Cynics and Stoics, in medieval Asia in the writings of Mazdak and the theological anarchism of the Mu'tazillite ascetics and Naidiyya Kharijites, in Medieval Europe among the Hussites, Adamites, and Anabaptists, and in the utopian philosophies that emerged during and after the Renaissance. The words anarchia and anarchos already appear in Homer's *Iliad* and Herodotus's *Histories*.

The first clear expressions of anarchism appear in the works of William Godwin and notably for the present context Peter Kropotkin's (1902/1976) *Mutual Aid.* For a review of the anthropology of anarchy, see Barclay (1990). The quality of and sheer quantity of data on early human settlements makes it hard to assess the evidence for primitive anarchism or communism. Theoretically, it seems plausible to assume that survival in relatively small "hunter gatherer" or "gatherer hunter" societies was dependent on some level of societal equality, equal justice, and communal living. We shall have to move on without feeling confident that these societies unequivocally established social forms we can draw on for our inspiration.

Bakunin declared "Machiavelli was right" when he claimed that "... what is permitted to the State is forbidden to the individual," but Bakunin developed an anarchism that questioned the legitimacy of political systems rooted in questions of ethics and political justice. In this way, Bakunin's anarchism was a departure from the Machiavellianism he had initially adopted (McLaughlin, 2007: 101–116).

For examples of how this might work in practice we can turn to small-scale societies such as hunter-gatherer societies. And this reveals a key ingredient of the anarchist agenda; an anarchist society must be organized around relatively small-scale, relatively autonomous communities. I noted earlier that the anthropological model for such a community is the band. Communities should to the greatest extent possible produce the resources to satisfy basic needs locally. Inevitably, resources like electrical power are more efficiently organized across community networks. The anarchists Proudhon and Kropotkin advocated federations.

Anarchist organizations should be voluntary in principle, not organized via dogmatic proclamations. They should be organized around the principle of permanent revolution to avoid bureaucratic stagnation and the iron law of oligarchy. They should be in flux, in becoming, but not so fluid that they become anemic and amoebic. Education should be lifelong, not confined to specific institutions; but schools are not excluded. Education should be devoted to creating an informed and active citizenry not patriots, nationalists, or gullible know-nothings easily manipulated by political and media bullies and con artists.

Some anarchists would like to eliminate all large-scale forms and functions. Better to say: Let us find ways in which the large-scale functions can be broken down into functions capable of being organized by small functional groups and then link these groups in a federal manner. The classical anarchist thinkers, envisaging the future organization of society, thought in terms of two kinds of social institutions: the territorial unit or commune, and the syndicate or workers' council. Commune is a French word which is the equivalent of the word 'parish' or the Russian word 'soviet' in its original meaning, but which also has overtones of the ancient village institutions for cultivating the land in common. Syndicate, another French word from trade union terminology, is the basic unit of industrial organization. Commune and syndicate were envisaged as small local units which would federate with each other for the larger affairs of life, while retaining their own autonomy, the one federating territorially and the other industrially.

The federal principle, which is at the heart of anarchist social theory, is worth much more attention than it is given in the textbooks on political science. Even in the context of ordinary political institutions its adoption has a far-reaching effect. Another anarchist theory of organization is what we might call the theory of spontaneous order: given a common need, a collection of people will, by trial and error, by improvisation and experiment, evolve order out of chaos – this order being more durable and more closely related to their needs than any kind of externally imposed order. Kropotkin derived this theory from observations of the history of human society and of social biology which led to his book *Mutual Aid*. It has been observed in most revolutionary situations, in the *ad hoc* organizations which spring up after natural catastrophes, or in any activity where there is no existing organizational form or hierarchical authority. This concept was given the name *Social Control* in the book of that title by Edward Allsworth Ross (1901), who cited instances of "frontier" societies where, through unorganized or informal measures, order is effectively maintained without benefit of constituted authority. Interesting examples of this phenomenon include the Pioneer Health Centre at Peckham, London founded by Drs. Scott Williamson and Innes Hope Pearse, and Aichhorn's (1925/1935) experiment with self-governing non-punitive communities of wayward children described in the book *Wayward Youth*.

Anarchism adopts a floating concept of leadership. Sometimes I direct, sometimes you direct; it all depends on our skills and circumstances. This occurs in the context of a voluntary mutuality as opposed to leadership imposed from above and based on power relationships. Leadership should flow, a concept opposed to hierarchical, authoritarian, privileged, and permanent leadership. Consider, for real world examples, Walter Gropius' concept of collaborative architecture, or the gang system worked out in Coventry UK (Melman, 1958). Melman cites examples to illustrate the distinction between "predatory competition" and mutuality in decision making by the "gang," the group of workers themselves. Another example comes from a study of "composite working" among coal miners in Durham UK (Trist, Higgins, et al., 2016; Herbst, 1962). Anarchism proposes that order can be brought to a system of autonomous work groups by drawing once more on the principle of federation. Anarchists can ground their thinking on autonomy and spontaneity in theories of deinstitutionalization and cybernetic theories of self-organizing systems. A sociologically coherent anarchist theory of social organization can be constructed on the foundations of autonomous work groups, spontaneous order, workplace democracy, and the federation principle.

2   Social Anarchism

Social anarchism would be a transparent oxymoron were it not for the existence of varieties of anarchism that emphasize individualism, individual will, the free market or libertarian socialism, and some forms of anarcho-communism. Historically, individualist and social anarchism can be found knotted up and acting on each other, revealing their tensions in the works of anarchist champions such as William Godwin, Josiah Warren, and notably Max Stirner and Benjamin Tucker. The "social-individualist" distinction turns on whether free people will enter into voluntary associations with each other or prefer to live in isolation. This distinction dissolves once we realize that we are children of the cooperative principle in evolution. On the varieties and traditions of individualist anarchism, see Freeden (1998).

Social anarchism is compatible with the radically social nature of human beings, a species, as we've seen, that arrives on the evolutionary stage always, already, and everywhere social. Individuality is a product of culture, not evolution. The social anarchist's commitment to "community" as the context for supporting individual growth, freedom, and creativity is consistent with sociological and evolutionary realities. Kropotkin is the locus classicus for this conception of anarchism. It does not raise the community above the individual but makes the community the context for every effort to advance the individual. Of all its possible associations, its association with mutualism is the one I advocate. This also allows its easy integration into the secular humanist worldview.

The industrial revolution of the 1800s knotted various streams of economic organization that had crystallized beginning as early as the 13–1400s in Europe with the result that the mutual exploitation of humans by humans reached new heights compared to all prior human history. One of the turning points in our contemporary awareness of the limits of this mutual exploitation came with the publication of Rachel Carson's (1962/2002) *Silent Spring*. If anarchism comes down to "no Gods, no Masters," and humanism comes down to "do no harm, do good," and if anarchism and humanism are compatible with secularism – no Gods, no transcendental, supernatural, or spiritual realities – then anarchism fits easily into the secular humanist worldview.

3   Coda

You don't have to be a strict Marxist to recognize that history is a narrative of classes, conflicts, and contradictions (Collins, 1975). Marxists, however, have been in the vanguard of theorists proposing ways to resolve these contradictions. One such theory was built into the 1975 Preamble of the Constitution of the People's Republic of China:

> These contradictions can be resolved only by depending on the theory of continued revolution under the dictatorship of the proletariat and on practice under its guidance.

On the one hand this sounds like a standard piece of ideological propaganda indicated by the phrase "Marxism-Leninism-Mao Tse Tung Thought" (page 8 of the preamble). On the other hand it seems to echo Jefferson's remarks on rebellion refreshing the tree of liberty. A rational theory of continuous revolution should guide the anarchist society, although it would be haunted by French writer Jean-Baptiste Alphonse Karr 's (1849) oft quoted remark, "plus ça change, plus c'est la même chose" – the more things change, the more they stay the same.

> COUNTER POINT: "So the more things remained the same, the more they changed after all. Nothing endures. Not love, not a tree, not even a death by violence" John Knowles (2003: 7). For example:
> (1)   Body Temperature: 98.6? Not so fast. Body temperature is individual; it varies according to age, sex, height, weight and other factors, and fluctuates throughout the day (Ley, Heath, et al., 2023).
> (2)   There are nine planets in our solar system? Not so fast. In August 2006 the International Astronomical Union downgraded the status of Pluto to that of "dwarf planet" (Tyson, 2009).
> (3)   Snowflakes Are Not as Unique as We Thought (Kennell, 2015).
> (4)   Groundbreaking Study Reveals Your Fingerprints Aren't as Unique as We Thought (Starr, 2024).

4   Conclusion: Once Again, What Is to Be Done?

How do we get from here – today's world of existential threats at all levels – to a society organized around the anarchistic sociological imagination? It seems like – and may indeed be – an impossible task. We can, of course, try to build on the models of relatively well-functioning global networks – the airline industry for example, or certain mutual defense networks, or the European Union. Vijayendra (2022) has proposed achieving this by way of a Transition Towns movement (Hopkins, 2014; Thomas, 2018). Krznaric (2024) argues that history is a reservoir of lessons in how to manage crises and leverage the instabilities of contemporary existential threats.

The world is actually already an arena for hundreds of intentional anarchist, permacultural communities. India has long been a nation of such experiments, from alternative energy movements beginning as early as the 1960s to self-managed communities in our own era. Such experimental communities can be found in the Mexican state of Chiapas, the Syrian autonomous region of Rojava, and the eco-villages of Russia. These movements are fragile and opposed by a robust "fourth industrial revolution" being pursued by the ruling classes. All we can know for certain in this moment is that we are at a crossroads, one way leading to death by existential threat, the other to at least a brief reprieve from our ultimate extinction.

PART 4

Paradigm for Transition

∵

CHAPTER 14

What Is Real, after All?

"We humans," writes Glen Crouch (2024), "have an odd penchant for catastrophizing our species and our world. ... we also like to tell stories about a coming, possible utopia and lots of stories about a coming dystopia, or that we're already in a dystopia. We aren't. Of more recent times, there is talk of a techtopia. These topics make for some interesting memes, debates, movies, books and so on. None of them will come to be." Have I been catastrophizing in this book? Are we living through a mere episode or is there something truly different about our era that escapes earlier cries of "catastrophe" and announcements about the arrival of dystopic times? I don't think this is just another episode. The existential threats we face today are different by orders of magnitude from any we have faced in the human past. They are different in part because of the global populations and planetary ecologies that are at risk. And they are different enough, they are dystopic enough, to have provoked anti-natalist movements that go beyond mere philosophies about the worthlessness of life that were already abroad in ancient times.

The world we live in is ablaze with wars in the Middle East, in the Ukraine, and elsewhere; border and territorial disputes threaten local and worldwide conflicts in the Near and Far East. The TV shows we watch are interrupted all day and all night by ads featuring horrible illnesses and diseases that promote drugs with terrifying side effects. The news accosts us from all directions with stories of melting ice bergs, ocean currents gone awry, pollution, plastic in our water and in our bodies, climate change, the lack of compassion in our governments and their failure to protect the disempowered, global corporations lying to protect their profits at the cost of human lives and ecological damage, threats to non-normative life styles and to decision-makers we don't like. Trump's rants take up all the air in the room while like the Teflon Don he avoids prison. The Supreme Court mocks public desires. Fragile democracies across the world are threatened by authoritarian leaders and populations itching for dictatorships and theocracies. How can we possibly hope to solve existential threats in this context? I've introduced some more or less plausible ways we might achieve this. But their plausibility is weak in an age of alternative facts, post-truthism, anti-science and conspiracy theories. Should we join the anti-natalists? Should we escape into our own shells of immediate pleasures and distractions aided by drugs and alcohol? Is there a rational choice we can make in the face of the overwhelming odds against saving humanity and the world?

There is no reckoning with our capacity to procreate knowing that the lives we bring into the world will in the best of cases sooner or later suffer and die. Biology, physics, chemistry, evolution, and society are the walls of our imprisonment. Why shouldn't we try to escape?

1   A Reiteration

In the epigraphs that introduced Chapter 2, we read Goethe's observation that "Few people have the imagination for reality;" and T.S. Eliot's observation that "Humankind cannot bear very much reality." I also introduced "delulu," the idea that our thoughts can attract a specific desired reality, delulu is mostly about seeing life through a rose-tinted, excessively romanticized lens: "Nothing good ever comes from thinking realistically," says a TikTok business coach and dedicated delulu spreader. "You need to think that you are the baddest bitch and everyone is obsessed with you. If you think they're obsessed with you, they are."

> The world is everything that is the case.
> L. WITTGENSTEIN

> Reality is all that there is.
> S. RESTIVO

> APHORISM: No one will ever figure out why there is anything at all. As for the rest of it, it's cosmic accidents all the way down.
> S. RESTIVO

2   Reality Redux 2

A secular humanist anarchist society (SHAS), like any society, has to provide a context for a culture, a system of humans interacting with each other and their environments to produce and sustain a viable system of artifacts (technology), socifacts (social organizations and institutions), mentifacts (ideas and concepts), emotifacts (feelings, emotions), and ethifacts (values, ethics, and morals). I expand by two – emotifacts and ethifacts – the cultural categories introduced by Bidney (1953). Like any society, SHAS would have to deal with the common good in terms of providing responses to, using a simple decomposition, the seven life (organic) forces, the five inorganic forces, and the three general forces. The seven organic forces are: Respric (respiration, breath),

Nutric (food, nutrition), Bevric (fluids, drinks), Thermic (temperature control), Dormic (sleep, rest, recovery), Excric (excretion), and Eroic (the sensual, the sexual, reproduction, pleasure). The five inorganic forces are: Gravic (gravity), Atomic (atomic), Chemic (chemical), Electric (electricity), and Magnic (magnetism). The three general forces are Transic (movement), Zonic (space), and Horic (time). Together these forces are called the "Prime Inceptors." They are universal and invariant. These terms (with my "Eroic" added) were introduced during the 1950s and 1960s by the anthropologists Burt and Ethel Aginsky (Aginsky and Aginsky, 1978: 63ff).

All human cultures must contend with the prime inceptors for self-perpetuation. For the greater part of human history cultures have dealt with the prime inceptors in ways that have led to territoriality, greed, enmities, aggression, and warfare. We are at an inception point; everything that has gone before has led to a humanity and a planetary ecology in danger from a multiplicity of converging existential threats. I have outlined a possible way to move forward. In this final chapter I argue for grounding SHAS in the Eroic force, making society more responsive to the significance of sensual and sexual behavior as forces that can mitigate fractures in the social fabric that can lead to aggression and violence. One could argue that there is an eighth force, Waric (warfare, aggression, violence, conflict). If this is an eighth force, then it is a force, that is not necessary to the self perpetuation of the species or any given society. In that sense it is a weak force whose power exceeds that of stronger forces in society. The cooperative principle in evolution and the radical social nature of humanity mean that it is possible in principle to live without random out of control conflicts. The Eroic force will have to be given its due and more if we are going to build a sustainable world from this point on.

INTERVENTION: I get my health care through the OneMed health care service. They send out occasional memos to members on health matters. Today they sent one out on: *HUMAN TOUCH CAN IMPROVE YOUR HEALTH:* "Marvin Gaye said it best, Sexual healing is something that's good for me. And he was right: Physical touch can make you happier, lower blood pressure, lessen anxiety, and even boost immunity. So whether you're getting up close and personal with your summer crush or just hugging friends and family, remember that human interaction and touch are important – and good for your health." I noted earlier that because we are the most radically social of the social species, touch is more important in social life than we have realized. Damming it up is a major cause of violence, from the everyday violence of bullying, mugging, and spousal assaults to terrorism and even war. There was more to our 1960s slogan of MAKE LOVE NOT WAR than may be at first apparent. What if the relationship in the slogan is causal? MORE LOVE LESS WAR. Sound too romantic, too idealistic for you? Maybe a little anthropological science will help: see Montagu, 1972.

3   The Garden of Epicurus

In 307/306 BCE the Athenian philosopher Epicurus bought a house with a garden just outside Athens along the road from the Dipylon gate to the Academy (Cicero, *De Finibus* 5.1.3). Other great founders of philosophical schools had chosen public areas for their teaching: Plato established his school near the Academy, Isocrates and Aristotle taught in the Lyceum, Zeno often met his students in the Stoa Poecile. In contrast, Epicurus' hedonistic and materialistic philosophy flourished and grew amidst the privately owned groves of his Garden. The Garden itself – apart from the city, a private space, and pleasurable – became a symbol for the detachment and hedonism of the Epicurean school. Nothing of the Garden's layout is known, but its closeness to the canalized Eridanus River must have provided plentiful water for irrigation of its trees and plants. After Epicurus' death the Garden was passed down to his followers (Diogenes Laertius, 10.10 and 10.17). We may imagine that Epicureans seeking relief from the disturbances of the city gathered in the Garden's groves for many centuries (Morison, n.d.; Furley, 1996; Wycherley, 1978/2016).

We cannot seek relief from the world as it is, from its disturbances. Perhaps those of us who are not prepared to give up our lives could retreat into a life characterized by some form of hedonism giving ourselves up to the Eroic force. Is there some way this could actually contribute to mitigating the existential threats we face? Could this be part of localizing anarchistic actions that might spontaneously self-organize, federate and globalize? Frankly, I have no idea if or how this might work. But if having more fun isn't a solution, perhaps it's a way to weather the storms surely coming our way. Let's explore a bit.

4   Realistic, Not Rational, Hedonism

I am not envisioning a society in which people do nothing but engage in sensual and sexual pleasures. SHAS will have industry, but on a smaller scale than in the industrial age, locally rooted for the most part, and greener than we have now. We have to pull back from concretizing the green environment that sustains life. Realistic hedonism is not designed to give the Eroic force dominance, but rather to give it a more prominent, a more central role in our everyday lives. What has brought me to this point?

Think about it. We are drawn almost magically and unceremoniously out of a void and thrown into a life we didn't choose, into circumstances we didn't choose. And after a lifetime that could end in the womb or in as many as 100 years we are unceremoniously tossed back into the void. To have lived and died is essentially to have never lived at all.

And what a life! Violence is everywhere, waiting to take us indiscriminately at any moment either by way of biology, accident, planetary violence, or human aggression. We have a radical politics because the world is awash in fear and theft, a hunger for gold that surpasses our thirst for milk, and a commitment to inventing, making, and storing weapons of all sorts while creating havoc by deploying and using only a minor fraction of what we produce. We suppress sex across all our institutions, even to the extent of trapping the need for touching in the most restrictive taboos, while we flood the world with violence in our media because apparently we don't get enough of it in our everyday lives. This is the real world I have lived in and in which I have become associated with a radical agenda designed to make the world a better, a more humane, a more compassionate experience for humanity. That reality demonstrates that the radical activities of generations of communists, socialists, and anarchists have not made a difference on the scale of society.

I am grateful for the fact that of all the kinds of human beings I could have become I became a learner and an educator. I did something good in a world mired in evil. And this book is a continuation of that life of learning and educating in a new context, one which has seen the emergence of an anti-natalist movement (de Girard, 2006; Lochmanová, 2020).

Better a hundred times not be born;
But if we must see the light,
The least harm is still to return
Where you come from, and the sooner the better!
Sophocles (d. 406/405BCE)
Well-being is in heaven; But we are on earth,
Where all is but annoyance, worry, and grief.
William Shakespeare, Richard II. England, XVIth century.
Men must weep at their birth, and not at their death.
Montesquieu, Persian Letters. France, 18th century
Life is a burden to me, I desire death and I abhor existence.
Oh ! That I am never born!
J.W. von Goethe, Faust. Germany, 19th century
Nietzsche (1889/1968: 29) expressed this in terms of the "Problem of Socrates:"

> In every age the wisest have passed the identical judgement on life: it is worthless.

I have come more and more to see the sense in the anti-natalist movement. But I have been moved like others like me by a question that has haunted and motivated radicals since 1863: What is to be done?

5   What Is to Be Done?

Russian philosopher, journalist, and literary critic Nikolay Chernyshevsky's novel *What is to be Done?* (Что делать?, Chto delat, literally "What to do?") was published in 1863. The novel was written while Chernyshevsky was imprisoned in the Peter and Paul fortress in St. Petersburg. The novel is a platform for advocating industrial production in socialist cooperatives, a message designed to show Russian workers the way to socialism. Rakhmetov transcends his minor role in the story by embodying philosophical materialism, Russian radicalism, and a society characterized by an earthly "eternal joy." The book's title became a motif in radical literature from that time on, most notably in Lenin's *What is to be Done* (1902/2020). So now I ask again: What is to be done?

The bulk of this book has offered one three-fold answer: embrace reality, safeguard truth, protect the freedoms of science and reason. But we realists are obliged to consider another answer, one that might become in a sense a new radical politics, a transformation of our traditional response to "What is to be done?"

6   A Different Beginning

My approach to reality in this book has basically followed an engineering paradigm. If you want to achieve A what do you have do and do you have options to choose from? For example, if you want to build a bridge across the East River in New York City, there are a variety of designs you can examine that might work, such as arch bridges, beam bridges, or suspension bridges. The existing bridges tell you what designs work. In New York City, the Brooklyn Bridge is a cable-stayed/suspension bridge; the Manhattan and the Williamsburg Bridges are suspension bridges; the Queensboro Bridge is a cantilever bridge. If all you had on hand was thousands and thousands of toothpicks and an enormous amount of Elmer's glue, you could not build a bridge across the East River. You need a bridge design, the relevant materials, and trained crafts people, skilled workers. This is the reality test that tells us how to achieve building a bridge across the East River. There is always the possibility of a creative leap to a new design, but toothpicks and glue will never work.

This book has been about how to meet the dangers of existential threats and address the general plights that face humanity, the planet, and individual human beings. Relying on theological and narrowly scientific worldviews would be more fruitful than using toothpicks and glue to build a bridge but just as futile in the end. The secular worldview cannot guarantee a full-fledged solution, but not applying it means we will definitely fail. Exercise cannot guarantee that you won't die young or won't develop dementia; but it's your best bet to a long healthy mentally alert life.

Reality won't tolerate any and all lifestyles if the goal is to maximize the lifespans of humanity and the planet in ways that support and sustain quality lifestyles and reasonable life chances. But given how short and often brutal our lives are, and given how terrifying and mysterious it all is, the alternative to trying to do something about existential and everyday threats is to just have as much fun as you can for as long as you can, and in the extreme perhaps support the anti-natalism movement. My own life has been a contradiction of tensions between living hedonistically and writing and acting in support of survival with quality, improving our life chances, and choosing life and planetary sustaining lifestyles. Is hedonism in the face of the real world's nature and demands a reasonable lifestyle choice?

I have defended a pluralistic, open ended, science-in-becoming perspective on reality, but someone like William Blake might object to my radical disenchantment: "Art," he wrote, "is the Tree of Life, Science is the Tree of Death." I acknowledge objections to radical disenchantment but stand by my concerns about the dangers of being awed.

7   Intervention: The Problem of Meaning

In the midst of all the chaos and terror that is our universe it is understandable that some people refuse to put up with it and take their own lives. There are even those who have dedicated themselves to bringing humanity to an end. The Voluntary Human Extinction Movement (VHEMT.org, founded in 1991) calls for universal abstinence in order to bring about the gradual voluntary end to the human race. Their goal is the prevention of environmental degradation. There is a related movement that seeks to end humanity on moral grounds. Anti-natalism is the view that humans should abstain from procreation on moral grounds. Already among the ancient Greeks we find examples of the argument that it would have been better not to be born. I am not unsympathetic to this movement. However, that is not the direction I am going to pursue. I want to consider whether those of us who choose to stay can find meaning in the middle of this firestorm of meaninglessness. This search is haunted by the myth of Sisyphus.

In the Greek myth, the gods punish Sisyphus for conning others and cheating death. Sisyphus' punishment is to roll a large boulder up a hill only to have it roll back every time it nears the top of the hill. So it's up the hill over and over for eternity. The myth is an allegory for human life which is laborious and futile. In his *The Myth of Sisyphus*, Camus (1991) writes that our deepest desire is for familiarity and clarity; but what the world offers us is unreason, senselessness, meaninglessness, and ultimately absurdity. The danger of focusing on the reality given to us by the profundity of the surface is that it constantly distracts us from the absurdity and the futility of it all. And this distraction gives rise to clichés: "everything happens for a reason;" "God (or the Universe) has a plan;" the dead go to a "better place" where they are "at peace;" "no door closes that another one opens;" "I was put here for a reason." For the reality of the profundity of the surface to work for us, for science to comfort us, we must, Camus concludes, learn how to laugh.

Meaning only exists in one place; among our friends and in our communities. It is still possible to find kindness, compassion, empathy, and a shared feeling of belonging here and now. Don't look up at the stars, that will only scare you into believing in heaven or being awed by your insignificance. A few rational ones will look up and not see the stars as "above" them. Don't look to leaders, especially political and theological ones. They will only lead you astray or scare you into apathy. Look around you. Find those who retain some of the cultural DNA of cooperative, kind, compassionate, loving humanity. Cultivate them. Live with them. Love them. It won't be easy to find or live with them. We all carry the sociopath virus of civilization. But love, compassion, and kindness can, *may*, stay the virus in its latent state. Love, be kind, be compassionate, show empathy. It will, *may*, sustain you in the midst of the doom that sits on the horizon, or looms next to you like your shadow. It will diminish the power of that doom and allow you to live, really live. I do not rely here on a romantic concept of love, but on love as a manifestation of the cooperative principle in evolution.

We want to know what it all means; what is the meaning of life? We find ourselves born into a world we do not choose, burdened with stress, anxiety, the need to find resources for survival, surrounded by the most horrible incidents of humans harming each other, spending precious resources on weapons of minor and mass destruction, confronted by nature's terrifying disregard for us, burying us in volcanic ash, destroying our towns with hurricanes and tornadoes and earthquakes, and in the end we die. The overwhelming proportion of humanity's creative energies and powers have been dedicated to and corrupted by violence and the myths of traditional religions and the gods. We have not endeared ourselves to each other or the very principles of life. We are prisoners of biology and evolution. We are inevitably ruled by, surveilled by, our fellow humans; controlled by too many rules and laws that do not benefit us but are enforced by others of our kind who control the means of violence.

If you are going to find meaning anywhere, it's going to be in your community, in your networks. And it is going to involve sex or more generally sensual pleasures. We haven't learned the first thing about sex. The first thing is that sex is everywhere all the time, like gravity (labelled "Sexity" as we saw earlier). In fact, it is the Eroic force that is everywhere. Until we learn this lesson, we will continue to make life miserable for humanity. Lesson number two is that sex, as a manifestation of the Eroic force, comes in many forms, is multidimensional, and more complex than anyone has yet imagined. Lesson number three is that sex exists for humans of all ages, keeping in mind that sex is a particularly focused form of sensuality. One must be sensual first. Lesson number four: touching is the alpha and omega of life. In an important sense, nothing else matters without it. Now what?

Are there sensual and sexual issues of consent and violence because we don't yet understand sex? Imagine a world in which movies, video games, and stories featured love, romance, sex in all of their consensual combinations and permutations and contained no violence, no guns, no mayhem. What would that say about that world? And what does it say about our world that this is not the case with us? Why shouldn't we pursue pleasure above profits, money, territory, above all else?

What about the problem of evil that is a central concern in the debates between atheists and theists? It should be clear by now that we don't need a God to identify and to struggle against evil. Furthermore, the problem of evil is not the problem of extreme evil represented by Genghis Kahn and Hitler, or by Manson and Bundy but rather the problem of mundane evil represented by the school-yard bully, the mugger, the spouse abuser, and emotional violence.

No one will ever figure out why there is anything at all. As for the rest, it is cosmic accidents all the way down. One can generate a curious but telling cognitive paradox by trying to imagine how much time passed before one was born (which is impossible) and then imagining how much time will pass after one dies (which is also impossible, but not in the same way). This shows that we know nothing about time. The paradox is that this exercise makes us feel as if we are on the threshold of perhaps the greatest discovery of all time (so to speak!) and, simultaneously, as if we are on the threshold of going mad. What makes sense to me is that there is no time for us before we are born, and no time passes for us after we die. It is interesting to note that just as some scientists claim there is no reality, some claim time is an illusion.

If we want to get philosophically serious about hedonism, we can explore the various types of hedonism: folk, value, prudential, motivational, normative, hedonistic egoism, and hedonistic utilitarianism. The bottom line, however, is to consider that hedonism identifies pleasure and pain as the earth, air, water, and fire of human behavior, its basic elements. Pleasure and pain are not just two important elements, they are the only elements that matter.

8   We Are Not Oysters

In the Platonic dialogue *Philebus*, Socrates and Protarchus discuss the virtues of a life without pleasure but one marked by consciousness and knowledge versus a life of pleasure without a mental life, a life like that of the oyster. But there can be no pleasure without consciousness; humans are not oysters.

9   Origins

Arguably the earliest record of hedonism occurs in the Barhaspatya sutras' Caravaka tradition in Indian philosophy (from ca. 600BCE). Right action brings pleasure and is worth pursuing even if sometimes accompanied by pain. Aristippus, a Socratic philosopher (ca. 435–356BCE), founded the Cyrenaics who argued that pleasure was the ultimate good. Their viewpoint can be captured in a Cartesian mode: corpus voluptas ergo sum. Epicurus (ca. 341–271BCE) argued for what is known as "normative hedonism." His goal was not so much the pursuit of pleasure as the avoidance of pain. This involves individuals following their own paths to happiness in ways that do not interfere with the paths of others. Some of the famous philosophers who supported hedonism include Bentham (1748–1832), J.S. Mill (1806–1873), and G.E. Moore (1873–1958). The basic argument against hedonism is that pleasure is not the only path to the good life. Living in the reality that is the subject of the greater part of this book can also define the good life, and one that is richer, more complex, and more diverse. Most of the contemporary arguments against hedonism, and prudential hedonism in particular (hedonism focused on well-being), rely on a simulation model such as Robert Nozick's "experience machine." This is like many philosophical arguments not sociologically credible; it is a thought experiment that has no substantial foundation in the social and cultural realities of being human.

10   Hedonism Then

I am not interested in hedonism in a general sense, that is, in a sense that encompasses pleasurable experiences in general. I want to focus on erotic pleasures. The reason is that we are surrounded by an erotic force (Eroic) in the same way that we are surrounded by a gravitational force. Why focus on the Eroic force?

Humans arrive on the evolutionary stage always, already, and everywhere social. Before their arrival the tinkering process of evolution had invented cooperation as an adaptive mechanism already with cellular cooperation. In humans, the cooperative principle was a mitigating force against violence and given the fundamental role of touching for survival, I find reason in the anthropological conjecture that early humans practiced community sex. I argue further that there is an inverse relationship between the scale and frequency of sensual and sexual activity across and within cultures and the scale and frequency of violence.

The standard model of early humans is expressed in the Flintstone paradigm of the nuclear family and the evolutionary biology of mating, marriage, and reproduction. One of the first wrenches thrown into the works of the standard model was Morgan's *Ancient Society* (1877). Morgan's study of the Iroquois revealed a hunter-gatherer society organized in large polyamorous (to use the modern term) family units. Engels (1884) drew on Morgan's work and comparative materials from around the world in developing his argument for "primitive communism." Polyamory and active (i.e., enforced) equality were widespread in the "Stone Age" ("fierce egalitarianism," Lee, 1988). Overlapping and intersecting sexual and other relationships meant stronger group cohesion and greater security in an uncertain world (Ryan and Jetha, 2010; and see Starkweather and Hames, 2012; Beckman and Valentine, 2002; Dyble,. Salali, et al., 2015).

11   The Transition

How do we get from here to there? There is some evidence that we have already or will soon reach one or more tipping points on the existential threats timelines. We may already be faced with a situation in which all we can realistically do is echo Voltaire: "Comptez que le monde est un grand naufrage, et que la devise des hommes est, sauve qui peut" (Voltaire, 1792). I find it difficult in the face of a realistic appraisal of our current situation to imagine that there is a path to an anarchistic world order in which people practice realistic hedonism. Are there any hopeful signs?

Biological evolution is a slow gradual process marked by episodes of punctuated equilibrium. That is, evolution occurs primarily through short bursts of intense speciation, followed by lengthy periods of stasis or equilibrium. Cultural evolution may also follow this pattern but with shorter periods of equilibrium. If that's the case, a "short burst of intense speciation" might produce a path to the anarchistic-hedonistic global order. Where would we look for evidence for such an imminent punctuation?

If we were able to take a bird's eye view of Europe during the 17th century, we would see "gentlemen scientists" working in homemade labs bubbling up in England and elsewhere. Their activities would seem harmless enough unless we looked forward to the 18th century and backward to the 15th century. Copernicus was born in 1473, Galileo in 1564, Kepler in 1571, and Newton in 1643. The scientific revolution occurred between 1543 and 1687 according to one standard periodization. Copernicus' *De revolutionibus orbium coelestium* (*On the Revolutions of the Heavenly Spheres*) was published in 1543 and Newton's *Principia* was published in 1687. The concept of a scientific revolution emerged in the period of the Enlightenment in the work of Jean-Sylvain Bailly (1736–1793; Cohen, 1976). So between 1450 and 1690, the old order of the universe inherited from the Greeks and Arabs was swept away and a new order of the universe was established. This could be viewed as a "short burst of intense speciation." Its emergence would not have been evident on viewing the Copernican era and the era of gentlemen science, but that "bubbling" rapidly became a revolution.

Suppose we take a bird's eye view of our planet's cultures looking back to the 1960s, focusing on the 2020s and looking with our futurist telescopes to the 2050s. Are there any signs of "bubblings" that might portend a revolution in the directions of an anarchistic-hedonistic society? There are indeed such signs though they are weak; the radicalism of the 1960s did not achieve all that it hoped for, but its achievements echo on in the continuing calls for social equality, social justice, and ecological sanity. In our own time we see here and there bubbles of polyamory, LGBTQIAPK actions, activities, and communities, renewed interest in and actions in support of women's reproductive, marital, and political rights, and increasing numbers of. "nones," the religiously unaffiliated. There is a powerful worldwide authoritarian wave of opposition to these developments but the very existence of the bubbles of anarchistic-hedonistic actions, activities, and communities offers some hope, however small, of an impending "short burst of intense speciation."

12   The Erotics of the Revolution

> You cannot buy the revolution. You cannot make the revolution. You can only be the revolution. It is in your spirit, or it is nowhere.
>
> It's always easier not to think for oneself. Find a nice safe hierarchy and settle in. Don't make changes, don't risk disapproval, don't upset your syndics. It's always easiest to let yourself be governed.
>
> URSULA LEGUIN (1974)

Those of us who are alive today may live to see our fellow humans and the planet die along with us; we may die natural, accidental, and self-inflicted deaths; or we may live long enough to see the beginnings of a resurrection, a new renaissance, a new enlightenment taking over humanity and the planet; or we may live to see those new beginnings crushed by waves of authoritarianism. A realistic appraisal of our situation does not bode well for our future. I have never looked at the world through rose colored glasses and I can't now. If you sympathize with my message, the answer to What is to be Done? is simply to do your best to behave anarchistically and hedonistically in your own lives. Maybe you will find yourself helping to fuel the new renaissance, the new enlightenment. If you do you can die knowing you did your best to live a good life, a life of love, compassion, and community. Anarchism has promoted ideas about sex and love that are compatible with a realistic hedonism.

Historically, the struggle for women's rights became paired with free love movements and a call for sexual freedom. Most of the prominent anarchists (Bakunin, Goldman, Warren, but notably not Proudhon) supported the fight for women's rights and opposed the patriarchy. Oscar Wilde (1891), in the wake of writing *The Soul of Man Under Socialism*, became disenchanted with authoritarian socialism and declared himself less a socialist and more something like an anarchist. He actively campaigned for homosexual emancipation with Mackay Carpenter and others. Anarchists were prominent in the movement for sexual liberation, and free love. The free love movement developed a strong presence in the Victorian era and sought to get the state and religion out of the business of regulating sexual, romantic, and marital relationships. The movement soon blossomed into a movement for full scale liberating social change. As the nineteenth century was left behind, the early twentieth century was witness to further developments in this movement. Greenwich Village in

New York became a center for feminist and socialist activities led by women like Edna St. Vincent Milay, Margaret Anderson, Emma Goldman and the "New Life Socialists" Edward Carpenter, Havelock Ellis, and Olive Shreiner.

These movements were largely led by individualist anarchists. Ernest. Lucien Juin-Armand (aka Émile Armand, 1872–1963) was one of the leaders of this movement. He advocated free love, naturism, and polyamory. His concept of "camaraderie amoreuse" (Manfedonia and Ronsin, 2000) proposed free association between anarchist individualists of different sexes and genders, one that could be freely annulled. He promoted standards of sexual hygiene to protect those so engaged from such risks as rejection, possessiveness, indifference, and prostitution (and see Armand, 1930/2009). Malatesta (1853–1932) says in *Love and Anarchy*, "Let's eliminate the exploitation of man by man, let's fight the brutal pretention of the male who thinks he owns the female, let's fight religious, social and sexual prejudice, let's expand education and then we will be happy with reason if there are no more evils than love. In any case, the ones with bad luck in love will procure themselves other pleasures, since it will not happen like today, when love and alcohol are the only consolations of the majority of humanity" Malatesta (1903–1905/1975: 63; trans. from the Spanish). And let's not forget Emma Goldman (1869–1940). Goldman demanded independence for women, their right to support and live for themselves, the right to love whomever and as many as they pleased. She demanded freedom for both sexes, "freedom of action, freedom in love and freedom in motherhood" (Wexler, 1984: 94). Goldman wrote (Falk, 2019: 102) "Free love? As if love is anything but free." Man can buy brains, subdue bodies, conquer whole nations but love cannot be bought, subdued, or conquered:

> Man has chained and fettered the spirit, but he has been utterly helpless before love. High on a throne with all the splendor and pomp his gold can command, man is yet poor and desolate, if love passes him by. ... If the world is ever to give birth to true companionship and oneness, not marriage, but love will be the parent.

And yet progressive ideas about sex and love are no guarantee that you will escape the turbulence of these activities in the context of a social order dominated by conservative views on these matters, as we can see from Goldman's letters (and notably those related to her relationship with Ben Reitman: Falk, 2019).

It is interesting to speculate on whether the attention to issues of diverse ways of doing sex and gender is a *fin de siècle* phenomenon, as suggested by Showalter (1990). Showalter writes about the 1880s and 1890s as an era of "sexual anarchy," challenges to conventional ideas about femininity and masculinity, and the invention of "feminism" and "homosexuality." There may indeed be some connection between the turbulence that accompanies the dawn of a new century and challenges to conventional norms, values, and beliefs. And yet, there is something deeper, darker, and more chaotic about our *fin de siècle* compared to the last one. "Free Love" in the anarchist sense is radically distinct from "sexual liberation as individualized non-stop self-gratification." History offers us many lessons and alternatives in erotic "codes [and] otherness of borders and boundaries" (Alexander, 2011: 40). Alexander (2011: 41) writes, in her appreciation for Alexander Berkman (1870–1936), that while he championed same-sex intimacy,

> he did not accord sex a significance over and above other physical and emotional expressions as the *only* "truth" of passion. He made a political commitment while inhabiting the borderland. In resisting the totalizing commodification of sex, and its perpetual, impossibly perfectible cash-cow copulating machinery, let us, in remembering what Alexander Berkman had to say about desire, rediscover the borderland.

In the wake of Foucault's call for a counter-productivity to resisting the disciplining of sexuality, Preciado (2000) produced a *contrasexual manifesto*. As I understand this, it is like Foucault's program, a mechanism, a technology of resistance and a platform for the voiceless. It opposes the taken-for-granted world of the binary homogeneity of bodies with the practice of de-heterosexualising. I understand this to be grounded in the reality of sexual activities around the world and across histories and cultures that demonstrate alternatives that put the lie to the "given naturalness" of heterosexual male and female bodies. Preciado dramatically represents this counter-discourse by "quoting the dildo:"

> The dildo is one among many organic and non-organic machines such as hands, whips, penises, chastity belts, condoms, and tongues. Therefore, "quoting the dildo" means implying the possibility of ceasing to assign the power of the phallus (the Law/Name of the Father) to an arbitrary organ. This arbitrary organ – the penis – then ceases to be the signifier of sexual/gender difference.
>
> ECKERT, 2011: 78

This takes thinking outside the box into an entirely new dimension of thinking, emotions, and practice. It offers us an erotic paradigm for confronting our global crises with new tools for survival. Free love, sexual freedom, a new erotic paradigm cannot be simply a matter of political efforts within the existing cultural framework. It must question that framework itself, break with the assumed to be untouchable institutions of marriage, the military, the state, the economy itself. Anarchists must tie their erotic paradigm to thinking analytically about social structures and producing new ones (Butler, 2011: 99). In the end, we are obliged to see the connection between love as an evolutionary mechanism, as a manifestation of the cooperative principle in evolution and the political economy of revolutionary action (cf. LeGuin, in Davis, 2011: 106):

> If anarchism is about changing relationships throughout life, then sex education could be just as much a focus of anarchist practice as G8 summits, poverty or climate change (inasmuch as any of these are really separate). ... What practices shift patterns in consciousness and in relationships, undermining domination, nurturing connection, in particular locations?
>
> HECKERT, 2011: 161

13   Doomerism?

Could the existential threat doom-sayers be wrong? Consider Bryan Walsh's (2023) defense of the necessity of progress:

> If I wanted to convince you of the reality of human progress, of the fact that we as a species have advanced materially, morally, and politically over our time on this planet, I could quote you chapter and verse from a thick stack of development statistics.
>
> I could tell you that a little more than 200 years ago, nearly half of all children born died before they reached their 15th birthday, and that today it's less than 5 percent globally.
>
> I could tell you that in pre-industrial times, starvation was a constant specter and life expectancy was in the 30s at best.
>
> I could tell you that at the dawn of the 19th century, barely more than one person in 10 was literate, while today that ratio has been nearly reversed. I could tell you that today is, on average, the best time to be alive in human history.

The problem for me is that it could indeed be the best time to be alive in human history for at least some segments of humanity, and yet I feel overwhelmed not by the statistics of progress but by the devastation in our headlines every day. I am more impressed by the tornadoes, earthquakes, volcanoes, poverty beyond what is captured in government statistics, injustices that assault us in every moment, than I am by rainbows, and daffodils, and glitzy technologies. When I see the pundits glorying in the growth of our GDP or GNP, I wonder what the costs of the products embodied in those acronyms are: what's the GDDP, or GNDP: what's the gross domestic or national disproduct? Even the most hopeful headlines come with dark overtones. Elizabeth Kolbert (2024) titled her collection of essays "H is for Hope: Climate Change from A to Z." But while the book is described as "inspiring" and "humorous," the humor is dark and the message is in part "alarming."

For those of you in my generation, especially those of you who identify as "children of the 1960s," much of what I have written that is critical and pessimistic may have a familiar ring. Indeed, there are echoes of Tom Hayden's (1967) perspectives on the America and the world of the 1960s. For those with a historical sensibility, the 1860s in Russia produced its own "children of the 1860s." Once more, Tom Hayden (1967: 4):

> So here we stand, limp, questioning, even scared. Our jokes run something like the cover of a recent Liberation: scrawled in the manner one finds covering rest room walls: "What can we do now?" and the huge bold answer, "Get ready to die." It is not as though we can dismiss the world; some of us know people who have, who already have contracted radiation disease. It is not as though we can change things. Mills [C. Wright Mills] was pretty accurate with his description of the monolithic power elite. It is not as though we even know what to do. We have no real visionaries for our leaders, we are not much more than literate ourselves. And it is not as though, I also fear, we even know who we are.

And then he goes on to voice my own sense of things, so eerily similar more than half a century later and part of the motivation for writing this book:

> What has made me so strangely sensitive when my brothers seem so acquiescent, what has made me call insane what the experts call the "hard facts of power politics," what has made me feel we are on the threshold of death when others say we are on the New Frontier, and why have I turned with trembling and disgust from the Americans who do recognize peril and recoil into shelters full of the comforting gadgets the culture has produced? A more blinding situation is difficult to imagine. War [i.e., World War III] would be cathartic – though the release would be grimly brief.

Are we in just another "panic era" that proves we are not doomed since we have survived earlier ones? Indeed, predicting doom is an ancient game and we seem to be very good at surviving the predicted moments of humanity's demise. The twentieth century has witnessed more than one such era. In the 1920s, machines were the demons of doom, but humanity survived Rossum's Universal Robots (Čapek, 1922/2004). H.G. Wells gave us doomerism in *The Way the World is Going* (1928). The 1930s brought fear of fascism and new unfathomable heights of humanity's inhumanity; the 1940s and 1950s brought the ultimate doomsday promise of the atomic bomb. The 1960s saw waves of panic, from adumbrations of our contemporary fears about AI to fears of famines and the population explosion;

Is history a series of suicide notes or a record of our survival, as one character, Harper, queries in Jeanette Winterson's 2009 novel, *The Stone Gods*? (2024). He reads our history of recurring panics as hopeful, a history that give us reason for optimism: the 1920s saw this coming but they could not predict that we are surviving. But then Harper ends his essay with four haunting words: "At least for now." And there's the rub. Optimism is fueled by the fact that we are still here. But we're not here in the same way we were "here" during earlier panics. What the optimists are missing is the sheer weight, the sheer scale, the sheer speed, the shortening timelines of the existential threats we face. In that sense, "at least for now" is hardly reason to celebrate our survival, a survival that is not being experienced equally across localities, regions, nations, the social classes, sexes, genders, and ethnicities; in some areas, for some peoples, the bells are already tolling.

How do we navigate the reports that support a form of doomerism, or doomism (climate change damage is "dramatically worse than previous estimates," Dienes, 2024b) from claims that it's not too late to save the planet? How do we distinguish the reality of doomerism from the reality of anti-doomerism? "Doomism robs people of the agency and incentive to participate in a solution to the climate crisis" (Hockenos, 2024). Hockenos objects to Kohei Saito's (2024) claim that climate change cannot happen in a market economy. We've already seen that the concept of market economy, like that of capitalism itself, is ideological and not an economic reality. Hockenos has to believe in the ideology in order to defend the idea that we already possess the mechanisms and policies for achieving climate neutrality. Ideology cannot trump reality, so Hockenos is wrong. We cannot rely on market mechanisms and capitalism to get us out of this mess. We need something dramatically different and that's why I have argued that we need to turn to anarchism and hedonism.

Whether its "panic eras" or doomers versus anti-doomers, reality undermines any reassurances that my panegyric to hedonistic anarchy might engender. Nonetheless, its success via, for example, Transition Towns, would give us a more peaceful and pleasurable world to live out our lives in.

There is another paradigm that has been designed to help achieve the goals of a hedonistic anarchist society, The Stories for Life paradigm (Short, 2024). It helps address the classic question from the left, "What is to be done?" and suggests a path that takes us from here ("Capitalism is crashing. Society is dividing. Democracy is degrading. Climate is tipping. Ecology is vanishing. Disease is spreading. Inequity is rising. Protest is pervading") to there ("Stories for Life" narratives are a way of birthing and seeding new stories that may "bring us back together and help people recognize that we're entangled with all life ... and begin to see cultural stories that completely help us, reframe what success is all about in this culture, what it is to be human, what is our relationship with the natural world").

It will take more than stories to achieve these goals. But if we interpret telling new stories to mean reformulating the themes that drive our novels, our movies, our TV shows, our songs, our entertainment industry, our teaching modules, our consumer habits this story telling paradigm's power to change things will be enhanced. At the end of the day, the two-fold message of this book can be stated in the form of two questions: (1) In whatever time we have left, can we do better? And (2): In whatever time we have left, can we do better, by actualizing the ever present power of the cooperative principle in evolution, and of love as a manifestation of this principle?

14   Conclusion: The Walls of Our Imprisonment

For reasons beyond my ability to reconstruct, I had a naïve fondness, a passion, for reason, logic, and science in childhood. It bothered me, for example, if someone in class – whether it was a student or the teacher – skipped or mispronounced a word while reading from a book. I "felt" people making mistakes about what I understood as matters of fact. My earliest recollections of church and religious matters is that I found them troubling to say the least. Something about the experience didn't "feel" right. These moments adumbrated my later fascination with everything scientific, with the facts and laws of every science. At a deeper level, I was sensitive to a kind of ordering, the need to smooth things out. If there was such a thing as being born to something, I was born to theory.

In my teens and early college years I suppose I was more scientistic than scientific, more naïve realist than critical realist. In my professional years, I became associated with networks of scientists, philosophers, and intellectuals who helped sharpen my ideas and forged me into a skeptical critical materialist scientific thinker. One of the complications of that sharpening was the revelation that there was a lot more chaos in the worlds of science, theory, and truth than I – or many others – had imagined. The complexities of that sharpening have guided me throughout this book. They have lent a certain positive, optimistic tone to my writing. I have defended forms of science and realism I believe take into account the critics of science as an all-encompassing worldview. But all of my life my positive unfettered pursuit of truth, my defense of science, objectivity, materialism, and realism have been shadowed by a deep pessimism.

Approaching my 85th birthday and shadowed by intimations of my mortality, I find myself navigating between the Charybdis of optimism and the Scylla of pessimism. This is an interesting trial because these monsters stand on opposite sides of the Strait of Messina which divides Sicily, the land of my father's parents, and Calabria, my mother's homeland. What this means for revealing the author behind this book was brought home to me recently when I came across this blog post (The Honest Sorcerer, 2024: final paragraph):

> Science has enabled our species to overshoot the natural carrying capacity of the planet, and made us believe that we are above all living beings. That we are the masters of this Universe. Giving up that dream will be unbearably hard for many (especially for those in power), but that doesn't necessarily infer that life will lose its meaning. There will be – in fact, there [are] – so many other things to live for than to plunder the planet and get rich. Friends, family, community. Or just living together with animals of the forest. Dancing, singing, playing a flute, telling stories around a campfire, cooking, gardening, arts and crafts were always … [and continue to be] perfectly possible without science and modernity. The biggest psychological or I dare to say … eschatological challenge ahead of us will be to find this new meaning in the decades ahead, even as science and technology slowly breaks down around us.

Humans have always been good at imagining Edens. But we are not destined for Edens. We may have better futures ahead of us then the present but if so our only access to them will be by way of the forms of science and realism I have defended in this book. There is optimism there. At the same time, those forms of science and realism fuel a deeper pessimism. That pessimism in turn is fueled by the long-term evolutionary destiny driving our present visions. Converging tipping points appear to be drawing our long-term destiny closer and closer to our present. We are asking the question "What is to be done?" from inside a series of walls of imprisonment.

Society, Peter Berger wrote (1963: 92), is "the walls of our imprisonment." It is only one of the walls of imprisonment our lives unfold through; the physical world, the chemical world, and the biological world are the other walls of our imprisonment. The physical world imprisons us with the fewest degrees of freedom; the chemical world imprisons us with slightly more degrees of freedom, and the biological world with still more degrees of freedom. Society offers us the greatest number of degrees of freedom. The influence of these interpenetrating degrees of freedom on us is that in the later and more complex stages of our evolution we find ourselves engaging in choice behaviors that give us the illusion that we have free will. Computers exhibit choice behavior but we don't consider them free willing agents. We could, perhaps, but then we would be more inclined to view ourselves as machines.

Earlier, I introduced the concept of bootstrap physics. Perhaps we live in a bootstrap social world, which like a bootstrap physical world is the way it is because it could not be any other way. We face the future imagining that we can make the world over in Edenic ways when in fact the world will never be other than the way it is, as a reality in becoming within the walls of its and our imprisonment. It's not that the world doesn't change in accordance with its own dialectical dynamics. It's that we are wrapped up in those dynamics and cannot alter their directions.

Is there more to this dismal picture of being imprisoned by the reality we look to for answers to our problems of everyday existence and existential threats to humanity and planet Earth? Peter Berger (1963: 93), after informing us that society is the walls of our imprisonment asks if there are "some escape tunnels from this gloomy determinism." I have already identified an escape tunnel, that of open systems. The more complex and diversified a system is, the more open to outside influences it is, the less determined it is. It will always be lawful; that aspect of imprisonment cannot be breached. What can we identify in the open system of society that can fuel our optimism about the possibility that directed change is possible? Following Berger, we can look to certain sociological concepts that have sufficient play in them to allow for changes in our thoughts, behaviors, and emotions individually and collectively. One such concept is social role. In the normal course of events, we go through life stepping into social roles with predetermined constraints. Some social roles are systemically more closed than others; the role of garbage collector has fewer degrees of freedom than the role of professor. But in a complex society, all social roles are constantly interacting with each other and eating away at each other's constraints. As societies increase in complexity, social roles develop increasing degrees of freedom. Social identities become less fixed, providing more room for plays and ploys. It becomes possible to circumvent the roles' pre-programmed constraints, to sabotage them, to withdraw from them, to re-program them.

History offers us numerous examples of walls of imprisonment being broken and new social forms emerging. This is the case for revolutions. How do these breaks happen? Basically, and in the simplest terms, "outward acts against the old order are invariably preceded by the disintegration of inward allegiances and loyalties" (Berger, 1963: 130). More routinely, individuals who sabotage the system by withdrawing from it may find other like-minded individuals and create a counter-society (e.g., sect, cult, subculture, counterculture, "inner circle"). Other option drawing on Goffman (1961a,1961b) include manipulating or "working the system" and playing a role tongue-in-cheek (role distancing). These and other examples come under the general category of "society as drama" (Berger, 1963: 122–150).

The physical walls of imprisonment are less forgiving than the walls of social imprisonment. If you take on the role of a jumper on the Golden Gate Bridge, once you jump your death is inevitable. If the initial impact doesn't kill you, you will drown or die of hypothermia. There are no negotiations during the fall, no compromises to call for. If, by contrast, you take on the role of a professor you will find many different ways to mold the role. The administrations who define the role may rein you in, but in general they do not have the same level of non-negotiable power of natural laws to constrain you. In the more extreme cases, their power can indeed be as uncompromising as natural laws. But the social system of universities will tolerate a great deal of role diversity in the interest of the smooth running of the organization. Marx (1852/1937: 15) famously described our situation this way:

> Men make their own history, but they do not make it as they please; they do not make it under self-selected circumstances, but under circumstances existing already, given and transmitted from the past. The tradition of all dead generations weighs like a nightmare on the brains of the living. And just as they seem to be occupied with revolutionizing themselves and things, creating something that did not exist before, precisely in such epochs of revolutionary crisis they anxiously conjure up the spirits of the past to their service, borrowing from them names, battle slogans, and costumes in order to present this new scene in world history in time-honored disguise and borrowed language.

In other words, we find in thinkers from Marx to Berger and Goffman a recognition that we are bound in walls of imprisonment but at the same time we have a sense that there are escape tunnels. Those of us committed to making the world a better, safer, more sustainable and humane home for humanity are obliged to act as if there are escape tunnels. Some scientists have recently been countering the doomers with studies demonstrating the resilience of the planet in response to climate change and other existential threats. Carbon emissions, it appears, are no longer rising but we must act quickly if we are going to avoid climate catastrophes (Mann, 2021). Climate Analytics (Fyson, Grant, et al., 2023; Infan, 2024) reported last year that the worst of human impacts on climate might be behind us. Greenhouse gas emissions may have peaked in 2023. China, the world's largest carbon emitter, installed more solar panels in a year than the United States has installed in its entire history; more electric vehicles were sold worldwide than ever before, and so on. The bald eagle crisis of the 1960s was resolved by eliminating DDT from the environment. Otters, whales, manatees, and grizzly bears were almost driven to extinction in the early 1900s by the fur trade. Banning the fur trade brought the populations of these animals back from the edge of extinction. The Gorongosa National Park in Mozambique has recovered from the ecological disaster it was headed for in the mid-1990s once the government stepped in to curb poaching for ivory and other black market activities (Carroll, nd).

We are now looking at Berger's and Goffman's perspectives on social change and the resilience defenders in the context of being thrown into the Alcatraz of walls of imprisonment: the boundaries of Earth's planetary ecology. The examples of resilience tend to be drawn from local and regional contexts and evidentiary sources. This seems to make escape tunnels increasingly less likely to be found and if found to lead to dead ends. Nevertheless, my final piece of wisdom is to fight today for humanity, the planet, yourself and your community and we may all live to fight another day. I have been reminded by my friend Peter Denton (2001) of Bertrand Russell's lesson for our times. Profoundly skeptical of the human capacity for reasoned action, in his own life he demonstrated the "unshakeable connection between science and hope."

My knee jerk response was that it would be bad faith if I let the sentiment of "hope" be the last word in this book. And then I remembered that I am a sociologist, especially after I took notice of sociologist Harriet Bulkeley's remark that "Hope is a practice." She was quoted in an encouraging essay demonstrating the need for a sociological perspective on the climate crisis (Hoffman, 2024). Hoffman underlines the importance of bringing social scientists into the climate crisis dialogue and activism arena. Unlike climate natural scientists, climate social scientists are "experts in humanity's efforts to address climate change." Already by 2009, The American Sociological Association and the National Science Foundation had jointly published a summary of an important workshop on the issue of climate change research. It examines a critically important dimension of earth's climate variation: Basic research on social determinants affecting global climate change (for more recent activities in the sociology community, see ASA, (2021). The American Sociological Association has a Section on Environmental Sociology dedicated to "reshaping the study of sociology:"

> Radiation, genetically modified crops, toxic waste, biodiversity loss, climate change. Facing the challenges of the 21st century requires more than sound scientific understanding and technological solutions. Too often missing from the debate is knowledge of the complex social, economic, and political relationships that drive society in destructive directions. Environmental Sociology brings together the tools of social sciences and applies them to these key issues of our day. Examining environmental issues in turn is reshaping the field of sociology.

I began this book by writing that it has been as hard to write this book as it has been hard to live my life, and it has been as easy to write this book as it has been easy to live my life. Now I find that it is as hard to end this book, and as easy, as it has been hard and easy to end my life. No one, to my knowledge ever escaped Alcatraz. I won't escape the last walls of imprisonment that I am up against. I have faced all of my walls of imprisonment cloaked in more or less naïve, more or less sophisticated garbs of the anarchism of mutual aid. My final words are worthless in the long run. In the short run, their message is a childlike cry to "do good, be good," practice the anarchism of mutual aid, a social form in which science is one with the ethos of humane living.

The Reality Fallacies as the Foundation of the Iron Laws of Reality

The Transcendental Fallacy (the theologian's fallacy) is that there is a world or that there are worlds beyond our own – transcendental worlds, supernatural worlds, worlds of souls, spirits and ghosts, gods, devils, and angels, heavens and hells. There are no such worlds. They are symbolic of social categories and classifications in our earthly societies and cultures. There is nothing beyond our material, organic, and social world. Death is final; there is no soul, there is no life after death. It is also possible that the so-called "many worlds interpretation" in quantum mechanics is contaminated by this fallacy as the result of mathegrammatical illusions. The world, the universe, may be more complex than we can know or imagine, but that complexity does not include transcendental or supernatural features.

The Subscendental Fallacy (the logician's fallacy) is that there are "deep structures" or "immanent structures," genetic or neuronal, that are the locus of explanations for language, thought, and human behavior in general. Such "structures" are as ephemeral and ethereal as transcendental and supernatural worlds. They lead to conceptions of logic, mathematics, and language as "free standing," "independent," "history, culture, and value free" statements. And they support misguided sociobiological, neurological, and genetic explanatory strategies.

The Private Worlds Fallacy (the philosopher's fallacy) is that individual human beings harbor intrinsically private experiences. The profoundly social nature of humans, of symbols, and of language argues against intrinsically private experiences (as Wittgenstein, Goffman, and others have amply demonstrated).

The Internal Life Fallacy. When we engage in discourses about surrogate counters, imitation, and artificial creatures that mimic, we need to remind ourselves that we are working in an arena of analogies and metaphors. Such efforts carry a high emotional charge because they take place at the boundaries of our skins. Analogy and generalization, if they can be shown to have constructive scientific outcomes, need not obligate us to embrace identity in, for example, building robots. Robots will not have to have "gut feelings" in the identical sense humans have gut feelings because they are organic machines. Even this "fact" needs to be scrutinized. What we "feel" is given to us by our language, our conversations, our forms of talking. At the end of the day, feelings may not at all be straightforward matters of bio-electro-chemical processes. Electro-mechanical creatures will turn out to be just as susceptible to an internal life as humans once they have developed language, conversation, and forms of talk. This implies a social life and awareness. Roboticists may already have made some moves in this direction with the development of signal schemas and subsumption-based hormonal control. The development of cyborgs and cybrids may make this issue moot.

The Psychologistic Fallacy is that the human being and/or the human brain is/are free standing and independent, that they can be studied on their own terms independent of social and cultural contexts and forces. This is also known as the neuroistic error (Brothers, 2001: 3; and see Brothers, 1997). It is the idea that mind and consciousness are brain phenomena. Human beings and human brains are constitutively social. This is the most radical formulation of the response to this fallacy. A more charitable formulation would give disciplinary credibility to neuroscience and cognitive approaches to brain studies. These approaches might produce relevant results in certain contexts. Then there might be fruitful ways to pursue interdisciplinary studies linking the social sciences to the neurosciences.

The Eternal Relevance Fallacy is that ancient and more recently departed philosophers should be important and even leading members of our inquiring conversations about social life. An act of intellectual courage is needed to rid us of Plato and Hegel. Once they are eliminated, an entire pantheon of outmoded and outdated thinkers, from Aristotle to Kant, will disappear from our radar. This move might also go a long way to eliminating the worshipful attitude intellectuals often adopt to the more productive and visible members of their discourse communities. The caveat here is that some ancient and some modern thinkers (departed ones, as well as some who are still with us) who can be claimed for philosophy are still extremely valuable for us. Marx, Nietzsche, and Wittgenstein come immediately to mind.

The Corollary Intellectual's Fallacy is that philosophers as philosophers (and psychologists as psychologists) have anything at all to tell us anymore about the social world. In the wake of the work of sociologists from Emile Durkheim (1995/1912) to Mary Douglas (1966), all the central problems of traditional and contemporary philosophy resolve into (not "reduce to") problems in sociology and anthropology.

The Fallacy of neque demonstra neque redargue/neither provable nor unprovable is that one can neither prove nor disprove some claim, proposition, or statement. Consider: One can neither prove nor disprove the existence of God. This has not kept theologians, philosophers, and mathematicians from

Anselm to Gödel from proposing proofs for the existence of God. While all proofs build conclusions into premises, God proofs are notoriously poorly constructed in this sense. The fallacy has, on the other hand, kept social thinkers and social critics from proposing proofs for their beliefs about God as a delusion, a myth, and so on. In fact, proofs are situated, contingent, contextualized, community matters, and indeed, social constructions and social institutions. Therefore, within the world of Durkheim's Elementary Forms of Religious Life (1912/1995) and what follows a proof that God does not exist is clearly possible.

The NOMA Fallacy. This is the fallacy, made famous by S.J. Gould, that science and religion are non-overlapping magisteria. Once we admit social science into the science and religion dialogue this fallacy takes effect.

1   Classic Fallacies from Philosophy

The fallacy of misplaced concreteness, described by philosopher Alfred North Whitehead, involves thinking something is a 'concrete' reality when in fact it is an abstract belief, opinion or concept about the way things are. The fallacy refers to Whitehead's thoughts on the relationship of spatial and temporal location of objects. Whitehead rejects the notion that a real, concrete object in the universe can be described simply in spatial or temporal extension terms. Rather, the object must be described as a field that has both a location in space and a location in time. This is analogous to lessons learned from E.A. Abbott's *Flatland* (1884). Humans cannot conceive of a line that has width but no breadth. Similarly, humans cannot conceive of an object that has spatial but not temporal position (or vice versa):

> among the primary elements of nature as apprehended in our immediate experience, there is no element whatever which possesses this character of simple location. ... [Instead,] I hold that by a process of constructive abstraction we can arrive at abstractions which are the simply located bits of material, and at other abstractions which are the minds included in the scientific scheme. Accordingly, the real error is an example of what I have termed: The Fallacy of Misplaced Concreteness.
>
> WHITEHEAD (1925), p. 58. also see WHITEHEAD
> (1919, Part III), and WHITEHEAD (1920).

A category mistake, or category error is a semantic or ontological error by which a property is ascribed to a thing that could not possibly have that property. For example, the statement "the business of the book sleeps eternally" is syntactically correct, but it is meaningless or nonsense or, at the very most, metaphorical, because it incorrectly ascribes the property, *sleeps eternally*, to *business*, and incorrectly ascribes the property, *business*, to the token, *the book*. The term "category mistake" was introduced by Gilbert Ryle in his book *The Concept of Mind* (1949) to remove what he argued to be a confusion over the nature of mind born from Cartesian metaphysics. It was alleged to be a mistake to treat the mind as an object made of an immaterial substance because predications of substance are not meaningful for a collection of dispositions and capacities.

References and Further Readings

Part 1. What to Read While You're Waiting to See if and How the World Will End

The fall of Rome casts its shadow over every generation. There are many causes that have been posited to explain the fall of Rome, of the Sumerians, of the Assyrians, and of other civilizations – from despotism to moral decay. It seems clear, however, that all of these "falls" had in common some kind of extreme climate change.

Buehlman, C. (2012), Between Two Fires (New York: Ace).

Cooper, P. (2024), Fall of Civilizations (New York: Hanover Square Press).

Fleming, R. (2021), The Material Fall of Roman Britain, 300–525 CE (Philadelphia: University of Pennsylvania Press).

Hoban, R. (2012) Riddley Walker (New York: Bloomsbury).

McCarthy, C. (2006), The Road (New York: Alfred A. Knopf).

Weisman, A. (2022), The World Without Us (London: Picador).

Part 2. Text References

Abbott, E. (1884/1952), Flatland (New York: Dover).

Aginsky, B. and E. Aginsky (1978), Anthropotentialism and Language, Preliminary edition (Provo, UT: Brigham Young University Language and Intercultural Research Center).

Aichhorn, A. (1925/1935), Wayward Youth (New York: Viking).

Albert, M. (1991), Capitalisme contre capitalisme (Paris: Seuil).

Aldous, J. (1972), "An Exchange Between Durkheim and Tönnies on the Nature of Social Relations," American Journal of Sociology, 77, 6: 1191–1200.

Alexander, J. (2011), "Alexander Berkman: Sexual Dissidence in the First Wave Anarchist Movement and its Subsequent Narratives," pp. 25–44 in J. Herkert and R. Cleminson, eds., Anarchism & Sexuality (New York: Routledge).

Algeo, J. and A. Algeo (1988), "Among the New Words," American Speech, 63, 4: 235–236.

Almond, G., M. Chodorow, and R.H. Pearce (1985), Progress and its Discontents (Berkeley: University of California Press).

Al-Rodhan, N. (2017), "Post-Truth Politics, the Fifth Estate and the Securitization of Fake News," Global Policy Journal.

Alterman, E. (2004), When Presidents Lie (New York: Viking).

Andersen, H.C. (1837/1992), The Emperor's New Clothes (New York: Atlantic Monthly).

Andersen, T. (1994), "Economic Black Holes – The Dynamics and Consequences of Accumulation," Post-Keynesian Archive: https://ideas.repec.org/p/wop/pokear/_017.html.

Anderson, D. (2018), Overcoming the Threat to Our Future (Bloomington, IN: Xlibris US).

Arendt, H. (1951), The Origins of Totalitarianism (New York: Harcourt Brace and World).

Arendt, H. (1972), Crises of the Republic: Lying in Politics, Civil Disobedience, On Violence, Thoughts on Politics and Revolution (New York: Harcourt Brace Jovanovich).

Armand, E. (1930/2009), La révolution sexuelle et la camaraderie amoureuse (Brooklyn, NY: ZONE books).

Artis, Z. (2024), "Unveiling Big Oil's Campaign of Lies," Natural Resources Defense Council: https://www.nrdc.org/bio/zanagee-artis/unveiling-big-oils-campaign-lies.

Atari, M., Haidt, J., et al. (2023), "Morality beyond the WEIRD [Western, Educated, Industrialized, Rich, and Democratic]: How the nomological network of morality varies across cultures," Journal of Personality and Social Psychology, 125, 5: 1157–1188.

Athope, D. (2021), "Yes, YO Too, Can be an Anarcho-Humanist," https://damienmarieathope.com/2021/07/yes-you-too-can-be-an-anarcho-humanist/(section of "social anarchism").

Atrill, V. (2018), http://www.macnicolasset.com/wp-content/uploads/2018/06/Black-Hole-Economics.pdf.

Axelson, U. and I. Makarov (2020), "Informational Black Holes in Financial Markets," April: https://personal.lse.ac.uk/makarov1/index_files/informationalBlackHoles.pdf.

Axford, C. (2024), "The Fruitless Search for the Source of Consciousness," Medium, January 9: https://craig-axford.medium.com/the-fruitless-search-for-the-source-of-consciousness-b2d81baf807b.

Baer, N. and M. Hennefeld (2017), "Prophets of Deceit: Post-Truth Politics and the Future of the Left," https://publicseminar.org/2017/04/prophets-of-deceit.

Bakunin, M. (1953), "The Immorality of the State," in G.P. Maximoff, The Philosophy of Bakunin (New York: The Free Press).

Bamford, S. (2012), "A Framework for Approaches to Transfer of a Mind's Substrate," International Journal of Machine Consciousness, 4, 1: 23–34.

Barclay, H. (1990), People Without Government (London: Kahn and Averill).

Baron, M. (2023), "We Want Objective Judges and Doctors; Why not Journalists too?" March 24, The Washington Post: https://www.washingtonpost.com/opinions/2023/03/24/journalism-objectivity-trump-misinformation-marty-baron/?campaign_id=9&emc=edit_nn_20230515&instance_id=92584&nl=the-morning&regi_id=182486231&segment_id=132967&te=1&user_id=ce4a91076d1b09877746bf0fa0404d3a.

Barrass, C.S. (2019), "Beauty is Terror," Medium.com: https://medium.com/@coletteslaterbarrass/beauty-is-terror-341f45ff54cf#_ftn1.

Beaudreaux, D. (2011), "The Great Fact," Pittsburgh Tribune-Review, 27 April 2011.

Beavan, A., M.R. Domingo-Sananesa, and J.O. McInerneya (2014), "Contingency, repeatability, and predictability in the evolution of a prokaryotic pangenome," Proceedings of the National Academy of Sciences, 121, 1: 1–10.

Beckerman, S. and P. Valentine, eds. (2002), Cultures of Multiple Fathers: The Theory and Practice of Partible Paternity in Lowland South America (Gainesville, FL: University Press of Florida).

Bejan, A. (2020), Freedom and Evolution: Hierarchy in Nature, Society and Science (New York: Springer).

Bellos, A. (2010), Here's Looking at Euclid (New York: The Free Press).

Benson, O. and J. Stangroom (2006), Why Truth Matters (New York: Continuum).

Berger, P. (1963), Invitation to Sociology (New York: Anchor).

Bernal, J.D. (1939), The Social Function of Science (New York: Macmillan).

Bernal, J.D. (1964), "After Twenty-Five Years," pp. 209–228 in M. Goldsmith and A. Mackay (eds.), Society and Science (New York: Simon and Schuster).

Benedict, R. (1946), The chrysanthemum and the sword (Boston: Houghton Mifflin).

Berkowitz, A. (2016), Governing Behavior: How Nerve Cell Dictatorships and Democracies Control Everything We Do (Cambridge, MA: Harvard University Press).

Bidney, D. (1953), Theoretical Anthropology (New York: Columbia University Press).

Bird, D.K., G. Gisladottir, and D. Dominey-Howes (2010), "Volcanic risk and tourism in southern Iceland: Implications for hazard, risk and emergency response education and training," Journal of Volcanology and Geothermal Research, 189, 1–2: 33–48.

Bohm, D. (1976), Fragmentation and Wholeness (Jerusalem: Van Leer Jerusalem Foundation).

Bohm, D. (2002), Wholeness and the Implicate Order (New York: Routledge). Rob.

Bohm, D. (2016), Causality and Chance in Modern Physics (New York: Routledge; orig. publ. 1958).

Boston, R. (2016). "Humanists and the Rise of "Post-Truth America."" The Humanist:thehumanist.com/magazine/january-february-2016/church-state/human ists-rise-post-truth-america.

Boswell, J. (1791/2008), The Life of Samuel Johnson (New York: Penguin).

Boulding, K. (1970), A Primer in Social Dynamics (New York: The Free Press).

Brothers, L. (1997), Friday's Footprint: How Society Shapes the Human Mind (New York: Oxford University Press).

Brothers, L. (2001), Mistaken Identity: The Mind-Brain Problem Reconsidered (Albany, NY: SUNY Press).

Brown, H. (1954), The Challenge of Man's Future (New York: Viking).

Bubula, M. (2024), "It's Called 'Artificial' Intelligence For a Reason: Data Vs. Decisions," Forbes.com, January 25: https://www.forbes.com/sites/forbesagencycouncil/2024/01/25/its-called-artificial-intelligence-for-a-reason-data-vs-decisions/?sh=51cd34251293.

Büchner, G. (1836/2005), Lenz (Brooklyn: Archipelago Books).

Burke, E. (1757/2017), "The Sublime," pp. 489–91 in B. Goldblatt, L.B. Brown, and S. Patride, eds., Aesthetics, 4th ed. (New York: Routledge; and see Kant, 1790/2007; Zizek, 2009, and Slade, 2007).

Butler, J. (2011), "On Anarchism: An Interview with Judith Butler," pp. 93–99 in J. Heckert and R. Cleminson, eds., Anarchism & Sexuality (New York: Routledge).

Calhoun, J.B. (1962), "Population Density and Social Pathology," Scientific American, 206, 3: 139–148.

Call, L. (2011), "Structures of Desire: Postanarchist Kink in the speculative fiction of Octavia Butler and Samuel Delany," pp. 131–153 in J. Heckert and R. Cleminson, eds., Anarchism & Sexuality (New York: Routledge).

Cajori, F. (1894), A History of Mathematics (New York: Macmillan).

Campbell, D.T. (1960), "Blind variation and selective retentions in creative thought as in other knowledge processes." Psychological Review, 67, 6: 380–400.

Camus, A. (1991), The Myth of Sisyphus and Other Essays (New York: Vintage).

Čapek, K. (1922/2004), RUR (New York: Penguin).

Carhart-Harris R.L. (2018), "The Entropic Brain – Revisited," Neuropharmacology, 142: 167–178.

Carhart-Harris, R.L. and K.J. Friston (2019), "REBUS and the Anarchic Brain: Toward a Unified Model of the Brian Action of Psychedelics," Pharmacological Review, 71, 3: 316–344.

Carrier, R. (2022), "Why the Fine Tuning Argument Proves God Does Not Exist," Richard Carrier Blogs, June, 23: https://www.richardcarrier.info/archives/20661.

Carroll, S.B. (n.d.), "We're Not Doomed. Here's How to Revive Planet Earth," BigThink. com: https://bigthink.com/series/explain-it-like-im-smart/the-resilience-of-nature/.

Carson, R. (1962/2002), Silent Spring (New York: Houghton Mifflin Harcourt).

Chalmers, D. (2022), Reality: Virtual Worlds and the Problems of Philosophy (New York: W.W. Norton).

Chancellor, E. (2022), "Central banks get sucked into financial black hole," Reuters, October 14: https://www.reuters.com/breakingviews/global-markets-breakingvi ews-2022-10-14/.

Chew, G. (1992), quoted on, p. 32 in H. Margenau and R.A. Varghese, eds., Cosmos, Bios, Theos: Scientists Reflect on Science, God, and the Origins of the Universe, Life, and Homo Sapiens (Chicago: Open Court).

Christie, P. (2020), Unnatural Companions: Rethinking Our Love of Pets in an Age of Wildlife (Washington DC: Island Press).

Clark, N. E. and | R. Chongtay (2020), "Technological Mediation for Disaster RiskContingencies and Crisis Management," Journal of Contingencies and Crisis Management, 28:411–415.

Cohen, A.P., D. Azrael, and M. Miller (2014), "Rate of Mass Shootings Has Tripled Since 2011, Harvard Research Shows," Mother Jones: https://www.motherjones.com/polit ics/2014/10/mass-shootings-increasing-harvard-research/.

Cohen, I. Bernard (1976), "The Eighteenth-Century Origins of the Concept of Scientific Revolution." Journal of the History of Ideas, 37, 2: 257–88.

Collingridge, D. (1980), The Social Control of Technology (New York: St. Martin's Press).

Collins, R. (1975), Conflict Sociology (New York: Academic Press).

Collins, R. (1979/2019), The Credential Society – Legacy edition (New York: Columbia University Press).

Collins, R. (1998), The Sociology of Philosophies (Cambridge, MA: Harvard University Press).

Collins, R. and M. Makowsky (2010), The Discovery of Society (New York: McGraw-Hill).

Cooley, C.H. (1909/2018), Social Organization: A Study of the Larger Mind (London: Forgotten Books).

Cornwall, Kauffman, et al., eds. (2023), Evolution "On Purpose": Teleonomy in Living Systems (Cambridge, MA: MIT Press).

Crouch, C. (2005), "Models of Capitalism," New Political Economy, 10, 4: 439–456.

Cox, J.W., S. Rich, et al. (2024), "More than360,000students have experienced gun vio-lence at school since Columbine," Washington Post, January 4 https://www.washing tonpost.com/education/interactive/school-shootings-database/.

Craig, W.L. (2016), "In What Sense is it Impossible for the Universe to Come from Nothing?" Reasonable Faith blog: https://www.reasonablefaith.org/writi ngs/question-answer/in-what-sense-is-it-impossible-for-the-universe-to-come -from-nothing.

Crimethinc.com (2020), "Exercise: What Would an Anarchist Program Look Like?" 11/ 02: https://crimethinc.com/2020/11/02/exercise-what-would-an-anarchist-program -look-like

Crouch, C. (2004), Post-Democracy (Cambridge: Polity).

Crouch, G. (2024), "Utopia, Techtopia or Dystopia? None of the Above," The Digital Anthropologist <gilescrouch@substack.com, February, 19.

Curry, O.S., D.A. Mullins, and H. Whitehouse (2019), "Is It Good to Cooperate? Testing the Theory of Morality-as-Cooperation in 60 Societies," Current Anthropology, 60, 1: 47–69.

Darwin, C. (1859/2017), The Origin of Species (New York: Macmillan Collectors Edition).

Davis, L. (2011), Anarchism & Sexuality (New York: Routledge).

Deacon, M. (2016), "In a World of Post-Truth Politics, Andrea Leadsom Will Make the Perfect PM," The Telegraph, July 9: https://www.telegraph.co.uk/news/2016/07/09 /in-a-world-of-post-truth-politics-andrea-leadsom-will-make-the-p/.

Delisle, J.R. (2014), Dumbing Down America (New York: Routledge).

DeLong, J.B. (2022), Slouching Towards Utopia: An Economic History of the 20th Century (New York: Basic Books).

Denton, P. (2001), The ABC of Armageddon: Bertrand Russell on Science, Religion, and the Next War, 1919–1938 (Albany, NY: SUNY Press).

Denton, P. (2016), Live Close to Home (Victoria, BC: Rocky Mountains, Ltd.).

Denton, P. (2022), The End of Technology (Dubuque, IA: Kendall Hunt).

Derber, C., ed. (1962), Professionals as Workers: Mental Labor in Advanced Capitalism (Boston: G.K. Hall).

Dienes, T. (2024a), "Risk experts warn of global catastrophe predicted to occur within next decade: 'Risks could hit the point of no return'" The Cool Down.com, February 29: https://www.thecooldown.com/green-business/experts-global-catastrophes-warning/.

Dienes, T. (2024b), "Researchers find economic damage from climate change to be dramatically worse than previous estimates: 'It's a worrying thought,'" https://www.thecooldown.com/outdoors/economic-impact-warming-world-gdp-loss/.

Dick, P.K. (2011), The Exegesis of Philip K Dick, edited by P. Jackson and J. Lethem (New York: Houghton Mifflin Harcourt).

Doherty, E. (2022), "America's Belief in God Hits New Low," Axios.com: June, 17: https://www.axios.com/2022/06/17/belief-god-low-gallup-poll.

Douglas, M. (1966), Purity and Danger (London: Routledge and Kegan Paul).

Drake, F. (1961), "Project Ozma," Physics Today, 14, 4: 40–46.

Drezner, D.W. (2016), "Why the Post-Truth Political Era Might Be Around For a While," The Washington Post: https://www.washingtonpost.com/posteverything/wp/2016/06/16/why-the-post-truth-pollitical-era-might-be-around-a-while/

Duke, D.W. and W.S. Pritchard, eds. (1991), Measuring Chaos in the Brain (London: World Scientific).

Dumé, I. (2022), "Schwinger effect seen in graphene," Physics World, March 25: https://physicsworld.com/a/schwinger-effect-seen-in-graphene/.

Dunn, R. (2021), A Natural History of the Future (New York: Basic Books).

Durkheim, E. (1912/1995), The Elementary Forms of Religious Life (New York: The Free Press).

Dworkin, A. (1987), Intercourse (New York: The Free Press).

Dyble, M., G.D. Salali, et al. (2015), "Sex equality can explain the unique social structure of hunter-gatherer bands," Science, 348, 6236: 796–798.

Eckert, L. (2011), "Post(-)anarchism and the Contrasexual Practices of Cyborgs in Dildotopia, Or: The War on the Phallus," pp. 69–92 in J. Heckert and R. Cleminson, eds., Anarchism & Sexuality (New York: Routledge).

Egan, M. (2024), "AI could pose 'extinction-level' threat to humans and the US must intervene, State Dept.-commissioned report warns," CNN BUSINESS, March

12: https://www.cnn.com/2024/03/12/business/artificial-intelligence-ai-report-ext inction/index.html.

Ellis, E.C. (2024), "The Anthropocene Condition: Evolving Through Social-Ecological Transformations," Philosophical Transactions of the Royal Society B, January. 379, 1893: 1–11.

Emerson, S. (2020), "Consciousness is Anarchy: What Form of Government is Your Brain," Subtle Salmon, Substack.com, December 26: https://subtlesalmon.subst ack.com/p/consciousness-is-anarchy.

Engels, F. (1884/2010), The Origin of the Family, Private Property and the State (New York: Penguin).

Esser, F. (1999), "Tabloidization of News: A Comparative Analysis of Anglo-American and German Press Journalism," European Journal of Communication, 14, 3: 291–324.

Etkin, W. (1964) Social Behavior and Organization Among Vertebrates (Chicago: University of Chicago Press).

Falk, C. (2019), Love, Anarchy & Emma Goldman (London, Rutgers University Press).

Faure, P. and H. Korn (2001), "Is There Chaos in the Brain? I. Concepts of Nonlinear Dynamics and Methods of Investigation," Comptes Rendus de l'Académie des Sciences – Series III – Sciences de la Vie, 324, 9: 773–793.

Feldman, N. (2022), "Commentary: A Texas judge just took 'religious freedom' too far," Union Bulletin, September 17: https://www.union-bulletin.com/opinion/opinion_ columns/commentary-a-texas-judge-just-took-religious-freedom-too-far/article_5 a76b7b6-35d8-11ed-9c3b-eb44d22ea813.html.

Feyerabend, P. (1978), Science in a Free Society (London: Verso).

Fleck, L. (1939/1979), Genesis and Development of a Scientific Fact (Chicago: University of Chicago Press).

Follman, M. (2022), Trigger Points: Inside the Mission to Stop Mass Shootings in America (New York: Harper/Collins).

ASA, (2021), "Why the Environment Needs A Course Correction Now," Footnotes, Vol. 49, Issue 3.

Foucault, M. (1976/1997), "Il faut défendre la societie," p. 145 in M. Bertrani and A. Fontana, eds., Cours au Collège de France, 1975–1976 (Paris: Seuil/Gallmard).

Francis, R. and A. Moström (2023), "Amanda Moström 'itsanosofadog * It's an arse of a dog,'" roseeaston.com: https://www.roseeaston.com/exhibitions/itsanosofadog-its -an-arse-of-a-dog.

Freeden, M. (1998), Ideologies and Political Theory (Oxford: Clarendon Press).

Freud, S. (1933/1995), New Introductory Lectures in Psychoanalysis (New York: W.W. Norton).

Fromm, E. (1956), The Art of Loving (New York: Harper and Row).

Fuller, S. (1988), Social Epistemology (Bloomington IN: Indiana University Press).

Fuller, S. (2018), Post-Truth Knowledge as a Power Game (London: Anthem).

Furley, David John. "Epicurus" in the Oxford Classical Dictionary. Third Edition. Oxford 1996.

Fyson, C., Neil Grant, et al. (2023), "When Will Global Greenhouse Gas Emissions Peak?" Climate Analytics, November 22.

Harari, Y.N. (2024), NEXUS: A Brief History of Information Networks from the Stone Age to AI (New York: Random House).

Gao, A., M. Protsiv, and J. Parsonnet (2023), "Defining Usual Oral Temperature Ranges in Outpatients Using an Unsupervised Learning Algorithm," Journal of the American Medical Association, Internal Medicine, 183, 10: 1128–1135.

Garis, H. de (2005), The Artilect War: Cosmists vs. Terrans (Berlin: Etc Publications).

Gatto, J. (2017), Dumbing Us Down: The Hidden Curriculum of Compulsory Schooling (Gabriola Island, BC: New Society Publishers).

du Gay et al. (1997), Doing Cultural Studies: The story of the Sony Walkman (Thousand Oaks, CA: Sage).

Gazzaniga, M. (2011), Who's in Charge?: Free Will and the Science of the Brain (New York: Ecco).

de Giraud, Théophile (2006), L'art de guillotiner les procréateurs (Nancy, FR: Le Mot-Qui-Trompe); English trans: https://theophiledegiraud.e-monsite.com/medias/files/antinatalist-manifesto-raw-translation-by-google-1.pdf.

Glass, B. (2021), The Anthropocene Epoch: When Humans Changed the World (New York: DBG publishing).

Goddard, P. and A. Dagleish (2023), The Death of Science: The Retreat from Reason in the Post-Modern World (Bristol, UK: Clinical Press, Ltd.).

Godwin, W. (1793/1971), Enquiry Concerning Political Justice (New York: Oxford University Press).

Goetzel, T. and B. Goetzel, eds. (2015), The End of the Beginning: Life, Society, and Economy on the Brink of the Singularity (Los Angeles: Humanity+ Press).

Goffman, E. (1959), The Presentation of Self in Everyday Life (New York: Anchor Books).

Goffman, E. (1961a), Asylums (New York: Anchor).

Goffman, E. (1961b), Encounters (Indianapolis, IN: Bobbs-Merrill).

Goggin, G. (2006), Cell Phone Culture: Mobile technology in everyday life (New York: Routledge).

Gopalakrishnan, A. (2016), "Life in Post-Truth Times: What We Share With the Brexit Campaign and Trunp," The Times of India, June 30th, Editorial page, no page number.

Gorney, R. (1972), The Human Agenda (New York: Bantam Books).

Green, J. (2021), The Anthropocene Reviewed: Essays on a Human-Centered Planet (New York: Dutton).

Geertz, C. (1973), The Interpretation of Cultures (New York: Basic Books)

Geertz, C. (2000), Available Light: Anthropological Reflections on Philosophical Topics (Princeton: Princeton University Press).

Gumplowicz, L. (1885/1990), Outlines of Sociology (New Brunswik, NJ: Transaction Books).

Gurr, T.R., ed. (1989), Violence in America, 3rd ed. (Thousand Oaks, CA: Sage).

Gutenschwager, G. (2013), "From Epicurus to Maslow: Happiness Then and Now and the Place of the Human Being in Social Theory," CADMUS, 1, 6: 66–90.

Hagmann, P. (2005), From Diffusion MRI to Brain Connectomics, PhD thesis (Lausanne: Ecole Polytechnique Fédérale de Lausanne).

Haldane, J.B.S. (1923), Daedalus, or Science and the Future (London: Chatto and Windus).

Hall, E.T. (1966), The Hidden Dimension: An Anthropologist Examines Human Use of Space in Public and in Private (New York: Anchor Books).

Hall, P. and D. Soskice (2001), Varieties of Capitalism: The Institutional Foundations of Comparative Advantage (New York: Oxford University Press).

Hallett, H.F. (1947), "Dr. Johnson's Refutation of Bishop Berkeley," Mind, 56, 222: 132–147.

Haque, U. (2022), "This is What a Civilization Ending Feels Like: We've Had a Premonition of Civilization Ending – And its Driving Us Crazy," Eudaimonia and Co.: https://eand.co/this-is-what-the-beginning-of-the-end-of-a-civilization-feels -like-9e4da20463cb.

Harper, T.A. (2024), "The 100-Year Extinction Panic Is Back, Right on Schedule," New York Times, January 28, no page number.

Harsin, I. (2015), "Regimes of Post Truth, Post Politics, and Attention Economies," Communication, Culture, & Critique, 8, 2: 327–333.

Hart, M. (2021), "Dyson Sphere May be the Key to Human Immortality," Popular Mechanics, May 11: Nerdist.com: https://nerdist.com/article/human-immortal ity-dyson-sphere/; https://www.popularmechanics.com/space/a40230192/dyson -sphere-immortality/; https://nerdist.com/article/human-immortality-dyson-sph ere/; https://www.popularmechanics.com/space/a40230192/dyson-sphere-immo rtality

Hawkins, B. (2023), "Report: 1.2M Teachers, 100,000 Professors Now Under 'Educational Gag Orders,'" The74 (https://www.the74million.org/article/report-1-3m-teachers-100 000-professors-now-under-educational-gag-orders/).

Hayden, T. (1967), "A Letter to the New (Young) Left," pp. 2–9 in M. Cohen and D. Hale, eds., The New Student Left, Revised and Expanded (Boston: Beacon Press).

Heckert, J. (2011), "Fantasies of an Anarchist Sex Educator," pp. 154–180 in J. Heckert and R. Cleminson, eds., Anarchism & Sexuality (New York: Routledge).

Helfand, D. (2017), "Surviving the Misinformation Age," Skeptical Inquirer, 41 (3): 34–39.

Herbst, P. (1962), Autonomous Group Functioning (London: Tavistock).

Hesiod (2007). The Homeric Hymns, and Homerica (Loeb Classical Library #57N), (Cambridge, MA: Harvard University Press).

Hessen, B. (1931), "The Social and Economic Roots of Newton's 'Principia,'" pp. 151–212 in N. Bukharin et al., eds., Science at the Crossroads (London: F. Cass).

Hewitt, D. (2020), "A Critical Review of 'Post-Truth as a Power Game,' by Steve Fuller," Social Epistemology Review and Reply Collective, 8: 47–52.

Hobbes, T. (1642/1998), De Cive/The Citizen (Cambridge: Cambridge University Press).

Hobbes, T. (1651/2017), Leviathan (New York: Penguin).

Hockenos, P. (2024), "No, It's Not Too Late to Save the Planet," Foreign Policy: https://foreignpolicy.com/2024/06/02/climate-change-doomism-crisis-solutions-degrowth-sustainability/.

Hoffman, D. (2019), The Case Against Reality: How Evolution Hid the Truth from our Eyes (New York: W.W. Norton).

Hoffman, M. (2024), "Here's how climate social scientists are finding their way in the era of climate crisis," The Conversation.com: https://theconversation.com/heres-how-climate-social-scientists-are-finding-their-way-in-the-era-of-climate-crisis-229861.

Hofstadter, R. (1963), Anti-Intellectualism in American Life (New York: A. Knopf).

Hollingdale, R.J. (1968), "Introduction," pp. 7–17 in F. Nietzsche, (1889–1895/1968), Twilight of the Idols, bound with The Anti-Christ, 1895 (New York: Penguin).

Hooker, C. (1995), Reason, Regulation, and Realism: Toward a Regulatory Systems Theory of Reason and Evolutionary Epistemology (Albany, NY: SUNY Press).

Hopkins, R. (2014), The Transition Handbook (Newark, NJ: Green Books).

The Honest Sorcerer (2024), "The End of Science as a Useful Tool," May 20: https://thehonestsorcerer.substack.com/p/the-end-of-science-as-a-useful-tool.

Horizon Project (2023), "5 Senses – The Importance of the Sense of Touch:" https://horizonprojectinc.org/5-senses-the-importance-of-the-sense-of-touch/.

Howarth, T. (2024), "Auroras could soon pose serious threat to our electrical infrastructure, study reveals," Science Focus, July 10: https://www.sciencefocus.com/news/auroras-power-to-threaten-critical-infrastructure.

Hsu, J. (2014), "There's a 5% chance of AI causing humans to go extinct, say scientists," IFL Science, January 4: https://www.iflscience.com/evolution-may-not-be-as-random-as-previously-thought-72293.

Huffington Post (2013), "'Mind Uploading' & Digital Immortality May Be Reality y 2045-Futurists Say," June 18: https://www.huffpost.com/entry/mind-uploading-2045-futurists_n_3458961.

Infan, U. (2024), "We Might Be Closer to Changing Course on Climate Change Than We Realized," Vox.com:, https://www.vox.com/climate/24139383/climate-change-peak-greenhouse-gas-emissions-action.

Jacobs, G. (2006), Charles Horton Cooley, Imagining Social Reality (Amherst, MA: University of Massachusetts Press).

Jackson, B. and K.H. Jamieson (2007), un-Spun: finding facts in a world of [disinformation] (New York: Random House).

Jacob, F. (1977), "Evolution and Tinkering," Science, 196, 4295: 1161–1166.

Jacoby, S. (2008), The Age of American Unreason (New York: Pantheon).

Jaeggi, R. (2014), Alienation (New York: Columbia University Press).

Jarry, J. (2020), The Dunning-Kruger Effect is Probably Not Real, Office for Science and Society, McGill University: https://www.mcgill.ca/oss/article/criti cal-thinking/dunning-kruger-effect-probably-not-realhttps://www.mcgill.ca/oss /article/critical-thinking/dunning-kruger-effect-probably-not-real?fbclid=IwAR13 aDSHXbp-X5vsEoOOxLLsQbKNpxt77CnIqto5TllpIdoRehSOK4cRW1Q.

Jørgensen, P.S., Raf E.V. Jansen, et al. (2023), "Evolution of the polycrisis: Anthropocene traps that challenge global sustainability," Philosophical Transactions of the Royal Society B, 379: 1–17.

Jungk, R. (1958), Brighter than a Thousand Suns: A Personal History of the Atomic Scientists (New York: Harvest Books).

Justin, M., M.B. Hubert, et al. (2019), "Chaos in Human Brain Phase Transition," pp. 107–116 in P. Bracken, ed., Research Advances in Chaos Theory (London: Intechopen).

Kakutani, M. (2018), The Death of Truth: Notes on Falsehood in the Age of Trump (New York: Tim Duggan Books/Random House).

Kakutani, M. (2024), The Great Wave: The Era of Radical Disruption and the Rise of the Outsider (New York: Crown).

Kang, C. and A. Goldman (2016), "In Washington Pizzeria Attack, Fake News Brought Real Guns," The New York Times, https://www.nytimes.com/2016/12/05/busin ess/media/comet-ping-pongpizza-shooting-fake-news-consequences-html.

Kant, I. (1764/2003), Observations on the Feeling of the Beautiful and Sublime. Trans. John T. Goldthwait. University of California Press, 1961, 2003.

Kant, I. (1797/2007), Critique of Judgement (New York: Oxford University Press).

Kaushal, S.S., G.E. Likens, et al. (2023), "The Anthropogenic Salt Cycle," Nature Reviews Earth & Environment, 4: 770–784.

Keen, S. (2011), Debunking Economics: The Naked Emperor Dethroned (London: Zed Books).

Kelly, K. (2010), What Technology Wants (New York: Penguin).

Kennell, J. (2015), "Snowflakes Are Not as Unique as We Thought," The Science Explorer, December 3: http://thescienceexplorer.com/nature/snowflakes-are-not-unique-we -thought.

Kerner, S.M. (2023), "AWS exec downplays existential threat of AI, calls it a 'mathemati- cal parlor trick,'" VentureBeat, June 4: https://venturebeat.com/ai/aws-exec-downpl ays-existential-threat-of-ai-calls-it-a-mathematical-parlor-trick/.

Keyes, R. (2004), The Post-Truth Era (New York: St. Martin's Press).

Khanna, P. (2016), Connectography (New York: Random House).

Kirkpatrick, E. (2022), "Madonna Has a Sex 'Obsession,'" Vanity Fair, August 31: https: //www.vanityfair.com/style/2022/08/madonna-sex-obsession-regrets-borth-marria ges-sean-penn-guy-ritchiehttps://www.vanityfair.com/style/2022/08/madonna-sex - obsession-regrets-borth-marriages-sean-penn-guy-ritchie.

Klein, A. (2022), "Solar storms may cause up to 5500 heart-related deaths in a given year," New Scientist, June 17: https://www.newscientist.com/article/2324402-solar-storms-may-cause-up-to-5500-heart-related-deaths-in-a-given-year/#ixzz7WTzGgY2z.

Klein, N. (2023), "AI machines aren't 'hallucinating'. But their makers are," The Guardian, May 8, 2023: https://www.theguardian.com/commentisfree/2023/may/08/ai-machines-hallucinating-naomi-klein.

Knorr-Cetina, K. (1979), "Tinkering Toward Success: Prelude to a Theory of Scientific Practice," Theory and Society, 8: 347–376.

Knowles, J. (2003), A Separate Peace (New York: Scribner).

Kolbert, E. (2024), H is for Hope: Climate Change from A to Z (Berkeley, CA: Ten Speed Press).

Kolhatkar, S. (2023), "We Can Have Either Billionaires or Democracy, Not Both," CounterPunch: https://www.counterpunch.org/2023/12/05/we-can-have-either-billionaires-or-democracy-not-both/.

Korn, H. and P. Faure (2003), "Is There Chaos in the Brain? II. Experimental Evidence and Related Models," Comptes Rendus Biologies, 326, 9: 787–840.

Kotler, S. (n.d.), "Will we Download our Minds into New Bodies," Big Think: https://bigthink.com/the-well/immortality-steven-kotler/.

Kropotkin, P. (1902/1976), Mutual Aid: A Factor of Evolution (Boston: Extended Horizons Books).

Kruger, J. and D. Dunning (1999), "Unskilled and unaware of it: How difficulties in recognizing one's own incompetence lead to inflated self-assessments," Journal of Personality and Social Psychology, 77, 6: 1121–1134.

Krznaric, R. (2024), History for Tomorrow: Inspiration from the Past for the Future of Humanity (New York: Penguin).

Küng, H. (1978), Does God Exist? (New York: Doubleday).

Kuttner, R. (1983), "The Declining Middle," Atlantic Monthly, July: 60–71.

Lasswell, H.D. (1948), "The structure and function of communication in society," pp. 37–51 in L. Bryson, ed., Communication of Ideas (New York: Harper).

Lee, R.B. (1988), "Reflections on primitive communism," pp. 252–268 In T. Ingold, D. Riches, and J. Woodburn (eds), Hunters and gatherers 1 (Oxford: Berg); and see https://www.psychologytoday.com/intl/blog/freedom-learn/201105/how-hunter-gatherers-maintained-their-egalitarian-ways; and https://www.smh.com.au/lifestyle/were-just-swingers-after-all-20100730-10zsn.html; and on the matrilineal Mosuo of China, who have no word for "father," see https://www.theguardian.com/lifeandstyle/2010/dec/19/china-mosuo-tribe-matriarchy.

LeGuin, U. (1974), The Dispossessed (New York: Harper & Row).

Lehnertz, K., C.E. Eiger, et al. (2000), "Chaos in Brain?" Proceedings of the Workshop (Bonn, Germany: University of Bonn).

Leno, J. (2011), https://www.youtube.com/watch?v=KXWTQobaMaQ.

Lenin, V. (1902/2020), What is to be Done? (New York: International Publishers)

Lenski, G. (1974), Human Societies (New York: McGraw-Hill).

Lenton, T.M. (2013), "Environmental tipping points," Annual Review of Environment and Resources, 38, 1–29.

Lenton, T.M., S. Benson, T. Smith, T. Ewer, V. Lanel, E. Petykowski, ... and S. Sharpe (2022), "Operationalizing positive tipping points towards global sustainability," Global Sustainability, 5, e1.

Leonhardt, D. (2023), "The Case for Journalistic Independence," May 15, The New York Times: https://www.nytimes.com/2023/05/15/briefing/the-case-for-journalistic-independence-ag-sulzberger.html.

Leoni, E. (1982), Nostradamus and His Prophecies (New York: Gramercy).

Leopold, D. (2022), "Alienation," *The Stanford Encyclopedia of Philosophy* (Winter 2022 Edition), Edward N. Zalta and Uri Nodelman (eds.): https://plato.stanford.edu/archives/in2022/entries/alienation/.

Levin I. (1972), The Stepford Wives (New York: Random House).

Levin, P. (2024), "The Real Issue With Artificial Intelligence: The Misalignment Problem," The Hill.com, January 24: https://thehill.com/opinion/4427702-the-real-issue-with-artificial-intelligence-the-misalignment-problem/.

Lewis, N. (2010), "The Myth of Spiro Agnew's 'Nattering Nabobs of Negativism,'" American Journalism, 27, 1: 89–115.

Lewis, T. (2013), "The Singularity is Near: Mind Uploading by 2045?" LiveScience.com, June, 17: https://www.livescience.com/37499-immortality-by-2045-conference.html.

Levy, S. (2023), "How Not to Be Stupid About AI, With Yann LeCun," Backchannel, Dec. 22: https://www.wired.com/story/artificial-intelligence-meta-yann-lecun-interview/.

Ley, C., F. Heath, et al. (2023), "Defining Usual Oral Temperature Ranges in Outpatients Using an Unsupervised Learning Algorithm," Journal of the American Medical Association – Internal Medicine, 183, 10: 1128–1135.

Lobina, D. (2024), "The Folly of Seeing Agency in Contemporary Artificial Intelligence: Machine Learning (for that is what it is all about) as Pattern Finding Algorithms (Part 2 of 2)," 3 Quarks Daily.com, February 12: https: /3quarksdaily.com/3quarksdaily/2024/02/the-folly-of-seeing-agency-in-contemporary-artificial-intelligence-machine-learning-for-that-is-what-it-is-all-about-as-pattern-finding-algorithms-part-2-of-2.html.

Lochmanova, K. (2020), History of Antinatalism (Independently published).

Longino, H. (1990), Science as Social Knowledge (Princeton: Princeton University Press).

Londsdale, K. (1957), Is Peace Possible? (New York: Penguin).

Lynch, M. (2019), "How Dumbed Down Education is Creating a National Security Crisis," The Edvocate (https://www.theedadvocate.org/how-dumbed-down-education-is-creating-a-national-security-crisis/).

MacGregor-Reid, M. (2020), "Beauty, Terror, and the Sublime," blog: https://marymacgregorreid.wordpress.com/2020/04/15/beauty-terror-and-the-sublime/.

MacPherson, M. (2006), All Governments Lie! The Life and Times of Rebel Journalist I.F. Stone (New York: Scribner).

Maher, B. (2022), "How Dumb Are We?" (https://flip.it/H5Z_SI).

Malatesta, E. (1903–1905/1975), "El Problema del Amor," pp. 63–66 in E. Malatesta, Socialism Y Anarquia (Madrid: Editorial Ayuso).

Manfredonia, G. and F. Ronsin (2000), "Émile Armand and *"la camaraderie amoureuse"*: Revolutionary sexualism and the struggle against jealousy," 'Free Love and the Labour Movement' Second workshop in the series 'Socialism and Sexuality,' October 6: Amsterdam, International Institute of Social History.

Mair, P. (2013), Ruling the Void: The Hollowing Out of Western Democracy (London: Verso).

Mann, M. (2021), The New Climate Wars (New York: Public Affairs).

Marcus, G. and E. Davis (2019), Rebooting AI: Building Artificial Intelligence We Can Trust (New York: Pantheon).

Marx, K. (1852/1937), The 18th Brumaire of Louis Bonaparte (Moscow: Progress Publishers).

Marx, K. (1894/1981), Capital, Vol, 3 (London: Penguin).

Maslow A.H. (1954), Motivation & personality (New York: Harper & Row).

Maslow, A.H., J.J. Honigmann, and M. Mead (1970), "Synergy: Some Notes of Ruth Benedict," American Anthropologist, 72, 2: 320–333.

Maslow A.H. (1971), The farther reaches of human nature (New York: Viking).

McCloskey, D. (2016), Bourgeois Equality: How Ideas, Not Capital or Institutions, Enriched the World (Chicago: University of Chicago Press).

McCloskey, D. (2019), Why liberalism works: how true liberal values produce a freer, more equal, prosperous world for all (New Haven: Yale University Press).

McClure, P. (2024), "The Bad and the Ugly: AI is Harmful, Unreliable, and Running Out of Data," New Atlas.com: https://newatlas.com/technology/ai-index-report-negatives/.

McIntyre, L. (2015), Respecting Truth: Willful Ignorance in the Internet Age (New York: Routledge).

McIntyre, L. (2018), Post-Truth (Cambridge, MA: MIT Press).

McIntyre, L. (2019), The Scientific Attitude: Defending Science from Denial, Fraud, and Pseudoscience (Cambridge, MA: MIT Press).

McIntyre, L. (2021), How to Talk to a Science Denier: Conversations with Flat Earthers, Climate Deniers, and Others Who Defy Reason (Cambridge, MA: MIT Press).

McIntyre, L. (2023), On Disinformation: How to Fight for Truth and Protect Democracy (Cambridge, MA: MIT Press).

McLaughlin, P. (2007), Anarchism and Authority: A Philosophical to Classical Anarchism (Burlington, VT: Ashgate Publishing).

Meadway, J. (2022), "The 'fiscal black hole' is a dangerous myth to justify austerity," November 10, The New Statesman: https://www.newstatesman.com/thestagg ers/2022/11/fiscal-black-hole-myth-justify-austerity.

Melman, S. (1958), Decision Making and Productivity (New York: Wiley).

Mencken, H.L. (1982), A Mencken Chrestomathy (New York: Knopf Doubleday).

Merchant, C. (1980), The Death of Nature (New York: Harper/Collins).

Merton, R.K. (1961), "Singletons and Multiples in Scientific Discovery: A Chapter in the Sociology of Science," Proceedings of the American Philosophical Society, 105: 470–486; reprinted as pp. 343–370 in R.K. Merton (1973), The Sociology of Science (Chicago: University of Chicago Press).

Miller, A.I. (2002), Einstein, Picasso: Space, Time, and the Beauty That Causes Havoc (New York: Basic Books).

Millett, P. and A. Snyder-Beattie (2017), "Existential Risk and Cost-Effective Biosecurity," Health Security, 15, 4: 373–383.

Mills, C.W. (1959/2000), The Sociological Imagination, 40th anniversary edition (New York: Oxford University Press).

Misra, J. (2024), "What's Sociology? A Sociologist Explains Why Florida's College Students Should Get The Chance to Learn How Social Forces Affect Everyone's Lives," February 8: https://theconversation.com/whats-sociology-a-sociolog ist-explains-why-floridas-college-students-should-get-the-chance-to-learn-how -social-forces-affect-everyones-lives-222365.

Mollman, S. (2023), "Tech execs should face '20 years in jail' for letting A.I. bots sneakily pass as humans, says 'Sapiens' author," Yahoo/Finance, July 8: https://finance.yahoo .com/news/tech-execs-face-20-years-224939447.html; and see Thomson, N. (2023), "A conversation with Yuval Noah Harari about Artificial Intelligence," Linkedin, July 10: https://www.linkedin.com/pulse/conversation-yuval-noah-harari-artific ial-nicholas-thompson/.

Mondal, P., W.M. Miller, et al. (2023), "The Spread and Cost of Saltwater Intrusion in the U.S. Mid-Atlantic," Sustainability, 6: 1352–1362.

Montague, A. (1952), Darwin: Competition and Cooperation (New York: Henry Schuman).

Montague, A. (1972), Touching: The Human Significance of the Skin (New York: Perennial).

Morgan, L. (1877), Ancient Society (London: MacMillan).

Morison, W. (n.d.), "The Garden of Epicurus," International Encyclopedia of Philosophy: https://iep.utm.edu/garden/.

Nicolelis, M. (2011), Beyond Boundaries (New York: Henry Holt & Co.).

Nietzsche, F. (1881/2007), The Dawn of Day (New York: Dover).

Nietzsche, F. (1886/1989), Beyond Good & Evil (New York: Vintage).

Nietzsche, F. (1889–1895/1968), Twilight of the Idols, bound with The Anti-Christ, 1895 (New York: Penguin).

O'Leary, D. (2024) "A Biochemist Begins To Sense The Limits Of Materialism," Mind Matters, January 9: https://Mindmatters.Ai/2024/01/A-Biochemist-Begins-To-Sense-The-Limits-Of-Materialism/.

Omodeo, P.D. (2019), "The Political and Intellectual Entanglements of Post-Truth," ARCA, Universita Cal'Foscari, Venezia: http://www.publicseminar.org/2019/09/the-political-and-intellectual-entanglements-of-post-truth/

Ord, T. (2020), The Precipice: Existential Risk and the Future of Humanity (New York: Hachette).

Oresmus, W. (2022), "Google's AI passed a famous test – and showed how the test is broken," The Washington Post, June 17: https://www.washingtonpost.com/technology/2022/06/17/google-ai-lamda-turing-test/.

Overbye, D. (2003), "Zillions of Universes? Or Did Ours Get Lucky?" New York Times, October, 23: https://www.nytimes.com/2003/10/28/science/zillions-of-universes-or-did-ours-get-lucky.html.

Palmer, L.M. (1993), "Anarchy and the Condition of Contemporary Humanism," History of European Ideas, 16, 4–6: 577–583.

Pazzanese, C. (2016), "Politics in a 'Post-Truth' Age," Harvard Gazette https://news.harvard.edu/gazette/story/2016/07/politics-in-a-post-truth-age/.

Perrigo, B. (2023), "Margaret Mitchell: Chief AI Ethics Scientist, Hugging Face," TIME100AI, September, 7: https://time.com/collection/time100-ai/6309005/margaret-mitchell-ai/.

Pert, C. (1997), Molecules of Emotion (New York: Scribner).

Petursdottir, G., Reichardt, U., Bird, D. et al. (2020), "Super Case Study 3: Eyjafjallajökull eruption in 2010," pp. 305–410 in: A.C. Valles, M.M. Ferrer, K. Poljanšek, and I.K. Clark, (eds.), Science for Disaster Risk Management 2020: acting today, protecting tomorrow (Luxembourg: EUR 30183 EN, Publications Office of the European Union).

Pinxten, R. (2024), Humanism Revisited: An Anthropological Perspective (New York: Berghahn).

Piper, K. (2022), "AI experts are increasingly afraid of what they're creating," The Highlight, by Vox (online, November 28).

Pittendrigh, C. (1958), "Adaptation, Natural Selection, and Behavior," pp. 390–416 in A. Roe and G. Simpson, eds., Behavior and Evolution (New Haven: Yale University Press).

Plantinga, A. (1974), God, Freedom, and Evil (New York: Harper & Row).

Plantinga, A. (2000), Warranted Christian Belief (New York: Oxford University Press).

Polenberg, R., ed. (2002), In the Matter of J. Robert Oppenheimer (Ithaca: Cornell University Press).

Pollay, R.W. and T. Dewhirstm (2002), "The Dark Side of Marketing Seemingly "Light" Cigarettes: Successful Images and Failed Fact," Tobacco Control, 11: 118–131.

Pomerantsev, P. (2015), Nothing is True and Everything is Possible: The Surreal Heart of the New Russia (London: Faber & Faber).

Pomerantsev, P. (2019), This is Not Propaganda: Adventures in the War Against Reality (London: Faber & Faber).

Pope, Q. (2023), "My Objections to "We're All Gonna Die with Eliezer Yudowsky," Form. effectivealtruism.org, March, 20: https://forum.effectivealtruism.org/posts/46tXkg 838EZ6uie45/my-objections-to-we-re-all-gonna-die-with-eliezer-yudkowsky.

Postman, N. and C. Weingartner (1969), Teaching as a Subversive Activity (New York: Delacorte Press).

Postman, N. (1996), The End of Education (New York: Knopf).

Preciado, B. (2000), Manifesto Contra-Sexual (Madrid: Opera Prima).

Pyenson, L. (2021), The Shock of Recognition: Motifs of Modern Art and Science (Leiden: Brill).

Rafael, E.F. (2018), The Promise of an Anarchist Sociological Imagination: https://thea narchistlibrary.org/library/erwin-f-rafael-the-promise-of-an-anarchist-sociologi cal-imagination.html.

Rancière, R. and A. Tornell (2010), "Financial Black-Holes: The Interaction of Financial Regulation and Bailout Financial Regulation and Bailout Guarantees:" https://www .imf.org/external/np/res/seminars/2010/arc/pdf/lc.pdf.

Rapaport, J. (2024), "Super Solar Flares Could End the World in Blink of an Eye," GiantFreakinRobot.com: https://www.giantfreakinrobot.com/sci/super-solar-fla res-world-end.html.

Restivo, S. (2011), Red, Black, and Objective: Science, Sociology, and Anarchism (New York: Routledge).

Restivo, S. (2018), The Age of the Social (New York: Routledge).

Restivo, S. (2020a), Einstein's Brain: Genius, Culture, and Social Networks (New York: Palgrave PIVOT).

Restivo, S. (2020b), "Einstein's Genius Wasn't In His Brain; It Was In His Friends," Zócalo Public Square, February 20.

Restivo, S. (2022), "The Sociology of Objectivity," pp. 71–100 in S. Restivo, Inventions in Sociology: Studies in Science and Society (New York: Palgrave Macmillan).

Restivo, S. (2023), The Social Brain (Lanham, MD: Lexington Books).

Restivo, S. (2024), Beyond New Atheism and Theism (New York: Routledge).

Rilke, R.M. (2021), Duino Elegies (New York: W.W. Norton).

Robertson, N. (2023): https://thehill.com/blogs/blog-briefing-room/4342468-mass -shootings-in-us-hit-new-record/.

Rockstrom, J., J. Gupta, et al. (2023), "Safe and just Earth system boundaries," Nature, 619: 101–111.

Rodriguez, E.Q. (2023), "Introducing the Exoplanet Escape Factor and the Fishbowl Worlds (two conceptual tools for the search for extra-terrestrial civilizations)," Journal of the British Interplanetary Society, 76: 365–368.

Rose, S. (2023), "Five ways AI might destroy the world: 'Everyone on Earth could fall over dead in the same second'," The Guardian, July 7: https://www.theguardian.com /technology/2023/jul/07/five-ways-ai-might-destroy-the-world-everyone-on-earth -could-fall-over-dead-in-the-same-second.

Ross, E.A. (1901), Social Control (New York: Macmillan).

Rothblatt, M. (2003), Your Life or Mine (Surrey, UK: Ashgate).

Rothblatt, M. (2014), Virtually Human: The Promise – and Peril – of Digital Immortality (New York: St. Martin's Press).

Roszak, T. (1969/1995), The Making of a Counter Culture: Reflections on the Technocratic Society and Its Youthful Opposition (New York: Doubleday).

Rushkoff, D. (2023), "'We will coup whoever we want!': the unbearable hubris of Musk and the billionaire tech bros," The Guardian, November 25: https://www.theguard ian.com/books/2023/nov/25/we-will-coup-whoever-we-want-the-unbearable-hub ris-of-musk-and-the-billionaire-tech-bros.

Russell, B. (1925), Icarus, or The Future of Science (London: Kegan Paul, Trench, Trubner & Co.).

Ryan, C. and C. Jetha (2010), Sex at Dawn: The Prehistoric Origins of Modern Sexuality (New York: Harper Perennial).

Ryle, G. (1949), The Concept of Mind (Chicago: University of Chicago Press).

Sahlins, M. and E. Service (1960), Evolution and Culture (Ann Arbor: University of Michigan Press).

Saito, K. (2024), Slow Down: The Degrowth Manifesto (New York: Astra House).

Salaman, G. (1983), "Managing the Frontier of Control," pp. 46–62 in A. Giddens and G. MacKenzie, eds., Social Class and the Division of Labor (Cambridge: Cambridge University Press).

Saliers, D.E. (2002), "Beauty and Terror," Spiritus: A Journal of Christian Spirituality, 2, 2: 181–191.

Salvado, O. (2023), "AI guru Geoffrey Hinton says AI is a new form of intelligence unlike our own, so are we thinking about it the wrong way?" Startupdaily: https:// www.startupdaily.net/topic/artificial-intelligence-machine-learning/ai-guru-geoff rey-hinton-says-ai-is-a-new-form-of-intelligence-unlike-our-own-so-are-we-think ing-about-it-the-wrong-way/.

Salk J. (1973), The Survival of the Wisest (New York: Harper and Row).

Salk, J. and J. Salk (2018), A New Reality: Human Evolution for a Sustainable Future (Stratford CT: City Point Press).

Sanders, B. (2023), It's OK to be Angry About Capitalism (New York: Crown).

Sarfati, J. (1997), "The Universe is Finely Tuned for Life," Creation.com: https://creation.com/the-universe-is-finely-tuned-for-life.

Schiller, F. (1798–99/2017), "The Piccolomini," pp. 184–293 in F. Schiller, Wallenstein (Sunnyside, CA: Loki's Publishing).

Schmidt, V. (2002), The Future of European Capitalism (New York: Oxford University Press).

Schopenhauer, A. (1813/2015), On the Fourfold Root of the Principle of Sufficient Reason (Cambridge: Cambridge University Press).

Schumacher, E.F. (1973), Small is Beautiful (London: Blond and Briggs, 1973).

Sedlacek, T. (2011), Economics of Good and Evil (New York, Oxford University Press).

Sharpe, S., and T.M. Lenton (2021), "Upward-scaling tipping cascades to meet climate goals: plausible grounds for hope," Climate Policy, 21, 4: 421–433.

Shelley, M. (2018), Frankenstein: Original 1818 text (New York: Penguin Classics).

Shieber, J. (2023), "An Idle and Most False Imposition: Truth-Seeking Vs. Status-Seeking and the Failure of Epistemic Vigilance," Philosophic Exchange: https://www.researchgate.net/publication/372440555_An_Idle_and_Most_False_Imposition_Truth-Seeking_vs_Status-Seeking_and_the_Failure_of_Epistemic_Vigilance==.

Short, A. (2024), "Outdated Narratives Have Humanity in a Downward Spiral," CounterPunch, February 26: https://www.counterpunch.org/2024/02/26/outdated-narratives-have-humanity-in-a-downward-spiral/.

Showalter, E. (1990), Sexual Anarchy: Gender and Culture at the Fin De Siécle (New York: Viking).

Silva, J.R. (2023), "Global Mass Shootings: Comparing the United States Against Developed and Developing Countries," International Journal of Comparative and Applied Criminal Justice, 47, 4: 317–340.

Sismondo, S. (2017), "Not a Very Slippery Slope: A Reply to Fuller," EASST Review, 36, 2.

Sjöstedt-Hughes, P. (2021), Modes of Sentience (Cornwall, UK: Psychedelic Press).

Skarda, C.A. and W.J. Freeman (1987), "How Brains Make Chaos in Order to Make Sense of the World," Behavioral and Brain Sciences, 10: 101–195.

Skarda, C.A. and W.J. Freeman (1990), "Chaos and the New Science of the Brain," Concepts in Neuroscience, 2: 275–285.

Slade, A. (2007), Lyotard, Beckett, Duras, and the Postmodern Sublime (New York: Peter Lang).

Smith, A. (1776/1976), An Inquiry into the Nature and Causes of the Wealth of Nations, 2 vols. (Indianapolis: Liberty Press).

Smith, D. (1999), Writing the Social (Toronto: University of Toronto Press).

Snodgrass, L. (2017), "Academics Can't Change the World When They Are Distrusted and Discredited," The Conversation: https://theconversation.com/academics-cant-change-the-world-when-theyre-distrusted-and-discredited-77420.

Sobhani, M. (2022), Proof of Spiritual Phenomena (New York: Park Street Press).

Soresi, E. (2006), Il Cervello Anarchico (Milan: UTET).

Sorokin, P. (1954), The Ways and Power of Love (Boston: Beacon Press).

Sperber, D., F. Clement, et al. (2010), "Epistemic Vigilance," Mind & Language, 25, 4: 359–393.

Spencer, H. (1864), Principles of Biology (London: Willians and Norgate).

Sporns, O., G. Tononi and R. Kötter (2005), "The Human Connectome," PLoS Computational Biology, 1 (4): e42.

Starkweather K.E., Hames R. (2012), "A survey of non-classical polyandry," Human Nature 23, 2: 149–72.

Starr, M. (2024), "Groundbreaking Study Reveals Your Fingerprints Aren't as Unique as We Thought," ScienceAlert.com, January 15: https://www.sciencealert.com/gro undbreaking-study-reveals-your-fingerprints-arent-as-unique-as-we-thought.

Steiner, A. (2020), "The Next Frontier: Human Development and the Anthropocene," Foreword, pdf (Belarus: United Nations Development Programme).

Strauss, L. (1965), Natural Right and History (Chicago: University of Chicago Press).

Strogatz, S. (2023), "Are There Reasons to Believe in a Multiverse," Quanta Magazine, May, 17: https://www.quantamagazine.org/are-there-reasons-to-believe-in-a-mul tiverse-20230517.

Sulzberger, A.G. (2023), "Journalism's Essential Value" May 15, Columbia Journalism Review: https://www.cjr.org/special_report/ag-sulzberger-new-york-times-journali sms-essential-value-objectivity-.

Tarbell, I. (1904/1969), The History of the Standard Oil Company (New York: W.W. Norton).

Tartt, D. (1992), The Secret History (New York: A. Knopf).

Thomas, J.A., Mark Williams, and Jan Zalasiewicz (2020), The Anthropocene: A Multidisciplinary Approach (New York: Polity).

Thomas, M. (2018), "Essential Guide to Transition," https://transitionnetwork.org /resources/essential-guide-to-transition-v-1/.

Thomson J. (2023), "The Nietzsche Thesis," https://bigthink.com/thinking/the-nietzs che-thesis.

des Tocqueville (2013/1835–40), Democracy in America, 2 vols. (Poole, Dorset: UK).

Thurow, L. (1992), Head to Head (New York: Morrow).

Tollefsen, J. (2019), "Humans Are Driving One Million Species to Extinction," Nature, 569, 7755: 171.

Tolstoy, L. (1869/1996), War and Peace (New York: W.W. Norton)

Trist, E., G. Higgins, H. Murray, and A. Pollock (2016), Organizational Choice (New York: Routledge).

Tyson, N. deG. (2009), The Pluto Files: The Rise and Fall of America's Favorite Planet (New York: W.W. Norton).

United Nations (2017), Joint Declaration on Freedom of Expression and "Fake News," Disinformation and Propaganda: https://www.article19.org/resources/joint-declaration-on-freedom-of-expression-and-fake-news-disinformation-and-propaganda/.

Varoufakis, Y. (2024), Technofeudalism: What Killed Capitalism (London: Melville House).

Vijayendra, T. (2022), "What does it mean to be human? An Anarchist/Humanist Perspective," Countercurrents.org: https://countercurrents.org/2022/12/what-does-it-mean-to-be-an-anarchist-humanist-perspective/.

Voltaire (1792/2018)) Oeuvres Completes de M. de Voltaire: Tome Cinquante-Sixieme, Volume 56 (London: Forgotten Books).

Vopson, M. (2023), Reality Reloaded: The Scientific Case for a Simulated Universe (Hampshire, UK: IPI Publishing).

Vox, L. (2017), Existential Threats: American Apocalyptic Beliefs in the Technological Era (University of Pennsylvania Press).

Walby, S. (2015), Crisis (Cambridge: Polity Press).

Walsh, B. (2023): https://www.vox.com/the-highlight/23627382/progress-climate-change-poverty-global-health-doom-industrial-revolution-vaccines... March 20.

Ward, L. (1903), Pure Sociology (New York: The Macmillan Co.).

Weber, M. (1918/1946), "Science as a Vocation," pp. 129–156 in H.H. Gerth and C.W. Mills (translated and edited), From Max Weber: Essays in Sociology (New York: Oxford University Press).

Wells, H.G. (1928), The Way the World is Going: Guesses and Forecasts of the Years Ahead (London: Ernest Benn, Ltd).

West, S.M. (2023), "AI Now Managing Director Sarah Myers West Gives Remarks Before Heads of Agency, International Competition Network," AINOW, Oct. 18: https://ainowinstitute.org/news/ai-now-managing-director-sarah-myers-west-gives-remarks-before-heads-of-agency-international-competition-network.

Wexler, A. (1984), Emma Goldman: An Intimate Life (New York: Pantheon).

Whitehead, A.N. (1919), Enquiry Concerning the Principles of Natural Knowledge (Cambridge: Cambridge University Press).

Whitehead, A.N. (1920), The Concept of Nature (Cambridge: Cambridge University Press).

Whitehead, A.N. (1925), Science and the Modern World (New York: Macmillan Company).

Whitehead, C., ed. (2008), The Origin of Consciousness in the Social World (Exeter, UK: Imprint Academic).

Wiles, W. (2011), "The Mouse Universe of John B. Calhoun," Cabinet Magazine, 42: https://www.cabinetmagazine.org/issues/42/wiles.php.

Wilde, O. (1891/2001), The Soul of Man Under Socialism and Selected Critical Prose (New York: Penguin).

Williams, M. (2021), "Is the Universe Fine-Tuned for Life?" UniverseToday.com, November, 2: https://www.universetoday.com/153083/is-the-universe-fine-tuned -for-life/.

Wills, C. (2024), Missing Persons (New York: Farrar, Strauss, & Giroux).

Wilson, E.O. (2012), The Social Conquest of Earth (New York: Liveright).

Wilson E.O. (2014), The Meaning of Human Existence (New York: Liveright).

Wilson, E.O. (2016), Half-Earth: Our Planet's Fight for Life (New York: Liveright).

Wiggers, K. and Devin Coldewey (2023), "This week in AI: AI ethics keeps falling by the wayside," TechCrunch: https://lnkd.in/efgpWnS5.

Winner, L. (1977), Autonomous Technology (Chicago: University of Chicago Press).

Winterson, J. (2008), The Stone Gods (New York: Houghton Mifflin Harcourt).

WISEVOTER (2020), "Mass Shootings by Country:" https://wisevoter.com/country-.

Wittgenstein, L. (1922/1990), Tractatus Logico-Philosophico (London: Routledge).

Wolchover, N. (2019), "Why the Laws of Physics are Inevitable," Quanta Magazine, December 9: https://www.quantamagazine.org/how-simple-rules-bootstrap-the -laws-of-physics-20191209/.

Wright, E.O. and J. Singleman (1982), "Proletarianization in the Changing American Class Structure," American Journal of Sociology, 88, Supplement: 5176–5209.

Wycherley, R.E. (1978/2016), The Stones of Athens (Princeton: Princeton University Press).

Yen, A. (2024), "Meta, Google, and OpenAI Flouted Ethics to Harvest Data for AI Model Development: NYT," Daily Beast: https://www.thedailybeast.com/meta-google-and -openai-flouted-ethics-to-harvest-data-for-ai-modelsMeta, Google, and OpenAI Flouted Ethics to Harvest Data for AI Model Development: NYT; https://twitter.com /nytimes/status/1776673742527103211, April 6, 2024.

Yudowsky, E. (2023), "Pausing AI Developments Isn't Enough. We Need to Shut it All Down," Time.com, March 29: https://time.com/6266923/ai-eliezer-yudowsky-open -letter-not-enough/.

Zapporoli, L., M. Porta, and E. Paulesu (2015), "The Anarchic Brain in Action ...," Current Opinion in Neurology, 6: 604–611.

Zhu, R., J. Wang, et al. (2022), "Remotely mind-controlled metasurface via brainwaves," eLight, June 11: 2–10.

Zinn, H. (1980), A People's History of the United States (New York: Harper/Collins).

Zizek, S. (2009), The Sublime Object of Ideology: The Essential Zizek (London: Verso).

Additional Readings on Disinformation From The Special Issue of The Nordic Journal Of Media Studies, 5, 1: 2023.

"The return of propaganda: Historical legacies and contemporary conceptualizations," by Göran Bolin and Risto Kunelius: https://lnkd.in/ejBCty-i.

"Media studies, Le Bon's psychology of crowds, and qualitative-normative research on propaganda, 1880–2020," by Tarmo Malmberg: https://lnkd.in/e-G9Tre9.

"Guarding information's Other: Theorizing beyond information and communications technologies for disinformation," by Joseph M. Nicolaï: https://lnkd.in/edbhvjMd.

"Propaganda and the Web 3.0: Truth and ideology in the digital age," by Aaron Hyzen: https://lnkd.in/e3QDxJvZ.

"The transformation of propaganda: The continuities and discontinuities of information operations, from Soviet to Russian active measures," by Roman Horbyk, Yana Prymachenko, and Dariya Orlova: https://lnkd.in/em3Pg3mB.

"Raping turtles and kidnapping children: Fantasmatic logics of Scandinavia in Russian and German anti-gender discourse," by Maria Brock and Tina Askanius: https://lnkd.in/e-aHK3kG.

"Media criticism as a propaganda strategy in political communication," by Mattias Ekman and Andreas Widholm: https://lnkd.in/eWkr46fR.

"Fact-checkers and the news media: A Nordic perspective on propaganda," by John Grönvall: https://lnkd.in/eHjSdcSe.

"Persuasion through people: The rhetorical categories of documentary subjects in Michael Moore's films," by Ilari Kellokoski: https://lnkd.in/eJ2Vn7kD.

"The language of late fossil capital," by Leif Dahlberg: https://lnkd.in/esPhnu9J.

"What would a Swedish mine be without a party? On metals, minerals, and love during the "green" transition: Climate propaganda in The Swedish Mine advertising campaign," by Isabel Löfgren: https://lnkd.in/eMjrVEDh.

Nordicom at the University of Gothenburg hashtag#openaccess hashtag#scholarly-publishing hashtag#propaganda hashtag#media hashtag#commu.

Specialized Bibliographies

Bibliography on Mass Violence

Crews, G.A. (2016), Critical Examination of School Violence and Disturbance in K-12 Education (Hershey, Pennsylvania: Information Science Reference).

Finley, L. (2011), Encyclopedia of School Crime and Violence (Santa Barbara, California: ABC-CLIO).

Finley, L. (2014), School v (Santa Barbara, CA: ABC-CLIO).

Klein, J. (2013), The Bully Society (New York: New York University Press).

Lebrun, M. (2008), Books, Blackboards, and Bullets: School Shootings and Violence in America (Lanham, MD: Rowman & Littlefield Education).

Nash, J.R. (1992), World Encyclopedia of 20th Century Murder (Lanham, MD: Rowman & Littlefield). https://www.motherjones.com/politics/2014/10/mass-shootings-increasing-harvard-research/.

Restivo, S. (2021), "The Body Reimagined as a Node in a Nested Network of Social Ecologies: Body/Brain/Culture in the World," Round Table 3 (Dialogues). Knowledge in Praxis: The Social Construction of the Body, Post Porto Alegre, Brazil, International Sociological Association Forum, RC 54: The Body in the Social Sciences: Bodies in the Pandemic Context, 9/4/21.

Readings on Violence

Collins, R. (2022), Explosive Conflict (New York: Routledge).

Collins, R. (2009), Violence: A Micro-sociological theory (Princeton: Princeton University Press).

Review of Collins, R. Violence, 2009: "Covering infinitely recurrent strips of social action running from blustering confrontation to intimate physical attack, *Violence* is peppered with breakthrough insights, demonstrating the power of systematic theory and even concluding with that rarest of sociological contributions, a short list of eminently practical suggestions. The concept of 'forward panic' alone makes the book indispensable. This book is a milestone contribution to criminology, to micro-sociology, to the sociology of emotions, and to a field that knows no academic boundaries: the history of efforts to control violence. Randy Collins has developed a framework that should guide a generation of research."—Jack Katz, University of California, Los Angeles.

"I have no doubt that this book will be hailed as one of the most important works on violence ever written. After reading it, it is difficult any longer to imagine that all that is needed for violence to occur is a motive to engage in violence. Collins argues persuasively that the situation must also be right if violence is actually to occur."—Donald Black, author of The Social *Structure of Right and Wrong*.

"A masterful study of the microdynamics of violence. This book will undoubtedly provoke excitement and controversy among a wide group of readers, including educated nonspecialists as well as academics, journalists, law-enforcement professionals, and policymakers. Truly an original book."—Eiko Ikegami, author of *The Taming of the Samurai*.

Bibliography on Anarchism and Social Order

Albrect, G. (1994), "Ethics, Anarchy and Sustainable Development," Anarchist Studies, 2, 2: 95–117.

Bakunin, M. (1953), The Political Philosophy of Bakunin: Scientific Anarchism: selected Writings (New York: The Free Press).

Bakunin, M. (1974), Selected Writings (New York: Random House).

Braverman, H. (1974), Labor and Monopoly Capital: The Degradation of Work in the Twentieth Century (New York: Monthly Review Press).

Chomsky, N. (2015), Turning the Tide (Chicago: Haymarket Books).

Goldman, E. (1910–31/1996), Emma Speaks (New York: Humanities Press).

Goldman, E. (2008), A Documentary History of the American Years, Vols 1 & 2 (Champagne, IL: University of Illinois Press).

Goldman, E. (2024), A Documentary History of the American Years, Vol. 3 (Stanford: Stanford University Press).

Godwin, W. (1986), The Anarchist Writings of William Godwin (London: Freedom Press).

Kropotkin, P. (1970), Writings on Anarchism and Revolution (Cambridge, MA: MIT Press).

Kropotkin, P. (1885/1992), Words of a Rebel (Montreal: Black Rose Books).

Kropotkin, P. (1886/2020), The Place of Anarchism in Socialistic Evolution (Bristol, UK: Read & Co.).

Kropotkin, P. (1995), The Conquest of Bread and Other Writings (Cambridge: Cambridge University Press).

Kropotkin, P. (2020), The State: Its Historic Role (Bristol, UK: Read & Co.).

Malatesta, E. (1977), Errico Malatesta: His Life and Ideas (London: Freedom Press).

Pateman, C. (1976), Participation and Democratic Theory (Cambridge: Cambridge University Press).

Proudhon, P. (1840/1994), What is. Property? (Cambridge: Cambridge University Press).

Read, H. (1971), Anarchy and Order (Boston: Beacon Press).

Rocker, R. (2005), The London Years (Chico, CA: AK Press).

Wilde, O. (2001), The Soul of Man Under Socialism and Selected Critical Prose (New York: Penguin).

Bio-Sketches

Albrect (b. 1953) is an environmental philosopher and former professor at Murdoch University in Western Australia (retired 2014) and the University of Newcastle in New South Wales (retired 2008).

Bakunin (1814–1876), Russian social anarchist, one of the most influential revolutionaries of his era. Paul Avrich (1988), Anarchist Portraits (Princeton: Princeton University Press, p. 14): Bakunin was "a nobleman who yearned for a peasant revolt, a libertarian with an urge to dominate others, an intellectual with a powerful anti-intellectual streak."

Chomsky (b. 1928), the so-called "father of modern linguistics" and one of the founders of cognitive science Institute Professor Emeritus at MIT, and a prominent public intellectual with an international reputation as a political activist and social critic.

Goldman (1869–1940) was born in Lithuania and emigrated to the United States in 1885. She was prominent in the development of anarchism in North American and Europe in the early decades of the twentieth century. She founded the anarchist journal Mother Earth in 1906.

Godwin (1756–1836) was an English journalist and political philosopher, an early advocate of utilitarianism and is considered the first modern advocate of anarchism: Mark Philip (20 May 2006). "William Godwin," in E.N. Zalta (ed.). Stanford Encyclopedia of Philosophy. He married Mary Wallstonecraft in 1797 (who died that same year), and their daughter Mary Shelley married the poet Percy Bysshe Shelley and wrote Frankenstein (1818).

Kropotkin (1842–1921). Born into an aristocratic family of landowners, Kropotkin was a geographer, geologist, a student of evolution, and a proponent of mutual and anarcho-communism. Inspired interest in cooperation as a principle of evolution and understood anarchism as one of the social sciences.

Malatesta (1853–1932). Italian anarchist and revolutionary socialist, Malatesta was a radical journalist who supported insurrectionary "propaganda by deed" and later syndicalism. He spent most of his life in prison and exile. He toured in the US prior to and during World War I and returned to Italy in 1919. He was arrested by the Italian government and released a couple months before Mussolini came into power. He worked as an electrician during the last years of his life suffering from harassment and government censorship of his journal Pensiero e Volontà and repiratory illnesses which eventually killed him.

Pateman (b. 1940). Born and raised in England, Carole Pateman is an Oxford trained political scientist and Distinguished Professor Emeritus, political science, UCLA. Dr. Pateman has earned many distinctions as a feminist political theorist and critic of liberal democracy. She is a member of the British Academy.

Proudhon (1809–1865). Considered by some to be the "father of anarchism," he was a French socialist, political economist, and philosopher of mutualism. He also contributed to the development of sociology. He is claimed paradoxically by the individualist anarchists and the social anarchists. He is famous for the slogan "Property is theft."

Read (1893–1968). British born Read was art historian, literary critic, poet, and had an interest in existential philosophy. He considered himself an anarchist in the quietist tradition (Carpenter and Morris), but the anarchist community reacted negatively when he was knighted for his contributions to literature. More idealist than materialist he had many run-ins with Marxists.

Rocker (1873–1958). German anarchist and activist. In the 1920s he was associated with the syndicalist Free Workers' Union of Germany. He left Germany in 1933 and settled in the US where he became involved with the Yiddish Freie Arbeier Stimme, libertarian education, and support for the Spanish Revolution. Exposed to socialist writings by his uncle Carl Naumann, he eventually became a socialist.

Wilde (1854–1900). The Irish poet and playwright is widely known for such contributions as the novel, The Picture of Dorian Gray and the play The Importance of Being Ernest. He was an advocate of socialism, communism or "whatever one chooses to call it," and called for an end to private property, cooperation over competition. Artists would thrive best in a society without government. Wilde's homosexuality subjected him to various legal harassments throughout his life, including celebrity trials and imprisonment.

Index